Tell Me Why Dear Bennett

Memoirs of Bennett College Belles

Volume II

Compiled by
Dr. Juanita Patience Moss '54

Foreword by Dr. Esther Alexander Terry '61
Provost of Bennett College for Women

HERITAGE BOOKS
2012

HERITAGE BOOKS
AN IMPRINT OF HERITAGE BOOKS, INC.

Books, CDs, and more—Worldwide

For our listing of thousands of titles see our website
at
www.HeritageBooks.com

Published 2012 by
HERITAGE BOOKS, INC.
Publishing Division
100 Railroad Ave. #104
Westminster, Maryland 21157

Copyright © 2012 Juanita Patience Moss

Other Heritge Books by the author:
Anthracite Coal Art of Charles Edgar Patience
Battle of Plymouth, North Carolina (April 17–20, 1864): The Last Confederate Victory
Created to Be Free: A Historical Novel about One American Family
The Forgotten Black Soldiers in White Regiments During the Civil War
The Forgotten Black Soldiers in White Regiments During the Civil War, Revised Edition
Tell Me Why Dear Bennett: Memoirs of Bennett College Belles, Class of 1924–2012

Cover: "Through the Eye of the Lens"
Photograph by Wanda Edwards Mobley '83

Book Cover Layout Design
Compiled by Reba N. Burruss-Barnes

All rights reserved. No part of this book may be reproduced or transmitted in any form or by any means, electronic or mechanical, including photocopying, recording or by any information storage and retrieval system without written permission from the author, except for the inclusion of brief quotations in a review.

International Standard Book Numbers
Paperbound: 978-0-7884-5388-5
Clothbound: 978-0-7884-9476-5

THIS SECOND VOLUME IS DEDICATED TO THE MEMORIES OF RECENTLY DEPARTED BELLES WHO HAD CONTRIBUTED TO VOLUME I

<u>HELEN ELLISON NEWBERRY MCDOWELL '24</u>

(1904-2010)

<u>DR. MARGARET DEAN FREEMAN'30</u>

(1909-2011)

<u>JANICE DEJOIE '54</u>

(1932-2010)

Recited by

<u>DR. DAVID D. JONES</u>

(1 John 3:2-3, Psalm 115:12)

"Beloved, now are we the sons of God.

And it doth not yet appear what we shall

be like, but we know that when He shall appear, we shall be like Him.

For we shall see Him as He is.

And every man that hath this

hope in Him purifieth himself,

ever as He is pure.

The Lord hath been mindful of us.

He will bless us."

TELL ME WHY

Tell me why the stars do shine,

Tell me why the ivy twines,

Tell me why the sky's so blue,

Tell me, Old Benett

Just why I love you.

Because God made the stars to shine,

Because God made the ivy twine

Because God made the sky so blue,

God made Old Bennett

That's why "WE" love you.

TABLE OF CONTENTS

FOREWORD	7
INTRODUCTION	17
ACKNOWLEDGEMENTS	19
PROLOGUE	21
CHARTER DAY ADDRESS	22
PRESIDENTS OF BCNAA	29
BELLE LEGACIES	31
FAMILY LEGACIES	43
In Memoriam-Jeffries and Martin Belles	47
SPECIAL "BENNETT IDEALS"	63
1920s Memoirs	65
In Memoriam- Lucy Anderson Sadler '23	65
In Memoriam- Helen Newberry McDowell '24	73
FAVORITE BENNETT COLLEGE PRESIDENTS	75
1930s Memoirs	77
In Memoriam- Rose Withers Catchings '32	79
In Memoriam- Pauline Waters Smith '35	85
In Memoriam- Frances Jones Bonner '39	95
In Memoriam- Frances Lucas Enzlow '39	101
1940s Memoirs	105
In Memoriam- Alice Patterson Patience '40	105
In Memoriam- Mable Viviann Hargrave '45	105
In Memoriam- Sylvia Juanita Rock Greene '49	114
1950s Memoirs	128
In Memoriam- Alberta Copeland Lewis '51	131
In Memoriam- Shirey Cundiff Bethea '52	134
In Memoriam- Bishop Joseph Bethea	139
In Memoriam- Gwendolyn Harris Blount '52	141
WHITE BREAKFAST HISTORY	145
BENNETT BELL HISTORY	147
In Memoriam- Ellease Randall Colston '53	149
In Memoriam- Peggy Jeffries Foman '54	154
In Memoriam-Joye Stanley McClean Bridges '54	170
In Memoriam- Dr. David Dallas Jones	175

1960s Memoirs	*203*
50th Year Reunion- Class of 1961	*203*
In Memoriam- Audrey Wynn Spence '64	*231*
1970s Memoirs	*267*
1980s Memoirs	*287*
In Memoriam- Susie Williams Jones	*296*
1990's Memoirs	*397*
2000's Memoirs	*315*
In Memoriam- Dr. Willa B. Player	*327*
In Memoriam- Dr. Isaac Miller Jr.	*331*
2010's Memoirs	*335*
EPILOGUE	*361*
AFTERWORD	*363*
END NOTES	*365*
SOURCES	*380*
INDEX	*385*

FOREWORD

Dr. Esther Alexander Terry '61
Provost
Bennett College For Women

"Tell Me Why"

Why its alumnae fall so deeply in love with Bennett College has long been a question of discussion among those who have observed the enduring passion that exists between the college and her over 5,000 graduates. All agree that students experience something special at Bennett, even though that "something" is not easily identified. Whether it is their interaction with the succession of world famous personalities who come to speak at the College's ACES Programs, or the camaraderie that comes of living with and learning from their sister/women peers in the residence halls, or their ever-demanding professors who keep raising the academic bar in search of excellence, or the special leadership imprimatur of one or another of her distinguished presidents —whatever triggers it, it is quite obvious that sooner or later in their experience of Bennett, something grabs hold of her students' heartstrings and ignites the fire of a love affair that burns forever.

It is a subject befitting the hyperbolic language of the poet who asks:

"Tell me, Old Bennett, just why I love you,
 and answers:
Because God made the stars to shine,
Because God made the ivy twine,
Because God made the sky so blue,
God made Old Bennett. That's why I love you."

My Bennett sisters whose writings fill this exquisite little volume most certainly were not aiming to write poetry, but their stories and remembrances of their times at Bennett provide ample material for the poet's pen. Their writings reveal deep and abiding friendships, unmatched emotional support, true love and undying loyalty—unimpeachable evidence that over the life time of her existence, this "small but important College," this "oasis," has continued to be alma mater; and we, her daughters, continue to be bound to her and her mission *"...till the evening shadows fall, and we heed our last, clear call."* These stories speak for all of us in celebration of Bennett.

MESSAGE FROM THE 15th PRESIDENT
Dr. Julianne Malveaux

The Rotunda of the New Global Learning Center [1]

EXCERPTS FROM
SANKFOKA: WHAT DO WE LEARN FROM BENNETT'S PAST [2]

The Sankofa bird is one of the most important of the Andinka symbols that come from the Akan people of West Africa. It is also one of the most well known and most frequently invoked, the twist-necked bird looking backward while attempting to move ahead. One translation of the symbol is that "it is not taboo to go back to retrieve what you forgot." In other words, we must examine our roots before we move forward, reaching back to get the best of our past so that we are fully armed for the future. This is an important time for the Bennett College for Women team--our Trustees, faculty, staff, students, alumnae and community supporters—to ruminate on Bennett's past as we go forward, breaking new ground.

Bennett College for Women has always played an important role in producing scholars, activists, educators, and leaders. We are so much more necessary in an age that artist India Arie describes as "graceless," in an age when it is critical to replicate the energy of the Belles who picketed the Carolina Theatre, who stood with the brothers at Woolworth's in 1960, who supported Sandra Neely Smith '73 in her activism in 1979, who thronged to Jena in 2008. We claim the mantle of activism, and claim our participation in social justice movements that have transformed our nation.

So the Sankofa bird reminds us that this moment, while pivotal, is but another movement in the forward movement of Bennett College for Women. Just as the former slaves in an unpaved basement took a leap of faith to create this college, it is now necessary for our alumnae base to take a similar leap of faith to move the college to the next level.

It is such an exciting time for Bennett College for Women. We are on the brink of greatness. Our accreditation has been reaffirmed, we have broken ground on new buildings, we have dedicated new faculty in place, and our alums have achieved a new giving record. This is not the time to rest on our laurels, but instead to renew our commitment to this oasis, an educational institution where women are educated and celebrated.

Always on fire for Bennett,

Julianne Malveaux
President

MESSAGE FROM THE DIRECTOR OF ALUMNAE AFFAIRS

AUDREY DEMPS FRANKLIN'72

Lessons learned from *THE* weekend (2011):[3]

Alumnae Weekend is always a stressful time for me – first as NAA President and now as Alumnae Affairs Director. I always worry about whether alums will come, will they have a good time, will they donate the goal for the year, will we have enough seats for the classes…

This year started out the same, but somewhere along the way things shifted. I started feeling less stressed and smiling a little more (even singing in the shower one morning!!). I was trying to figure out what was different. Then I went to the White Breakfast that morning. While we were waiting for the event to start, the 50 year class lead coordinator (I won't call her out, but we all know who she is) began to grumble because she was ready to start. They summoned me and I went to her to find out what was going on. Before I could get a word out I was surrounded by the entire class. They were not concerned about the start time, they wanted to make sure their class mate was okay. It was obvious that if I blinked the wrong way, I would have 50 corsages tossed my way. Maybe even a few medallions!!

After that incident, I just observed that class more closely. I watched the way they interacted with each other, the ease they felt with each other, even the ones they had not seen in 25, 40 or 50 years. They knew so much about each other: whose husband was deceased, who had grandchildren, who always liked to dance, and whose birthday was that month. I also watched them laughing when no one on the outside could understand why.

That made me pause and look around at some of the other classes as they interacted—everyone was so happy to be back, but even happier to be in the company of their sisters at a time in a place called Bennett College. Memories of the good times we all had at Bennett made me just sit for a few minutes and then go immediately to my cell phone and call a couple of my classmates to say "Hi" and that I was thinking of them. It also made me realize that I have to do a better job of connecting with my classmates – a lesson we need to share with our younger sisters – not just the ones we "hung out with in school," but all of them. Even our little and big sisters – the circle can never be too large.

That night at the disco (because clearly wine and cheese were just menu items), I saw the mixing of all classes as they danced together, sang together and laughed together. I thought, well, this is what we should be doing. This is the good life.

You see, I came to realize that whoever sent me the e-mail about sisters had it right. They were talking about the sisterhood at Bennett—*"Time passes. Life happens. Distance separates. Children grow up; jobs come and go. Love waxes and wanes. Hearts break. Parents die. Colleagues forget favors. Careers end. But...Sisters are there, no matter how much time and how many miles are between you. When you have to walk that lonesome valley and you have to walk it by yourself, the women in your life will be on the valley's rim, cheering you on, praying for you, intervening on your behalf, and waiting with open arms at the valley's end. Sometimes, they will even break the rules and walk beside you…Or come in and carry you out."*

Alumnae weekend was over and back to the grind. I wanted to write a short piece about the weekend, but got caught up in the grind of day to day activities. I thought okay, I have too much work to do so I will do this next year. Fast forward to October, I was sitting in my office with Roslyn Smith '61, Iris Morton '61 and Johanna Polanen '61 and I had flashbacks of the weekend. I saw it again, how easily they talked to each other, how they genuinely liked each other, and me, too (I think). I was so overwhelmed with emotion, I just got up and walked out of the room, not wanting or being able to express the feelings I had at that moment about them and Bennett.

I then had a flashback from alumnae weekend Saturday night when I was extremely tired, doubting that the weekend went okay, that everyone had a good time, that the younger alums had as much fun as the older ones, that my classmates would be happy next year, and most importantly that Bennett would not just survive, but thrive. I just stopped and held my breath. I thought about those three Belles sitting in my office, about the ones who come over to assist whenever needed, the ones to come to ACES, the ones who mentor the students, the ones who work in chapters across the country recruiting and raising money, and the ones who send their checks (large and small). I just exhaled and smiled because I realized what I always knew was that Bennett was always going to be okay. It was going to be better than okay, it would be great. Why? Because the graduating class would one day be doing the same thing this 50 year-class was doing.

Would they love Bennett as much as we do? **YES**. Would they care about Bennett as much as we do? **YES**.

Because God made ole Bennett, that's why we love her.

It is as simple as that.

MESSAGE FROM
Dr. Lisa Johnson '81
President of the BCNAA [4]

Many have said to me, *"Tell Me Why* the alumnae of Bennett College love and care for her the way that they do?" In order to understand, you must open your heart in order to be 'Bennettized'!

Our Bennettization began when we first arrived and saw the beauty of the campus. It was impressive. The majestic magnolias, the well-manicured lawn of the unbroken green, the stately buildings all gave us a sense of peace and security. What a wonderful place to be nurtured and allowed to mature as we began our journey into womanhood.

The next thing we received was a hug from a student welcoming us to the campus instantly making us a part of the Bennett sisterhood. The bond between the girls, as the students were affectionately called by our 9th president David D. Jones, was tangible, it crossed the great divide of age and sororities. It is everlasting. Your Bennett sister lent you her most prized possession without question, was by your side at the birth of your child, would be there to celebrate your accomplishments and there24to support you when you lost a parent or spouse. She became your friend for life for she has known you since you were a teen and knows all your secrets. She shared her hat and gloves, helped you break curfew, saved you a place in line for meals and walked with you to A & T, Burger King, or Cook Out.

We were then embraced by the faculty and staff who became our extended family. They provided us with education and moral support as they nourished our souls, provided gentle discipline, pushed us to do our best. They let us know that every Bennett girl mattered. Drs. Willa B. Player, Charlotte Alston '54,

Georgia Latimer, Mrs. Louise G. Streat, and Yolande Johnson '83 were poised, elegant and graceful women who demonstrated the "Bennett Ideal." Drs. Hobart Jarrett, J. Henry Sayles, Michelle Linster, and Cristina Moreira encouraged us to do our best and strive for excellence. Nurse Alsie Tramwell '37, "Ma" Tucker and Mr. Garrison wrapped their arms around us when we needed them most. All of the faculty and staff were vested in us as much as our parents were and reminded us that with an education we could do anything.

All of us were indoctrinated to the values and traditions of being a Bennett Belle. We all remember our first Convocatum Est with our initial walk through the Bearden Gate as we wore our required white dresses, flesh tone stockings and black shoes. We didn't realize at the time that this would be the first of many occasions to enter the Pfeiffer Chapel to hear speakers such as Dr. Benjamin E. Mays, Dr. Martin Luther King Jr., Susan Taylor, Dr. Cornell West, Pearl Bailey, Mark Walton, Ntozake Shange, and Patricia Russell McCloud during required vespers and ACES programs. We all learned not to take short cuts in life by not walking on the grass, to always be properly attired when we went out and the safety in traveling in groups. We fondly remember our Big Sister/ Little Sister ceremony and the emotions of starting to say good bye two years later at Senior Day. Bennett College changed our perspective on life as we were taught to recognize injustice and how to express our displeasures in a dignified manner. We have demonstrated our civic responsibility by initiating and participating in protests at the Carolina Theater in 1937, at the F. W. Woolworth in 1960, traveling in 2007 to West Virginia to support Meagan Williams and to Jena, Louisiana in support of the Jena 6, and even on our own president's lawn.

We were taught, by example, the importance of giving back to our alma mater by our fellow alums. Ellease Colston '53, Tressie Muldrow '62 and Audrey Franklin '72 have reached out to many students to work for the NAA. Alumnae give of their time as they teach on campus and serve as mentors to matriculating students as well as to recent graduates. The class of 1953 set precedence by being the first to give over $100,000.00 to the college as they celebrated their 50th class reunion. The class of 1961 was next with their gift of over $165,000.00 in 2011. Many alumnae consistently give $1,000.00 to $25,000.00 yearly and their families regularly establish scholarships in memory of their loved ones in order to help our alma mater. Dr. Joyce Martin Dixon '56 showed this year that we don't have to wait until we depart this life to make a $1,000,000.00 gift to the college. She humbly reminded us, *"To whom much is given, much is required."*

I hope your heart is filled with a new appreciation of why we love our college. We want to insure that the legacy started in 1873 continues into the future, that the present students become global leaders and travelers as did their predecessors and we will support them on their way.

"The Lord has been mindful of us. He will bless us."

Dr. Lisa A. Johnson '81 presents citation from the National Alumnae Association to Alumna Dr. Joyce Martin Dixon '56 to honor her $1 million dollar gift to Bennett College for Women. (May 2011) [5]

INTRODUCTION

While attending Bennett College for Women, young women share many similar experiences, some of which remain forever with them. For instance, what Belle can forget chanting the harmonious *"Grace"* before meals? *"God is great and God is good."* On the other hand, so many experiences are unique to individual Belles and worth sharing.

Believing in emphasizing positives rather than re-living negatives, I asked Belles to share some of their fondest memories to publish in *Tell Me Why Dear Bennett: Memoirs of Bennett College Belles: Class 1924-2012*. Many alumnae have expressed their gratitude for such a book from which young Belles can learn the "her-story" of Alma Mater via the words of her daughters. After reading *TMWDB*, some alumnae have contacted long-lost friends and others simply are glad for the opportunity to reminisce about the precious time they had spent on Bennett's beautiful campus.

After a number of Belles asked me to compile a second volume because they had not submitted a memoir for the first, I agreed. Besides the interesting memoirs included in this second volume, a chapter has been devoted to Belle legacies as suggested by Zepplyn Stepp Humphrey '35/ '55. Also included are a number of memorials to deceased Belles, as well as tributes to others. In addition, a number of Belles shared their life after their sojourn at Bennett.

Please forgive any mistakes you may find, especially in the legacy categories. Certainly, none are intentional.

Dr. Juanita Patience Moss '54

2011 All-Bennett Banquet
NAA Presidential Awardee
May 7, 2011

Juanita Patience Moss '54

(Photo courtesy of Wanda Mobley '83)

Left: Dr. Lisa Johnson '81, President of BCNAA
Right: Dr. Julianne Malveaux, President of Bennett College

ACKNOWLEDGEMENTS

MANY THANKS TO:

1 Dr. Julianne Malveaux- 15th President of Bennett College
2 Dr. Esther Alexander Terry '61- Provost
3 Audrey Franklin '72- Director of Alumnae Affairs
4 Dr. Lisa Johnson '81- President of the NAA with her mother Mrs. Laverne Johnson
5 Wanda Mobley '83- Photographer
6 Nadirah Goldsmith '99- La Belle Boutique
7 Zepplyn Humphrey '35/ '55
8 Kenya Samuels Gray '99- Editor
9 Reba Burruss-Barnes- Publicist and Photographer
10 Mildred Copeland Simms '54- Class Coordinator
11 Ruth Reese Fiuczynski '56- Class Coordinator

And to the myriad others who lent support in any manner.

PROLOGUE
Dr. Gladys Ashe Robinson, Class of 1971
Senator, North Carolina Senate, District 28

NAA President (1985-1989)

In the midst of the sit-ins movements across America, six to seven years after women from Bennett College and men from NC A&T (mind you that I said "women from Bennett") began the sit-ins in Greensboro, arose a new generation of energetic women who were fed up with the segregated, less than equal conditions in their own communities. These women came, transformed from the children who witnessed their parents with heads bowed in the presence of white men- behaviors they practiced to keep food on the table --- to women who dared to look the white man in the eye and demand respect; transformed from young black girls whose mothers permed their hair to be acceptable to the white world - to young women once arriving on campus returned their hair to natural (called afros) saying "we like how we look;" transformed from wearing Liz Claiborne or rather Sears dresses and put on dai shikis and head wraps....reaffirming our kinship with the African continent.

This was our story, 44 years ago, the new Bennett College woman- of the latter 60's, continuing a legacy of female activism and leading "her-stories" of change.

Dr. Gladys Ashe Robinson '71
Charter Day Address at Bennett College for Women
March 17, 2011

Annie Merner Pfeiffer Chapel
(Dedicated in 1941)

Good morning, President Malveaux, dais guests, faculty, staff and my dear Bennett Sisters – Bennett Belles. It is my pleasure to be with you today on this Charter Day, 138 years since the founding of Bennett College and 85 years since Bennett became a College for Women. As your State Senator for the 28th district representing over 177,000 citizens, inclusive of Bennett College for Women, I thank you for your support this past November.

I greet you on behalf of the North Carolina General Assembly, and on behalf of our Governor, the Honorable Beverly Perdue.

We all know the history of Bennett College for Women. I trust that you, my Bennett Sisters, know how Bennett was founded as a co-ed school by newly emancipated slaves in the basement of what is now St. Matthews United Methodist Church, sustained with funding from the Freedman's Aid and Southern Education Society of the Methodist Church and anchored on land purchased by the church membership with a $10,000.00 donation from a New York businessman and its namesake, Lyman Bennett.

Presidents following Dr. David Jones were Dr. Willa Player, the first female president, and Dr. Isaac Miller where my story began and probably Dr. Miller's heartburn turned to ulcers. Assembled at the Belle tower in the summer of 1967 were hundreds of young, naïve, but vibrant Black women.

Five hundred miles from her hometown of Columbus, Georgia, came a valedictorian from a segregated high school in Columbus, where schools like Emory University came seeking the best and brightest of Negroes. But I refused to go - I chose Bennett – and so did most of my classmates. Our class of over 250 was comprised of student body leaders, valedictorians, and salutatorians of high schools across the south, east and west coasts of the United States. Our story was about choice – the choice we made about our future- or should I say the choice our parents made–that we should attend the women's college where girls are nurtured and challenged to become women leaders.

Bennett College for Women is a multifaceted story – a story of women leaders. Dr. Johnnetta Cole pinned the term "her-story," actually from a book of African proverbs. Bennett College for Women is a place where you create and leave your own story. My story is one of the many "her-stories" you will hear, and however different, the ending is the same.

The story of Bennett's beginning is <u>history</u> –men and women, people who were formerly enslaved (Julianne Malveaux) yearned for education as the path to freedom. Having recently bought their freedom, these people, our ancestors, built churches *such as my own – Providence Baptist Church, the first African American church built in 1866 down the street on Bluford on land owned by a free man. Those free men began schools in church basements.*

Our ancestors formerly enslaved believed that education was the only bridge you can rely on to get you over troubled waters. So- they built that bridge to get us to the other side where we could stand up and be counted, thereby leaving our footsteps in the sands of time for others to follow (Marie Evans). Although free, they were yet afraid of the white man's terror once he realized we were serious about education. But they took the chance- because they were convinced that the lack of knowledge is darker than the nights of terror they often witnessed.

From a church basement to a one building facility – history was tied to vision; vision for secondary education for Negroes; and some 47 years later, the vision for women to become educated, independent and leaders. "His-story" became "her-stories" - the role that only women could fulfill anchoring the home, educating their children, volunteering in the community, and, yes, leading the world to change.

As early as the 1800's, Lucy Craft Laney said "to women has been committed-- the responsibility of making the laws of society, making environments for children. She has the privilege and authority, God-given, to help develop into a noble man or woman the young life committed to her care. There is no nobler work entrusted to the hands of mortals."

A century and a half later, and 85 years since its founding as a woman's college, Bennett College for Women must continue to be the place where women seek and find educational excellence, life long learning opportunities, personal development and are prepared for leadership roles in a global society.

Lifelong learning for Bennett Belles was– about where the napkin goes; is the fork on the left-- and knife and spoon the right or visa versa –; how to dress – all of us received a list of what to bring to Bennett-most of us were smart, but poor, so clothing was limited. But everyone came with a white dress, black dress, leg color stockings and black shoes, white gloves, and a hat or *kerchief for your head on Sundays. That changed a few years later, but that's a "Glad-story" you will hear about later. Chapel was required on Tuesday and Thursdays at 11 a.m. and Sundays at 4 p.m. During those days, roll was taken by where we sat. - My name was Ashe and I sat on the front row, 4th seat from the right – I dared not be absent.*

There were horror stories and happy stories about chapel. Sundays were the best when we came to chapel in our dresses, gloves and hats or kerchiefs and listened to great speakers – of course like you I did not think they were so great all the time. Some years later, I was proud to say I had heard Benjamin Mays. But the fun was after chapel. When we exited the doors, handsome Aggies dressed in suits or shirts and ties lined the walkways just waiting for Bennett Belles. There were a few problems however. What if your boyfriend from Norfolk State happened to show up at the same time the Aggie boyfriend was there?

The life lesson there was how to keep your lies, I mean, "stories," straight. You see, lifelong learning was not just about the academics, but about social settings and cultural understandings and worldview- much of what we learned in chapel and in the classroom.

There were serious times. As young activists in the sit ins era, we felt that campus rules were too strict. Freshmen (or freshwomen as you say) had 9 p.m. curfews during the week and 10:30 p.m. on weekends; by the time you became a senior, you could stay out until 12 a.m. or a bit later on occasions as CIAA. Most of us exclaimed that we were staying out until 12 a.m. before we came to college; 9 p.m. curfews don't make sense.

By the time we were juniors, we were fully empowered to make changes; I dare not give the name of the junior class president? These activist women organized a sleep-in on the lawn of our college president's home. When he heard about the movement, Dr. Isaac Miller, a soft spoken guy was simply flabbergasted.

Now I don't suggest you try a sleep in on the president's lawn in protest; she would probably simply go back into the house, come back with a pillow and blanket and join you.

Of course we gave the president a list of our demands – later curfews -10:30 p.m. during the week, midnight on the weekends- no gloves and hats in chapel, no bed checks every night, allow us to ride in cars with our friends or boyfriends or whoever, and the list goes on.

Years after my graduation from Bennett, Dr. Miller would remind me of the heartburn he acquired – but not to his amazement, he said he knew I would become a leader. Today, when "her-story" is told about our radical class, I sometimes sigh and think that many traditions were good. But change has to occur. Bennett Women were and still are leaders of change. We defined the tipping point for our college environment and the community. Many of us were community activists, helping in the redevelopment of the area that surrounds Bennett-many of my days were spent in the community advocating for people and their rights. Our professors taught just that –Dr. Grandison, my psychology professor and advisor, told us that real learning was not on campus or just in the books; real experience was gained in the community.

True activism does not begin and end - it becomes a way of life – and so it was for many Bennett Belles. Not only did we help cafeteria workers and garbage workers strike for better wages – their wages were .25 per hour- but we got involved in political activism.

One of my fondest experiences was campaigning for then Attorney Henry Frye Sr., who had lost a first election to the North Carolina General Assembly, but with the volunteer efforts of students at Bennett, on his second campaign he was successfully elected to his first term in the NC House of Representatives. Now, we know him as retired North Carolina Supreme Court Justice, the first African American to occupy this seat, and I know him as a friend and mentor. I did not realize that my political career was being launched at that time.

My story is tied into our story; to the history of Bennett Seminary and the "her-story" of Bennett College for Women. Once asked what propelled me into community leadership, my answer was, "We were taught to be leaders at Bennett College for Women."

Malcolm Gladwell describes many situations where little things make a big difference in his book, The Tipping Point. "The Tipping Point," says Gladwell, "is the 'biography of an idea---- it is the best way to understand the emergence of fashion trends... the transformation of unknown books into best sellers, the rise of teenage smoking or any number of mysterious changes that mark everyday life---ideas, products, messages and behaviors spread like viruses.'"

Paraphrased – to me a Tipping Point is an idea, some thing or someone (you did not think so significant) that in the right time, place and situation – becomes the "impetus" to new and exciting beginnings or creations.

Bennett College for Women offers the Tipping Points - values, opportunities, academics, and leadership experiences at Bennett will be Tipping Points for your life and life's successes. They certainly were for me. Bennett taught me to not avoid the difficult, but the tipping point was to face and tackle the obstacles.

There is only one African American female in the North Carolina Senate, a body controlled by white mostly Republican men. This is not a challenge, but an opportunity to use this Tipping Point to speak for women like you, and women everywhere.

Bennett offers value added as one of the HBCUs preparing women as entrepreneurs, scientists, accountants, etc.

Bennett College for Women is a Tipping Point for women in STEM careers. **(Science, Technology, Engineering, Mathematics)**

Bennett College for Women was my Tipping Point; therefore, I am empowered with the knowledge, the skills and experience to advocate for the rights of African American and women of color, poor women, impoverished children and families.

Bennett was my Tipping Point; therefore, I am undaunted by a Republican majority who wants to reform legislation that addresses equity, and support for the poor, quality education for the least educated, healthcare for people who work all day but *can't go to the doctor; health care for college students who graduate in 4 or 5 years, without a job that offers health insurance.*

Because Bennett College was my Tipping Point, I can boldly proclaim, "We will not return to the pre civil rights era when separate and unequal was okay for some." Bennett College for Women remains the Tipping Point for me and 5000 other Belles.

A chapter of my story began where you sit today – The next chapter of "My-story" is to change "her-story" about women of color in North Carolina and America and the world; to change "her-story" of poor women and their children. "My-story" is to change the stigma of poverty that affects a growing percent of minority children, to change the story about lack of access to affordable health care. "My-story" is to change the story about a system where low-income and minority children still lack high quality education and educational equity, to change the story about workplace rights; and to write "her-story" that a Bennett College woman will make decisions about her education, her development, her future – that will change "his story" to "her-story" for women and families in this community, in this state, this nation, and across the entire world.

This is "my-story," "her-story," "your-story," and "our-story," Bennett Sisters. We must continue to move the chalice forward, to continue the legacy under which this institution was chartered as a college for women – because the hand that rocks the cradle has already sent her son to the White House and if your hand, your education, your leadership at Bennett College becomes your Tipping Point, that same hand will rule the world!

<u>Dr. Gladys Ashe Robinson '71</u>

Recipient of the BCNAA President's Award 2010

PRESIDENTS OF THE BENNETT COLLEGE NATIONAL ALUMNAE ASSOCIATION

1	*Alma Tarpley Taylor '30*	*1954-1957*
2	*Juanita G. Wells '37*	*1957-1959*
3	*Fannie Lee Hinnant '45*	*1959-1965*
4	*Maxine Haith O'Kelley '49*	*1965-1966*
5	*Elizabeth Alston Edwards '40*	*1966-1967*
6	*Marion Benton Tasco '60*	*1971-1975*
7	*Arney Hall Johnson '37*	*1975-1977*
8	*Bernice Johnson '51*	*1977-1979*
9	*Dr. Tressie Wright Muldrow '62*	*1979-1985*
10	*Dr. Gladys Ashe Robinson '71*	*1985-1989*
11	*Deborah Tillman Love '79*	*1989-1993*
12	*Dr. Tressie Wright Muldrow '62*	*1993-1997*
13	*Ellease Randall Colston '53*	*1997-2001*
14	*Dr. Marion Lee Bell '53*	*2001-2005*
15	*Audrey Demps Franklin '72*	*2005-2009*
16	*Dr. Lisa Johnson '81*	*2009-*

2011-2012 BCNAA Officers [6]
l.-r.: *Elayne Gibbs Jones '88, Recording Secretary;*
Deborah Tillman Love '79, Treasurer; Dr. Lisa Johnson '81, President;
Sandra Walker Johnson '86, Vice President;
Asha Pinkney Weithers '97, Financial Secretary
(not pictured- Kameelah Brown '00, Parliamentarian)

BELLE LEGACIES
Contributors To Volumes I and II

"Lighting the Way for So Many"
(Photograph by Wanda E. Mobley 2011)

PRESIDENTS
Dr. David Dallas Jones
   (Daughter) Dr. Frances Jones Bonner '39
   (Cousin) Gilberta Jeffries Mitchell '38
   (Cousin) Mary Maudelle Martin '49
   (Cousin) Virginia Jeffries Brown '48
   (Cousin) Maxine Haith O'Kelley '49
   (Cousin) Dr. Joyce Martin Dixon '56
   (Cousin) Edna Jeffries Pierce '56
   (Cousin) Barbara Ann Martin Burchette '58
   (Cousin) Margaret Hayes-Noel '58

Dr. Willa B. Player
   (Niece) Dolores Brown Smith '52
   (Niece) Barbara Brown Tazewell '56
   (Niece) Dr. Linda Brown '61

MOTHERS, DAUGHTERS AND GRANDDAUGHTERS
Alice Beville Dean 1885
   Dr. Margaret Dean Freeman '30
   Bessie Dean Clarke Riddick '34
      Lillian Clarke Lockery '50

Hallie Elizabeth Brown Cundiff (?)
   Shirley A. Cundiff Bethea '52
      Josefa E. Bethea Wall '87

Zepplyn Humphrey'35/'55
   Geneva Averett-Short '58
      Constance Blackwell '86

Doris Young Baldwin '48
   Linda Baldwin-Herring '74
      Carah Herring 2005
      Chemaye Herring 2008

GRANDMOTHERS AND GRANDDAUGHTERS
Alice Beville Dean 1885
   Lillian Clarke Lockery '50

Mary Jane Pope Hallmon '28
   Inga Graves Spinks 2005

Hallie Elizabeth Brown Cundiff
   Josefa E. Bethea Wall '87

Doris Young Baldwin '48
   Carah Herring 2005
   Chemaye Herring 2008

Gwendolyn Mackel Rice '61
   Toi Rice-Jones 2010

MOTHERS AND DAUGHTERS
Alice Beville Dean 1885
   Dr. Margaret Dean Freeman '30
   Bessie Dean Clarke Riddick '34

Novella Jeffries Martin (?)
   Mary Mernelle Martin '49
   Dr. Joyce Martin Dixon '56
   Barbara Ann Martin Burchette '58

Bessie Dean Clarke Riddick '34
   Lillian Clarke Lockery '50

Pauline Alston Donnell '35
   Gwendolyn Donnell Cobb '64

Lisbeth Ellen Edwards Berry '39
   Treda Sheryl Berry '73

Frances Lucas Enzlow '39
   Modgie Enzlow Williams '70

Cathryn Whitmore Morrow (?)
   Anna Morrow Bass '55

Alice Patterson Patience '40
   Dr. Juanita Patience Moss '54 (stepdaughter)

Doris Young Baldwin '48
   Linda Baldwin-Herring '74

Dorothy Arnold Hampton '48
   Karen Hampton Winfield '73

Shirley A. Cundiff Bethea '52
   Josefa E. Bethea Wall '87

Lovye Davis Oesterin '53
  Margrete Oesterlin Jean-Louis '91

Delores Cox Pittman '56
  Lisa Pittman Dennis '81

Margarie Mays Gibbs '57
  Elayne Gibbs Jones '88
  Shirley Louise Gibbs '90

Pauline Dixon Jeffries '57
  Paula Jeffries McKinney '82

Helen Becket Murray '59
  Tara Murray Richardson '87

E. Adell Taylor Dowdy '62
  Adrianne Dowdy Sweittenberg '85

Pensal Winston McCray '63
  Dr. Rispba McCray-Garrison '95
  Dr. Monique McCray-Osley '91
  Dr. Talia McCray '90

Dr. Judith Brooks-Buck '71
  Kimberly Buck Rouse '94

Winzell (Wendy) Ervin Neeley '70
  Angela Neeley 2003

Glenda Caldwell Dodd '72
  Dr. Melody Dodd 2002

Linda Baldwin Herring '74
  Carah Herring 2005
  Chemayne Herring 2008

Dyora Thomas Kinsey '75
  Dyora Michelle Kinsey '99

MOTHER-IN-LAW and DAUGHTER IN LAW
Cathryn Whitmore Morrow (?)
   Dorothy Dixon Morrow '54

SISTERS
Bettie Beville Cash ca. 1875
Alice Beville Dean 1885

Lucille Dean McKee '20
Dr. Margaret Dean Freeman '30
Bessie Dean Clarke Riddick '34

Louise Anderson '23
Lucy Anderson Sadler '23

Pauline Alston Donnell '35
Myrtle Alston '44
Dr. Charlotte Alston '54

Annie Green Ponds '43
Hattie Green Holmes '46

Cynthia McCottry Smith '45
Gloria McCottry (transferred)

Virginia Jeffries Brown '48
Edna Jeffries Pierce '56

Audrose Mackel Banks '49
Dr. Lyvonne Mackel Washington '53
Gwendolyn Mackel Rice '61
Marilyn Hortense Mackel, JD '65

Ouida Rush Hodnett '49
Joyce Rush Hunt '55

Mary Mernelle Martin '49
Dr. Joyce Martin Dixon '56
Barbara Ann Martin Burchette '58

Jeanne Martin Brayboy '51
Thomasina Martin Brayboy '53

Frances Rosetta Grier Brower '51
Fay Fagan '55

Alberta Copeland Lewis '51
Mildred Copeland Simms '54

Dolores Brown Smith '52
Barbara Brown Tazewell '56
Dr. Linda Brown '61

Dorothy Dixon Morrow '54
Pauline Dixon Jeffries '57

Peggy Jeffries Foman '54
Dr. Iris Jeffries Morton '61

Fay Fagan '55
Terrace Fagan-Mitchell '58

Geraldine Hughes Kiser '50
Othelia Mae Hughes '59
Opal Hughes Watkins '63

Marilyn Kimber Scales '54
Geraldine Kimber Rayford '58

Hazeline Taylor Harris '59
E. Adell Taylor Dowdy '62

Elizabeth Daise '61
Jacqueline Daise Lee '61

Valaida Wynn Randolph '62
Audrey Wynn Spence '64

Sylvia Jones '68
Dr. Norma Jones '73

Brenda Morgan Nicholson '69
Norma Lynn Morgan '71

Dr. Gladys Ashe Robinson '71
Lydia Ashe Mullins '81

Gwendolyn Hill '74
Sherrie Hill '77

Peggy Patrick Eakins '67
Veda Patrick Cook '71

Esther Canty-Barnes, Esq. '76
Loretta Canty Tann '78

Yulonda Green Cunningham '85
Nichelle Green McGill '89

Elayne Gibbs Jones '88
Shirley Louise Gibbs '90

Dr. Talia McCray '90
Dr. Monique McCray-Osley '91
Dr. Rispba McCray-Garrison '95

Carah Herring 2005
Chemayne Herring 2008

SISTERS-IN-LAW
Valaida Wynn Randolph '62
Audrey Wynn Spence '64
    Dr. Juanita Patience Moss '54

Dr. Lyvonne Mackel Washington '53
    Odella Washington Royster '58
    Alma Washington '60

Dorothy Dixon Morrow '54
Pauline Dixon Jeffries '57

Anna Morrow Bass '55
Sandra Jenkins Dixon '66
Dr. Joyce Martin Dixon '56

COUSINS

Sadie Morgan (?)
   Bettie Neville Cash (ca. 1875)
   Alice Beville Dean 1885

Gilberta Jeffries Mitchell '38
   Dr. Frances Jones Bonner '39

Dr. Frances Jones Bonner '39
   Gilberta Jeffries Mitchell '38
   Mary Mernell Martin '49
   Virginia Jeffries Brown '48
   Maxine Haith O'Kelley '49
   Edna Jeffries Pierce '56
   Dr. Joyce Martin Dixon '56
   Barbara Ann Martin Burchette '58
   Margaret Hayes-Noel '58

Mary Mernell Martin '49
Dr. Joyce Martin Dixon '56
Barbara Ann Martin Burchette '58
   Dr. Frances Jones Bonner '39
   Virginia Jeffries Brown '48
   Maxine Haith O'Kelley '49
   Clara Whitmore Burnette '51

Virginia Jeffries Brown '48
Edna Jeffries Pierce '56
   Grace Jones Knight '42
   Margaret Noel-Hayes '48
   Mary Mernell Martin '49
   Maxine Haith O'Kelley '49
   Dr. Joyce Martin Dixon '56
   Barbara Ann Martin Burchette '58
   Margaret Hayes-Noel '58

Honorable Yvonne Jeffries Johnson '64

Audrose Mackel Banks '49
Dr. Lyvonne Mackel Washington '53
Gwendolyn Mackel Rice '61
Marilyn Hortense Mackel, JD '65
Toi Rice-Jones 2010
    Michelle Mackel Brower '91
    Camille Mackel Alexander '96

Geraldine Kimber Rayford '49
Marilyn Kimber Scales '54
    Ruth Cropp Glenn '48
    Avery Massey '73
    Josefa Bethea Wall '87

Lillian Clarke Lockery '50
    Valerie Dean '69

Lovye Davis Oesterlin '53
    Ruth Reese Fiuczynski '56

Clara Whitmore Burnette '51
    Dorothy Dixon Morrow '54
    Pauline Dixon Jeffries '57
    Peggy Jeffries Foman '54
    Iris Jeffries Morton '61
    Paula Jeffries McKinney '82

Ruth Reese Fiuczynski '56
    Lovye Davis Oesterlin '53
    Margrete Oesterlin Jean-Louis '91

Dorothy Dixon Morrow '54
Pauline Dixon Jeffries '57
Paula Jeffries McKinney '82
    Clara Whitmore Burnette '51
    Peggy Jeffries Foman '54
    Dr. Iris Jeffries Morton '61
    Honorable Yvonne Jeffries Johnson '64
    Francine Dixon Johnson

Marion "Skeeter" Jeffries
Barbara Jean Guy
Dr. Mary D. Jacobs '67
Maxine Haith O'Kelley '49

Carolyn James Johnson '61
   Betty Harley '61

Desretta Veronica McAllister-Harper '62
   Treda Sheryl Berry '73

Maxine Bakeman Womble '62
   Sandra Kelly '63

Robbie Hamlett Dancy '63
   Yasmine Bowens 2011

Charlene Sanders Jones '65
   Dr. Joyce Dunn Garrett '65

Dr. Norma Jones Gray '68
Sylvia Jones' 68
Cheryl Summers '71
Linda Long Rousseau '74

Glenda Dodd Caldwell '72
Dr. Melody Caldwell 2002
   Shelia Hairston Reeves '72

Simone Janniere 2011
   Jordan Smith

GREAT AUNTS AND GREAT NIECES

Audrose Mackel Banks '49
Dr. Lyvonne Mackel Washington '53
Marilyn Hortense Mackel, JD '65
   Toi Rice-Jones 2010

Dr. Juanita Patience Moss '54
Valaida Wynn Randolph '62

Audrey Wynn Spence '64
   Simone Janniere 2011
   Jordan Smith

Dr. Gladys Ashe Robinson '61
Lydia Ashe Mullins '71
   Aisha Jefferson

AUNTS AND NIECES

Bettie Beville Cash ca. 1875
   Lucille Dean McKee '20
   Bessie Dean Clarke Riddick '34

Dr. Margaret Dean Freeman '30
   Lillian Clarke Lockery '50
   Valerie Dean '69

Cathryn Whitmore Morrow (?)
   Clara Whitmore Burnette '51

Gilberta Jeffries Mitchell '38
   Virginia Jeffries Brown '48
   Maxine Haith O'Kelley '49
   Mary Mernelle Martin '49
   Dr. Joyce Martin Dixon '56
   Edna Jeffries Pierce '56
   Barbara Ann Martin Burchette '58

Lisbeth Ellen Edwards Berry '39
   Desretta Veronica McAllister-Harper '62

Grace Jones Knight '42
   Sylvia Jones '68
   Dr. Norma Jones Gray '73
   Linda Long Rousseau '74

Nannie McAdoo Dick '42
   Lola McAdoo '58

Myrtle Alston '44
Dr. Charlotte Alston '54
   Gwendolyn Donnell Cobb '65

Dorothy Dixon Morrow '54
   Paula Jeffries McKinney '82

Dr. Joyce Martin Dixon '56
   Paula Jeffries McKinney '82

Dr. Gladys Ashe Robinson '61
Lydia Ashe Mullin '71
   Felicia Ashe '91

LEGACIES BY THE BUILDINGS

FAMILY LEGACIES

OUR FAMILY OF BENNETT BELLES
Submitted by
Lillian Clarke Lockery '50

Bettie Beville Cash (ca. 1875)
First Female Graduate of Co-ed Bennett College
Sister of Alice Beville Dean 1885
Aunt of Lucille Dean McKee '20, Margaret Dean Freeman '30,
And Bessie Dean Clarke Clark Riddick '34
Great Aunt of Lillian Clarke Lockery '34 and Valerie Dean '69

Seated 3rd from left: Sadie Morgan, Cousin of Betty and Alice Beville

Three Generations of Belles in 1950
l.-r. Lillian Clarke (Lockery) '50, Bessie Dean Clarke Riddick '34, Margaret Dean Freeman '30, Alice Beville Dean 1885

Our Generations – Our College
Submitted by Cousins
Geraldine Kimber Rayford '49 and Josefa Elizabeth Bethea Wall '87

When I, Josefa Elizabeth Bethea Wall, enrolled in Bennett College for Women in 1983, I became a part of the legacy of the connection between my family and the college. Not only was I the twelfth member of my family to decide to obtain my higher education at Bennett, I was also the daughter of a former pastor of St. Matthews Methodist Church where the college was founded. I grew up on the campus. Bennett College was my destiny.

The procession of my family to Bennett commenced with my grandmother, Hallie Elizabeth Brown Cundiff, and a distant male cousin, Leroy Cundiff, attending in the early 1920's. They greatly influenced the awareness of Bennett in the community and the county as a highly prestigious college for qualified young women.

It would be twenty years before the next family member began her matriculation. For the following five decades the procession continued. The most interesting facts about this legacy are the power of relationships and the connection to a small town. As my cousin Geraldine Kimber Rayford and I chronicled our family connection to Bennett, we determined that Mrs. Willa B. McCallum encouraged, counseled and guided students to enroll in the college. As a Bennett graduate, she worked with her husband who served as the principal of the local high school in Boonville, North Carolina. She was a very influential and an effective recruiter.

OUR FAMILY'S PROCESSION TO BENNETT COLLEGE

Hallie E. Brown Cundiff (1920s)
Leroy Cundiff (1920s)

COUSINS graduating from Yadkin County High School in Boonville, N.C., or its successor institution:

Geraldine Kimber Rayford, '49
   First from Yadkin County High School to attend Bennett

Shirley A. Cundiff Bethea, '52
   Daughter of Hallie E. Brown Cundiff
   Mother of Josefa E. Bethea Wall '87
      First cousin of Geraldine Kimber Rayford '49 and Marilyn Kimber Scales '54

Three Generations
Hallie Brown Cundiff
Shirley Cundiff Bethea '52
Josefa Bethea Wall '87

Louise Hinson Russell attended two years, Jonesville, N. C.

Marilyn Kimber Scales '54
   Sister of Geraldine Kimber Rayford '49
      First cousin of Shirley A. Cundiff Bethea '52

Ruth Thomasine Dobson '62
    Aunt of Cynthia Porter '82

Cynthia Porter Russell '82
    Niece of Ruth Thomasine Dobson '62

Ophelia Carter, Jonesville, N.C.
Ruth Cropps Glenn '48, Winston-Salem, N.C.
Avery Massey '73, High Point, N.C.
Josefa E. Bethea Wall '87, Reidsville, N. C.

Alma Mater Bennett – we thy daughters find thee fair;
loyally thy colors bear.

Three Generations

Hallie Brown Cundiff (?)
Shirley Cundiff Bethea '52
Josefa Bethea Wall '87

In Memoriam

My Mother and My Sisters
Novella Jeffries Martin   Mary Mernelle Martin, '49
Barbara Ann Martin Burchette, '58

Submitted by
Dr. Joyce Martin Dixon '56/ '81

One tradition in both the Martin and Jeffries families was for females to attend Bennett College. My youngest sister Barbara and I didn't wait for the College part. We were students in Bennett's pre-school and if that were not enough, our family lived on Bennett Street. Dad, a barber, worked in a shop on Gorrell Street and a relative, Dr. Jones (Prexy) and his friendly wife lived half way between our home and the barber shop. We made a path from Bennett Street through the Jones' yard to attend school or deliver Dad's lunch. I doubt if anyone explained to us what being a college president meant. We just loved receiving the warm greetings and hugs from Dr. and Mrs. Jones while strolling across their lawn. Twelve years later we would have received a lengthy lecture if one shoe had touched a blade of grass on or around the campus.

Novella Jeffries Martin

Dates of Mother's attendance at Bennett are unknown; however, fond recollections of the time she was there are etched in my mind. Mother, Dad and Mernelle were born in Burlington, North Carolina, and moved to Greensboro in 1932, two years before I was born. Prior to relocating, Mother had lived a full life as a teacher in Martin's School, a one room school house. We loved to hear her tell stories about the "olden days" because they were so different from life, especially school, in Greensboro.

For example, mature boys were responsible for keeping the wood box full because the stove was their only source of heat. And, older children were instructed to protect the younger ones, who in turn were taught to respect and obey older students and teachers. Mother's youngest brother was one of her students and many other children were related.

Our Mom attended every church and school program in which the three of us performed, and there were many. I have often thought the word "diversified "was defined to describe her. Professional and volunteer activities included: Home economist (she taught farmers' wives how to utilize their crops); registrar of our precinct; a member of a garden club and ardent supporter of the March of Dimes (MOD). Mernelle, Barbara and I were given our very own MOD collection cans, assigned neighborhood homes that were safe to approach, and marched right along beside her.

She was an excellent seamstress, compassionate beyond compare, and a good conversationalist. Then, she turned eighty! We witnessed a change that rivaled a 4th of July fireworks celebration. Did you see the movie *Driving Miss Daisy?* Mother became Miss Daisy. Her entertaining, and often overwhelming antics, left fond memories. Two things remained constant: the love of her family and, after 80, her role as "Leader of the Pack." She passed away peacefully in 1991 in Merritt Island, Florida.

Mary Mernelle Martin '49

Mernelle fit the profile of an older sister and reigned seriously. I shall never forget the time she was taking a child psychology class at Bennett and complained to mother, "Joyce and Barbara are different from children in the book." Mernelle was pretty, smart, an outstanding speaker, and a "tattle teller." Can you imagine your sister being a librarian at the college you attended? Oops, I'm getting ahead of myself.

My oldest sibling could have easily had a second career as a comedienne. She learned the alphabet at an early age. When Mother and friends spelled words, Mernelle wrote them on the chalk board under the bed and asked Dad about the words when he returned from work.

As a youngster, her goal in life was to become an usher. She was a born leader and developed an award-winning routine for classmates who majored in early childhood education. Guess who was always the teacher? Finally, the time arrived to practice the skills she had learned in the classroom. My sister decided on "Day One" that she had chosen the wrong profession. Those little adorable innocent children also flunked the child psychology textbook test. Her minor, library science, became her major. She attended Indiana University that fall and earned a Master's Degree in library science, then returned for another Master's, this time in audio visual aids.

Mernelle's first job was at the Bennett College Library, then Dudley High School, Fort Valley State College, and back to the Greensboro City Library. She was in great demand as a speaker for a variety of programs in and around the community, a member of Delta Sigma Theta Sorority, Inc., and other organizations. All of her involvement led to a fruitful life, but came in second to being a loving aunt for the niece and three nephews she adored. Mernelle was diagnosed with Alzheimer's disease at the age of fifty-six and moved to Florida with me where she lived for ten years.

Barbara Ann Martin Burchette '58

When Barbara was born, Mernelle did not want neighbors or friends to visit because she declared, "That is the ugliest baby I have ever seen." Barbara didn't wear that label long. Our youngest sister was Miss Dudley High, Dudley's May Queen, and Mary, the Mother of Jesus, in church and school nativity scenes. She was also my best friend. Her disposition matched her beauty. People still comment on my attractive sisters. Mother told me to develop my personality.

Barbara, the agile one, danced her way into the hearts of the community, Bennett's student body, faculty, and staff. Instead of a major in the arts, she, too, chose early childhood education as her major and taught first grade in Warren County where she loved every child as though he and she were her very own.

Barbara's instructors at our Alma Mater were an enviable team that is seldom witnessed. Requirements of future teachers were taught with originality, skill and the common sense approach for instructing bright-eyed students, many of whom would initially have problems being away from their mothers all day long. "Stay-at-home-moms" were the "norm" in those days.

When Barbara finished Bennett, she quickly engaged in an acquired talent that became a charming part of her life: usefulness was recognized in everything, whether near or far, and I do mean everything. Family and friends were given lists of items to save for use in her classroom that included things we normally discarded, like the small plastic trays that hold fruit and vegetables in supermarkets and empty paper towel tubes. I always hoped the boxes we gently packed and mailed would not be delivered to the wrong address.

Barbara married Bennie Robin Burchette, Sr., an Aggie, and they had two sons. Bennie Jr. lives in Germany with his wife, Adrianne, and two of their three children. The third works in Georgia. Reginald lives in Oklahoma with wife, Marquette, and four children. Barbara was also diagnosed with Alzheimer's disease. She passed away in Warrenton, North Carolina, in 1994.

The Mackel Family Legacies

Three Generations of Mackel Belles in 2010
r.-l.: Audrose Mackel Banks '49, Dr. Lyvonne Mackel Washington '53,
Gwendolyn Mackel Rice '61,
Marilyn Hortense Mackel, Esq. '65
Cousins: l.-r.: Toi Rice-Jones 2010, Michelle Mackel Brower '91
Missing: Camille Mackel Alexander '95

For three generations Mackel Belles have been making "her-story" at Bennett College from the mid-40s to 2010. We are four sisters, a granddaughter of one sister, and two cousins.

Our family legacy has been preserved in *Rosetta: An Autobiography* [8] by our mother Rosetta Libian Lloyd Mackel, an educator and homemaker. Even though for many years she would suffer from severe rheumatoid arthritis, she persevered to document important events and chronologies for future generations of the Mackel family.

She wrote about our father, Dr. Audley Maurice Mackel, a dentist and the son of a Natchez, Mississippi, funeral director. Both of our parents were consummate activists in their respective ways.

For example, Daddy was a civil rights leader who was active in the NAACP, serving on its national board during Brown vs. Board of Education. He was also the first President of the Bennett College National Parents' Association.

Mother was a child advocate, fighting for better schools and recreational facilities for black children. She organized the first Girl Scout Troops (black or white) in Natchez, majorette troops, the high school band, Parent-Teacher Associations, and advocated for better recreational facilities and health services before all-white Boards. She also founded the Women's Auxiliary of the National Dental Association.

With our family roots in the South we knew segregation well. Our father would not allow us to attend the "separate-but-equal" Mississippi public schools and so the first four of us attended boarding schools.

Due to threats because of his work with the NAACP, Daddy decided to leave Natchez for the safety of his family. We moved to Chicago where Marilyn, the youngest, would attend an integrated public school.

So after learning about our parents' activities even prior to the Civil Rights Movement of the '60s, one would have no doubt why this picture exists.

Gwendolyn Mackel Rice '61
Civil Rights Movement Participant
Greensboro, N.C.

MORE LEGACIES

Three Generations [9]
l.-r.- *Geneva Averett-Short '58, Constance Blackman '86, Zepplyn Stepp Humphrey '35/ '55*

Three Generations
Seated: Doris Young Baldwin '48,
Daughter Linda Baldwin Herring '74,
and Granddaughters (left) Chemayne Herring 2008 &
Carah Herring 2006 (right)

KINSTON, N.C. LEGACIES

Mother and Daughter
Lisbeth Ellen Edwards Berry '39
Treda Sheryl Berry '73

Patrick Sisters:
Peggy Eakins '67 and
Veda Cook '70

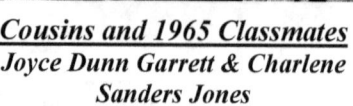

Cousins and 1965 Classmates
Joyce Dunn Garrett & Charlene Sanders Jones

Two Sisters in the Bennett College Choir 1950-51
(Holgate Library)
4th from right Jeanne Martin Brayboy '50;
3rd up steps on right- Thomasina Martin Brayboy '53

SISTERS

L: Tommy
R: Jeanne

SISTERS

(At Left)
Geraldine Kimber Rayford '49
&
Marilyn Kimber Scales '54

(At Right)
Alberta Copeland Lewis '51
&
Mildred Copeland Simms '54

Loretta Canty Vann '78
&
Esther Canty-Barnes
JD '76

Cousins at First Teaching Job
Peggy Jeffries Foman '54 & Dorothy Dixon Morrow '54

Mother & Daughters
l.-r.: Elayne Gibbs Jones '88, Margarie Mays Gibbs '75; Shirley Gibbs '90

Mother & Daughter
Glenda Dodd Caldwell '72
Dr. Melody Caldwell 2002

Two Generations
E. Adell Taylor Dowdy'62, Adrienne Dowdy Swittenberg'85,
Hazeline Taylor Harris '59

Sisters Wearing the Obligatory Bennett College White & Black Shirtwaist "Uniforms" (1960)
Audrey Wynn Spence '64, niece Brenda Moss, Valaida Wynn Randolph '62

Great Aunts & Great Niece 2007
Juanita Patience Moss '54, Simone Janniere '11, Valaida Wynn Randolph '62

Mother & Daughter
Kimberly Buck-Rouse '94 and Dr. Judith Brooks-Buck '71

Mother & Three Daughters in 2007[10]
l.-r.:Pensal Winston McCray '63, Dr. Rispah McCray-Garrison '95, Dr. Monique McCray-Osley '91, Dr. Talia McCray '90 and Monique's two daughters: Giselle (left) and Melanie (right)

Mother *Dyora Thomas Kinsey '75*
&
Daughter *Dyora Kinsey '99*

May Court 1954
Harris Twins: *First Row Dorothy & Gwendolyn '57*

Mother *Frances Lucas Enzlow '39*
&
Daughter
(photo courtesy of Reba Burruss-Barnes)

Sisters
Yulonda Green Cunningham '85
Nichelle Green McGill '89

Two Generations of Belles
Grandmother *Gwendolyn Mackel Rice '61 with*
Grandchildren and Great grandson
Granddaughter *Toi Rice-Jones 2010 with son*

SPECIAL BENNETT IDEALS

<u>Ellease Randall Colston '53 With Golden Belles of the Class of 1941</u>

PHENOMENAL "BENNETT IDEALS"

These thirteen Belles make up just a miniscule number of the many Bennett "Ideals" since Bennett became a college for just women in 1926. These Belles have been our mentors by setting the pace for us and we have looked up to them down through the years. Admiring their devotion to Alma Mater, we try to duplicate their fervor. Consider that due to their recruitment efforts and financial support, many students have been able to matriculate to Bennett College, even from foreign lands. They represent our corporate legacy of Bennett Belles.

1. **Helen Ellison Newberry McDowell '24, Washington, D.C.**
2. **Juanita Wells '37, Greensboro, N.C.**
3. **Dr. Frances Jones Bonner '39, Boston, MA**
4. **Dr. Margaret Dean Freeman '30, Philadelphia, PA**
5. **DuDonna Tate '39, Washington, D.C.**
6. **Edith Taylor Sheppard '46, Washington, D.C.**
7. **Nurse Alise Trammell '32, Greensboro, N.C.**
8. **Dr. Charlotte Alston '54, Greensboro, N C**
9. **Hattie Bailey '38, Chester, Pennsylvania**
10. **Lisbeth Ellen Edwards Berry '39, Kinston, N.C.**
11. **Rose Mae Withers Catchings '32, Montclair, N.J.**
12. **Zepplyn Short Humphrey '35/'55, Greensboro, N.C.**
13. **Ellease Randall Colston '53, Greensboro, N.C.**

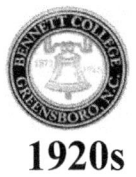

1920s

In Memoriam
Lucy Anderson Sadler '23
(1900-2007)

Excerpts from a taped interview in 2002, Coleman Falls, Virginia
"I" = the interviewers: Alvah Taylor Beander '73 and Juanita Patience Moss '54

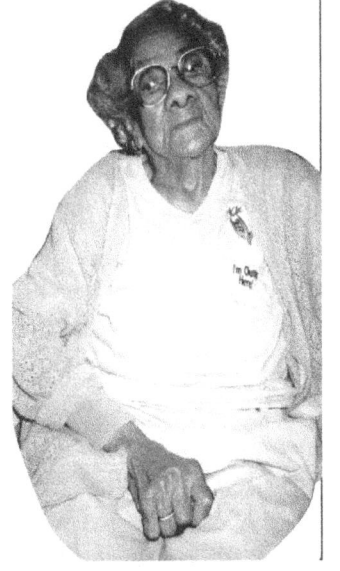

I. We are at the home of Mrs. Lucy Anderson Sadler, Class of 1923, Bennett College.
 Now, Mrs. Sadler, you will have to talk very loudly into the recorder so we can ask you a lot of pertinent questions.
 Okay.
I. Tell us where you lived when you were a little girl.
 Let's see. I was born in Tennessee.
I. Is that where you were living when you went to Bennett College?
 No, I was living here then. You see, my father had purchased 300 acres of land right over this mountain. That was my father's property.
I. Was this house next door to his house? Is that where you grew up?
 No, I said it was over the mountain from here. We lived in a big nine room house and we had 300 acres of land.
I. Your father was a farmer, then?
 Yes, my father was a farmer.
I. How did your father get the money to buy this big farm?

He was born over in back on the farm in Amherst. Over in Elon, I guess it is. Way back in the mountains somewhere. The house is right across the river.

My father said he was about 16 or 17 years old. He's always been a very thoughtful good person. He was real religious from a child up. Taught Sunday School and watched over children all of his life.

So about 16, he was sitting there one morning and said, "Lord, here I am. I have nothing. I have just my life before me and I want You to point me someplace to go to make some money."

So in talking to people he found out that down in Tennessee was where they were digging coal. So he went to the coal mine in Tennessee. In Nashville.

<u>I. And that's where he made his money?</u>
Yes. He had about 300 acres of land.
<u>I. He was a slave?</u>
Yes. He was in slavery until about 9.
<u>I. In what year did he die?</u>
I think he was at about 85.
<u>I. When did your mother die?</u>
My mother was 89.
<u>I. Did you have brothers and sisters?</u>
There were 14 of us.
<u>I. Where were you? What number child?</u>
The 6th
<u>I. Okay, now we are going to ask you the big question? How did you get enough money to go to college? What inspired you?</u>
I always wanted to go. We had a school teacher from Clarkstown. Her name was Ruth Tape and she was teaching school where we lived. She was boarding.

She said, "I'm going to another school when I leave here." And she was going to take up college down at Bennett College. So she went and took up two more years for her education. She was a very educated person. So she took it up and then she said, "I'd love for some of those children to come to Bennett because they were always smart children and I believe some of them would be good children in college."

And so she then invited us to try to see if we could come to Bennett College. And then my sister Lillian and I went to Bennett. We graduated in 1923.

I. And it was co-ed at that time? Boys and girls?

It was girls and boys when I was there. They changed it after that.

I. Right. 1926. Then it became a women's college.

Yes. I left in '23.

I. Now, when you went there had you finished high school?

Oh, no.

I. So you finished high school at Bennett?

No, I didn't finish high school. I went right on into my years-- like the first year of college.

I. What did you study there?

Well, we had everything there. Mean dormitory matrons.

I. Who was the president?

President Trigg. He lived in Clarkstown. He asked my Daddy would he send some children to Bennett College. And that's how we got to Bennett.

I. After Dr. Trigg left did Dr. Jones come right after?

Yes, I believe he did.

I. Did you ever meet him?

No, I don't think I ever met him. I went there once, but I think he had gone. They had a woman who was the president.

I. Now, your sister went to Bennett, too.

Yes.

I. Was she older or younger than you?

She was older. She's gone now.

I. After you finished from Bennett what did you do for a living?

Well, I taught school several years and after that I married and I didn't do very much after that. I worked in a hospital. I'd done enough.

I. Did you have 14 children, too?

Oh, my God, no. I had five kids. One son and four daughters. All living but one.

I. So, when you taught school what grades were you teaching?

I taught the third grade, but I taught by myself. I had 40-some students.

I. 40 students?

Yes, I got enough of school or something.

I. And they were great kids in those days.

I had to work on them with nothing but a switch. I was told that one girl is as mean as the devil since she was little. She was mean, but I didn't let her get away with nothing. No.

Another little boy got mad one day and shut the door cause I wouldn't let him go home when he wanted to. I said when the time comes, "I'm not going to let you go."

When the time came I wouldn't let him go. He was the last one. He slammed that door like he was going to break it off the handles. I said, "Okay."

The next day I told him, "You stay in because you about broke the door."

He said, "Well, we did break one off at home."

I told him, "That was at home. That's not here. You're not going to break any doors here. Uh-uh." School is too tough.

I. How did you get on to this property?

My husband.

I. This was your husband's property? What did he do?

He was just a farmer. He said he worked with electricity. I don't know. He did something 'cause he was a pretty smart man.

I. Tell us what Bennett was like when you went there.

Oh, it was a nice place.

I. What buildings were there?

They had the boys' dormitory and the house. The dining hall was off by itself. We didn't have a laundry. We had to wash our own clothes and iron them. But finally they got one and we moved away from that. But it was nice and I loved it. I had a big time. Some very strict matrons.

I. That never changed.

We had one named Miss Hippard. She was the meanest woman I ever seen in my life.

I. Where did you eat?
   We ate in the dining hall.
I. Was the chapel there?
   Yes. People up North donated the money.
I. Yes, the Methodist Church. Did you have a specialty when you graduated or did you get a diploma for teaching?
   Yes, I got a diploma for teaching. I went back to summer school for two summers.
I. When you would go to school did you go in a car or by train?
   We went on the train. Get on the train at 7:00 and get into Greensboro at 5 o'clock. I didn't like that.
I. Did you get on in Danville?
   No. We got on here in Lynchburg and when we got on it was about 7 o'clock in the morning and we got into Greensboro it was round about 5 o'clock in the evening. We rode the train all day. Now you can do it in two hours.
I. And you had to sit in a segregated coach, of course.
   Yes. A lot of girls got on in Reidsville after Christmas after the holiday. Had a good time.
I. Did you room with your sister?
   Yes, we always roomed together. One year there were nine of us in one room. When we got there we were a little late going in. But when we got there, they said, "Oh, yes. Let them come on in." And so nine of us stayed in that room. And we loved each other. We had one cot and three beds.
I. Was that Kent?
   No. Kent was not the name of our building. It was something else. Because Kent Hall was where these white people wanted to take care of some of the girls. That building was Kent Hall.
I. It was close to the street.
   Yes, because the white women stayed over there.
I. What white women?
   They had white matrons who took care of the children.
I. Children?
   Yes, like the matron of the thing.

I. So they stayed there?
Yes, some parents would rather their children stay with the white people . I didn't want to do that.
I. Was the library there? Carnegie Library?
Yes.
I. Did they take etiquette lessons? Or did you have tennis?
No, they didn't have tennis. We played volleyball. The boys played baseball. I wished we had that. I loved tennis.
I. Did you learn how to pour tea? Set a table?
No. No.
I. That must have come later because Bennett girls had to learn how to pour tea.
Yes, it must have been.
The only thing that used to vex me was when the school closed they would have that big banquet for all the people to come back. The older people. They'd be eating ice cream until 3 o'clock in the morning.

We was waiting on tables. They'd put big platters out. I could hardly carry them. I was a "little bit of somewhere." I would lift those big platters. My back hurt so much. In the morning I was so tired I couldn't walk.
I. Did you have to clean the dormitories?
Yes, we had to clean our rooms because they had inspections. I've see some people come and take a handkerchief. The girls would say, "Dust everything nice because they're coming." You'd have to take up something quick and dust.
I. What were the services like at the chapel?
Too much. Too many of them.
I. That didn't change, either. There were always girls who felt that way. Did you have Sunday vespers?
Oh, yes. And Wednesday night. She'd say, "Come on, girls."
She'd have us singing. I said, "Oh, me."
I hated vespers. Had to go.
I. Did you have dances?
No. No.
I. What did you do for social life?
They would have social things for us. Some kind of marches.

I think they had a few games.
I. Were the boys and girls allowed to do things together?
   Yes, in the chapel they'd let you.
I. In the chapel? There wasn't much you could do in the chapel.
   I remember once when we were in the senior class we wanted to go to the theater one night. There was 12 of us. We were seniors. One here and one there.
   We were well guarded tonight. Well guarded tonight.
I. Were you allowed to go off campus in the daytime by yourself?
   No, but I slipped off a few times.
I. You sneaked off?
   I had to go off. I had to go away a little while. Some girls lived on High Street.
   My sister said, "They're going to catch us." I said, "No, I had a good way of going off and getting back home."
I. What did you eat when you were down there?
   Gravy and grits in the morning. And then they served cabbage and beef. I had some beef that a-liked to kill me. I was never so sick in my life. We had gone to St. Matthew's. I guess it was the largest Methodist church in Greensboro. We didn't have school for two or three days.
   Bennett was a great school.
   We closed this delightful interview by reading to Mrs. Sadler the newspaper article "Boycott of '37."

Alvah Taylor Beander '73
Charter President of the Northern Virginia
Chapter of Bennett College Alumnae
2008 Achievement Awardee

To whom it may concern. Greeting;

Helen T. Ellison

Having honorably completed the High School course of study presented by Bennett College passed required examination therein and sustained a good Moral Character is awarded this DIPLOMA.

In Testimony Wereof, WE affix our signatures together with the public seal of the Institution this 28th day of May in the year of Our Lord 1924.

Frank Trigg, President
S.A. Peeler, President of the Trustees

(Courtesy of Juanita Page Cooke '52)

In Memoriam
Helen Ellison Newberry McDowell
(1904-2010)

Saving More Than She Spent
1924 Graduate Contributes $26,000.00 to Bennett College [11]

"With her mind set on getting an education, 15 year old Helen Ellison arrived at Bennett in 1920, from the small town of Abingdon, Va. Bennett was a co-ed high school at the time, and a high school education was not free. Just to be able to attend—a dream fulfilled-- cost her savings from cleaning an 11 room house at 25 cents per day, the dollars from her father selling his interest in his home place, and $26.00 from her two older brothers, who walked 30 miles to contribute their entire first month's salary of $13.00 each from their labors in a Virginia salt mine.

'That's why I help anybody who wants to go to school. Going to school is the only thing I ever really wanted to do,' said Helen E. Newberry McDowell, now 96 and living in Washington, D.C. She was the oldest girl of 14 children born to Lucy C. and Samuel Fletcher, and Helen said their family was as poor as Job's turkey (a turkey so poor he had to lean against a fence to gobble)."

In 2004 Helen Ellison McDowell endowed a scholarship at Bennett with a gift of $100,000.00.[12]

SOME MEMBERS OF THE CLASS OF 1924
(From the photograph album of Helen Ellison Newberry McDowall)

Helen Ellison

Bertanna Diggs (1921)

Helen J. Watson & Helen J. Ellison

Vertie Lee Bailey

FAVORITE BCFW PRESIDENTS
1926-2012

9th Dr. David D. Jones

10th Dr. Willa B. Player

11th Dr. Isaac Miller, Jr.

12th Dr. Gloria R. Scott

14th Dr. Johnnetta B. Cole

15th Dr. Julianne Malveaux

THE BENNETT IDEAL[13]
(Words by Carrie Robinson '33—Tune "Peggy O'Neil")

Bennett's Ideal
Is a girl who is real,
She's a friend ever loyal and true;
In work and in play,
By her simple way,
She makes herself known to you.
CHORUS
If she greets you with a smile,
She's the Bennett Ideal;
Always doing things worthwhile,
That's the Bennett Ideal.
If she places her cares on the shelf,
Thinks of others far more than herself
If from the start
She has love in her heart,
Then, she's the Bennett Ideal.

You've heard it said
She's a girl who's well bred,
For her college she'll stand any test;
Her motto is skill,
Her creed is good will,
And here's how you know her best;
CHORUS
If she smiles through thick and thin
She's the Bennett Ideal;
If she strives wholehearted to win,
She's the Bennett Ideal;
If she's honest and willing to share,
If she's eager to do and to dare,
Pep and vitality;
Sweet personality;
She's the Bennett Ideal.

1930s

"Prexy's First Class" 1930 [14]
First Four-Year Graduates

25th Class Reunion in 1955 [15]
l.-r.:
Maggie Simpson Matthews,
Alma Tarpley Taylor,
Ruth Artis Whitfield,
Dr. Margaret Dean Freeman

[16]

l.-r.: Ruth, Margaret, Maggie, Alma

Dorothy Ann Strothers Kennedy '30
26 Riverview, Lansing, MI 4915
_517-484-4719_

(Her birthday is August 4th, the same as of President Barack Obama who paid her a visit on her 100th when he was still an Illinois Senator.)

5-21-2010 [17]

Dear Juanita,

This letter is to let you know I have received my copy of "Tell Me Why Dear Bennett" and want you to know how much I am enjoying it. I also thank you for being so thoughtful to personally send it to me.

I have been recalling so many memories that I had forgotten as classmates, teachers, buildings. In fact I didn't remember my classmates that I graduated with. I am concerned why I didn't leave any photos of myself. I also wonder why I was not listed as a graduate. I am also trying to recall the names of my teachers. I also wonder how many of my classmates, teachers are still alive. I have so many questions.

Juanita, I know this is a rambling letter, but I am so thankful to you for having the dedication, vision, and patience to compile this history. Thank you for finding me (smile). You have done an outstanding job. The article you did on me makes me feel very happy and proud. I do wish I could have the opportunity to talk to you more about Bennett. However I do plan to keep in touch So thanks again.

          Love,
          Dorothy A. Kennedy '30
          (Your Bennett Sister)

In Memoriam

Rose Mae Withers Catchings '32
(1915-2009)
Former Trustee

Warm Corner In A Wide World

Catchings' Roles: Global, Local

BY DOUGLAS ELDRIDGE

Rose Mae Withers Catchings, a woman of considerable intellect and grace, has made the world her neighborhood during a long career with the YWCA and the Methodist Church.

Times photo by Douglas Eldridge

AMONG HER SOUVENIRS—Rose Withers Catchings stands in front of her fireplace, decorated with a painting of a Singapore street, a carving of a Zimbabwe chief, photos of grandchildren, and other artifacts from her years of work around the world.

Rose Mae Withers Catchings '32 in her Montclair, N.J. home [18]

An African Visitor With Rose Catchings on Bennett's Campus

Rose Mae Withers Catchings Personal Development Complex at Bennett College for Women

During the celebration of its 103rd anniversary, October 7-10, 1977, Rose Mae Withers Catchings '32 keynoted an assembly. A Bennett College trustee at the time, she was also the Executive Secretary, Ministry of Women's Office, World Division of the Board of Global Ministries of the United Methodist Church.

ZEPPLYN HUMPHRY '35/'55
REMEMBERING SOME OUTSTANDING PEOPLE ASSOCIATED WITH BENNETT COLLEGE

Adams, Dr. Alma- came to Bennett in 1973 as Art Director. Bringing many valuable skills with her, she has developed the Fine Arts Program into a variety of arts, including obtaining grants from many areas such as renovating Steele Hall into an Arts Museum on the top level and

Dr. Alma Adams

offices, classrooms and pottery facilities on the lower level. She has served on the North Carolina State Legislative Committee as a representative from Guilford County and has received funds from the state for Bennett.

Allen, Dr. Van S.- a biology professor who enhanced many Belles **to excel in their careers in medicine and other health care areas.**

Alston, Rev.- sent to Guilford County to establish a Methodist Episcopal Church in Greensboro, N.C. in 1865 in the community of Warnersville. After learning that the church was interested in establishing a school for Black ministers, St. Matthews offered it as the site.

In July, the announcement was made that a school to train Black ministers and young women as teachers would be built. So in October 1973, Bennett Seminary was opened in the unplastered basement of the church. Nearly 70 students enrolled the first year.

Throughout the northern Methodist Conferences, Bennett became well-known and through the generosity of a wealthy benefactor, Lyman Bennett, land was purchased for with $10,000.00 in southeast Greensboro.

Blair, Jean (Mrs. Jean Howard) '64- sister of Ezell Blair, one of the "A&T Four," served on the Bennett College Trustee Board.

Breathett, Dr. George- was a professor in Social Studies and a writer of Federal grants for many programs for the college. He was married to Florence Simpson '53 who worked in the Registrar's Office.

Brown, Betty '72- as the first Black and female to serve at the Public Defender's Office in Guilford County and later appointed as Attorney/Assistant Public Defender of Guilford Country.

Caldwell, Rev. Gilbert Haven, Sr.- one of the first graduates from the seminary and later became Dean of the Seminary part of the institution. His son, Gilbert, Jr., married a Bennett Belle, Grace Dungee '57.

***Eady, Fred*-** built up the theater program where Belles were inspired to perform, adding to the Performing Arts of the college. His wife Mary Mayfield '48 became the college registrar where she had worked as a student.

***Jones, Bishop Robert*-** brother of President David D. Jones, was able to raise funds from the southern Methodist Conferences. Jones Hall is named for him.

***Jones, Mrs. Susie Williams*-** the wife of Dr. David Dallas Jones. She served as a counselor as there were none then. Soon after the freshmen enrolled, Mrs. Jones would know their first names. As we passed her house where she would be sweeping her front walk or sitting on the porch, she would seek to talk with us. The President's house sat near the center of the campus at that time.

***Mack, Dr. Perry*-** added to this list with whom many still refer to him as a mentor.

***Peeler, Rev. Silas*-** another graduate of the Seminary, became the 9th Bennett College president after having taught for four years. His sister Joyce was a quartet member in 1920 and his granddaughter Yvonne is also an alumna.

***Player, Dr. Willa B.*-** French and Latin instructor, as well as the registrar in early years. She served in many other capacities and was active with students and alumnae, working with the Alumnae Association, local and national to encourage connection to the college following graduation. In 1955 she succeeded Dr. David D. Jones as president

Dr. Willa B. Player

Rogers, Lawrence- first superintendent of the college in 1929 and his wife Clara was the first dietician. They served through the years of their daughter Mary Ann's graduation in 1954 and even longer.

l.-r. Mrs. Susie W. Jones, Lawrence Rogers, Clara Rogers, Mary Ann Rogers Scarlette '54

Sayles, Dr. James and Mrs. Frederica Potts Sayles '47- were the cashier and office manager. They also supervised work-study students. Frank Bailey was the Account Manager. Dr. Sayles served as Dean of the Science Department for several years and after his retirement he was asked to remain serving as writer of grants to support that department.

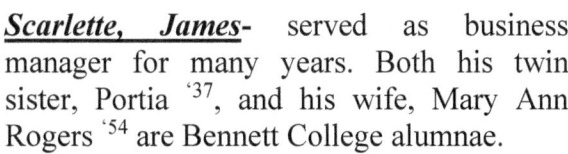

Scarlette, James- served as business manager for many years. Both his twin sister, Portia '37, and his wife, Mary Ann Rogers '54 are Bennett College alumnae.

James Scarlette

Smith, Mrs. Minnie B.- taught social science and later added Financial Aid. Later she was Dean of Women. She, like Mrs.

Mamie B. McLaurin, was a mother to many girls. "Ma Mac"/ "Mom Mac" was resident director and dorm director of Pfeiffer Hall for a while. Many faculty and staff served dual roles during the early days due to a lack of funds to hire for those positions.

Trent, William "Bill"- became a professor and the basketball coach in 1934. For two years Bennett College was the champion female team in North Carolina, even when playing against a professional team from Philadelphia, Penna.

Bill was appointed by Dr. F. J. Patterson to become the first director of the United Negro College Fund (UNCF). After retiring from Time-Life in 1976, he returned to Bennett as a consultant to President Isaac H. Miller, Jr. in the Office of Institutional Advancement.

During the late 1920s, his sister Altona Trent-Johns taught music at Bennett, was director of the choir, and traveled with President David D. Jones and the quartet to Black churches and northern Methodist Conferences to solicit funds and to recruit students.

The Women's Home Missionary Society supported Bennett College and in later years White Methodists would become trustee members who raised funds. Among them were Henry and Anne Pfeiffer whose Pfeiffer Foundation was responsible for several buildings, including the chapel built in 1941.

Mrs. Henry Pfeiffer
and Dr. David Dallas Jones
(1936) [19]

In Memoriam

Pauline Celeste Waters Smith '35
1915 - 1997
FIRST ALUMNA TRUSTEE
Submitted by her granddaughter
Robyn Smith
8140 Green Tree Drive, Elkridge, MD 21075
msualumni33@verizon.net

Pauline Celeste Waters Smith '35

My grandmother adored Bennett College and I remember her telling almost everybody who spent any time around her that she had gone there and how much she treasured the experience. I believe her father knew the President, Dr. Jones, and my grandmother remained friends with him long after graduation.

A very studious, serious straight-laced woman, she was everything you would imagine about the daughter of a Methodist minister. She recalled that the girls were required to wear hats and gloves to go to services. One of her classmates, the late Almira Wilson, remembered that there were only about 250-300 girls at Bennett during that time.

APPLICATION FOR ADMISSION
to
BENNETT COLLEGE FOR WOMEN
(Please fill blank in your own handwriting)

Date of application _____
Full name   Pauline Celeste Waters
Post office   Salisbury Maryland
Street and No. or R.F.D. No.   315 - E. Broad St.
Place of birth   Still Pond, Md.
Name of Parent or Guardian   Rev. & Mrs. Daniel Waters
Occupation   Household duties
Church affiliation   John Wesley M.E. Church
School last attended   Salisbury Colored High School
Highest grade completed   4th year High School
Name and address of Principal   Prof. Charles H. Chipman
211 - 2nd St., Salisbury Maryland
Course you wish to pursue _____
Time you expect to enter   September 14, 1931
Age   16   Condition of health _____
Who is responsible for your monthly bills?   Rev. Daniel Waters
315 E. Broad St., Salisbury Md.
Who is responsible for your behavior?   Rev. & Mrs. Daniel Waters
315 E. Broad St., Salisbury Md.

PHYSICIAN'S CERTIFICATE

The above named applicant is personally known to me and I certify that she is free from contagious diseases and in good health.

G. Herbert Dembly, M.D.
504 E. Church St. Salisbury, Md.

The above named applicant is known to be a person of good moral character and upright habits.

Signed   (Rev.) D. G. Waters   Pastor
Address of Pastor   315 E. Broad St Salisbury, Md.
Name and address of teacher   Mrs. Jeanette P. Chipman
211 - 2nd St., Salisbury Md.

My grandmother Pauline lived in Jones Hall and on Saturday nights "company" could visit and the girls could go on chaperoned dates. Many of the girls had boyfriends at North Carolina A&T, but my grandmother would have none of that! She was very religious, even back then: didn't drink and didn't party the way the others did.

When it was time to go home, everybody would take the train. Grandmother often told the story about how she was offered a job at a private Methodist boarding school in Jacksonville (Boylan-Haven) after graduation in 1935, and at the behest of the Dr. Jones, she went. She promised her parents she would stay in Florida only one year—but then she met her husband and ended up staying 50 years! She was very proud of being the first Bennett alumna to serve on the Trustee Board. I have included her original application to Bennett, as well as some other memorabilia.

She taught in the public schools of Duval County, Florida, for over 40 years. She was married to William Smith, who went on to become a prominent businessman in the Jacksonville community of the 1940's and 1950's, owning two pharmacies and a beauty products distributorship.

Pauline earned a Master's Degree in Education from New York University in 1960 and was active with Delta Sigma Theta Sorority, Inc. and several church related groups throughout her life. She loved God and her beloved Methodism. She enjoyed writing and was a dynamic teacher and public speaker. If my grandmother were any example of what a Bennett woman is, she was a fine example indeed.

She wrote a book about her life called *By God's Grace: A Personal Testimony.* Here is an excerpt:

"Of course, I was the first child in my family to go to college in 1931. I was sixteen years old.

The influence of a family friend and distant relative led me to attend Bennett College, a Methodist College in Greensboro, North Carolina instead of going to Morgan College in Baltimore, Maryland or Howard University in Washington, D. C. The clothes I took to Bennett were the same ones I brought home when I graduated with the exception of one new dress and one new coat.

Achieving scholastically seemed to be a natural thing for me to do I suppose out of respect for my parents' desires and accomplishments, but also because I believed God expected me to do my best in every way. Strangely enough, material things did not matter so much, though I am sure in the back of my mind I wanted a good husband, a happy family and a comfortable home.

I received financial aid by holding jobs all four of my years in college. There is one F on my report card because it was so hard for me to get out of the dining hall time that I over cut gym class. However, lack of new clothes and being a working student did not embarrass me or stop me from achieving. I was an honor student all four years, majoring in biology with a minor in mathematics. In fact I had been an honor student through elementary and high school. I was confident that my ability came from God. I also participated in the college choir, the drama club, student government, and the college paper."

Members of the Bennett College board of trustees. Left to right, front row: Mrs. W. H. C. Goode, Sidney, Ohio; Mrs. W. Raymond Brown, Herkimer, N. Y.; Mrs. Harry E. James, New York; Dr. Player and Bishop Edgar A. Love, of Baltimore, vice-chairman; second row: Mrs. Robert K. Gordon, Dillon, S. C.; Mrs. J. G. Meidenbauer, Buffalo, N. Y.; Mrs. H. C. Black, Johnson City, Tenn.; Mrs. Millard L. Robinson, New York; Mrs. J. N. Rodeheaver, Winona Lake, Ind., and Bishop Robert E. Jones, Sr., Waveland, Miss.; third row: Miss Muriel Day, New York; Miss Margaret Forsyth, New York; Mrs. Julius W. Cone, Greensboro; Mrs. Pauline Waters Smith, Jacksonville, Fla.; C. Everett Bacon, New York; and Dr. Prince A. Taylor, New Orleans; back row: Dr. J. A. Tarpley, Greensboro; Dr. Frederick D. Patterson, New York; and Dr Earl V. Tolley, Binghamton, N. Y.

1955 Trustee Board [20]

BENNETT COLLEGE
Greensboro, North Carolina March 1

OFFICE OF THE PRESIDENT

My dear Mrs Smith:

This is a letter of inquiry. If we should be able to get you nominated to the Bennett Board of Trustees could you accept? It would mean that you would need to attend Board meetings may be twice a year. The Board members usually bear their own expenses

BENNETT COLLEGE
Greensboro, North Carolina

OFFICE OF THE PRESIDENT

The other obligations you know about — from seeing your aunt, Mrs. Hargis, etc, and struggle for Bennett. I'm not sure that this can be done but please talk this over with Mr. Smith and let me know your reactions. Write me ℅ Bishop R. E. Jones, Waveland, Miss.

Yours sincerely
David D. Jones

55th Reunion of the Class of 1935 [21]
Pauline Waters Smith (right)
1990

The Trustees, Administration, Faculty, Staff,
Students and Alumnae of Bennett College
pay tribute to

Mrs. Pauline Waters Smith '35

in honor of her years of dedicated commitment
and outstanding service to Bennett College. She was a model for
Bennett women. She lived well, laughed often and loved much.
She was a true friend to Bennett.
Her life was an inspiration and her memory a benediction.

April 25, 1997

Dr. Gloria Randle Scott,
President
Bennett College

BENNETT COLLEGE
Greensboro, North Carolina

∞

Commencement Day Program

BENNETT COLLEGE CAMPUS
MONDAY MORNING, JUNE FIRST
NINETEEN HUNDRED AND THIRTY-SIX
AT TEN-THIRTY O'CLOCK

CANDIDATES FOR THE DEGREE OF
BACHELOR OF ARTS

Irene Delores Blackwell
Mildred Evelyn Cecil
Frances Juanita Clarke
†Katherine Virginia Galloway
Bertha Mae Herring
Cleo Vivian Lawson
Christabel Louise McKoy
Cecelia Rose Miller
Madge Elaine Moore
Margaret Christine Rhodes
Mary Payne Rhodes
Connell Willard Rosemond
Mayzell Thompson Rosemond
Maudelle Juanita Scarlett
Teanna Avatna Moir
Gussie Edna Tyler
Annie Dorothy Lipscombe
Alta Mae Wade
Sarah Elizabeth Walden
*L. Ferne Wood

CANDIDATES FOR THE DEGREE OF
BACHELOR OF SCIENCE

Dorothy Elizabeth Bailey
Evelyn Marguerite Foster
Lydia Mae Jetton
Sara Lucretia Phelps
Anne Chloetelde Porter
Mary Belle Sutton

HONORARY DEGREES

DOCTOR OF LAWS

Wallace E. Brown, A.B., D.D., L.H.D., Syracuse University;
Bishop of the Methodist Episcopal Church since 1924

DOCTOR OF HUMANE LETTERS

Mary McLeod Bethune, M.A. (Honorary), South Carolina State College; M.A. (Honorary), Wilberforce University; LL.D., Lincoln University; Winner of the Spingarn Medal for 1934; President of Bethune-Cookman College since 1904

*Valedictorian
†Salutatorian

*****Dr. Mary McLeod Bethune Received An Honorary Doctorate Degree*

A Tribute to Hattie Bailey '38
1617 W. Third St., Chester, PA
610-872-4985

THE BENNETT BANNER
Student Publication of Bennett College

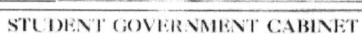

STUDENT GOVERNMENT CABINET

Front row l.-r.: Juanita Murray, Arney Hall, Hattie Bailey '38 (president), Dorothy Williams, Eleanor Johnson
Back row l.-r: Bettye Crump, Anne Kelly, Thomasina Atkinson, Jacqueline Myles, Dorothy Moore, Lucille Hargrave

(October 15-17, 1937) [22]
HEAD OF STUDENT GOVERNMENT ATTENDS CONGRESS
Miss Hattie Bailey Represents Bennett Student Group at National Negro Congress

---

Hattie Bailey '38 was one of eleven alumnae recognized at the second annual Celebration of Phenomenal Bennett Women on May 13, 1999. She is an active member of the Delaware Valley Alumnae Chapter.

In Memoriam

Dr. Frances Jones Bonner'39
Daughter of Dr. David D. and
Mrs. Susie W. Jones

Organizer of the Boycott of '37 [23]

Prior to the boycott of the famed "Greensboro-Four" [24] and the commemorated date of February 1, 1960, Bennett College students had successfully boycotted a downtown Greensboro theater in 1937. Their determination has to be applauded, for it was the first of many chinks needed to bring down the monolith of segregation. That incident was forgotten, though, because legal segregation would remain "alive and well" for nearly three decades longer.

Dr. Willa B. Player would support her "girls" *openly* during the Civil Rights Movement of the 60s; however, Dr. David D. Jones had to support his "girls" *discreetly* in the 30s. Miss Willa B. Player was a young Latin and French teacher at that time, as well as the registrar. Might she in the 60s have been remembering that long-ago nearly forgotten 1937 daring incident? Not only had Dr. Jones prepared her well for assuming the mantle of President of Bennett College, so, perhaps, had her memories.

Willa Beatrice Player

From *Bittersweet Memories of Home* [25] by Alice Patterson Patience '40:

"Long before there was a Civil Rights Movement, Bennett College students had staged a boycott against the local theater. The theater had been showing pictures that depicted the Negro only as a clown or a domestic. In their seats in the balcony Bennett students had accepted this, but when Hollywood changed its objective for Blacks to one of fairly compassionate understanding, the theaters would cut out those parts. The theater owners claimed that their white patrons would not have continued to come if blacks were shown out of their rightful positions in society.

This may or may not have been true. Who knows? But the girls (led by President Jones' daughter Frances and me) at Bennett College decided that they weren't going to go and sit in their segregated balcony and look only at Blacks being shown in inferior positions. So we boycotted. We canvassed the whole community and we ended up winning our boycott because the theaters were hit where it counted. They were not making any money, so finally they gave in. So Bennett girls went back up to the balcony and watched pictures they could approve.

From this incident I learned that courage comes in many forms and not always the obvious ones. The fact that Dr. Jones, president of the College, did not stop us, and he had to know what we were doing, means that even though openly in the deep South at that time he could not show approval, he did covertly approve of our actions.

That took courage. This man could have lost his job. This man could have been lynched. He could have been made a martyr at that time.

On the surface Dr. Jones acted as if nothing were occurring. You could not accuse him of anything. He did not participate, but he did not stop us. And once again, I have to admire people who find ways, not always the accepted ways, but ways to follow what their heart dictates.

Lisbeth Ellen Edwards Berry '39
523 Lincoln Street, Kinston, NC 28501
252-523-9805
Contact: Treda S. Berry, 704-562-4934

My favorite Bennett song is *"Tell Me Why."* The lyrics say *"Tell me, dear Bennett, why I love you"*. Let me tell you why I love Bennett College.

As a child of the Great Depression, attending college was a privilege and great accomplishment. I graduated from Adkin High School in Kinston, North Carolina in 1935. My father, John R. Edwards, a vendor of fish and vegetables and proprietor of several rental properties, died when I was two years old. My mother, Celia Hooker Edwards, was a teacher of a one-room school in the Post Oak community of Lenoir County during the week and cleaned for prominent people of the community on the weekends.

Even in those days, there were children in classes who played and were disruptive. However, I knew that achieving success meant that you must focus on the classes or tasks placed in front of you and not be distracted. As a result, my hard work in school gave me the opportunity to serve as the valedictorian of my high school class.

I credit my high school teachers, Mrs. Aiken and Mrs. Frye, for giving me both the inspiration to attend school and the educational preparation that served as the foundation for my collegiate experiences.

Upon graduation, I was awarded a scholarship to Bennett College to major in home economics. I naturally worried about the financial situation since my father had died when I was so young. However, despite being a widow with another young child to raise, my mother assured me that "everything would be all right" and Bennett would be a great place for me. With a wardrobe of dresses that she lovingly designed and the encouragement of Aunt (pronounced *"Aint"*) Novell Jones, I began my journey.

I left for Bennett College with a scholarship and just enough money for the taxi to campus. With money depleting quickly, I was fortunate to receive a job in the campus pantry at Wilbur Steele Hall which, at that time, was the dining hall. Dishwashing was one of my responsibilities, and there were also extra jobs available for sweeping and mopping the bathrooms in the dormitory. Even students who were not in a work-study program had to perform "duty work" in the dormitories at Bennett.

I took advantage of every opportunity for financial assistance that came my way. At the time of my enrollment, Bennett offered both a four-year plan and a five-year plan of study. Being frugal, and with the assistance of student jobs, I proudly completed my degree under the four-year plan with the distinguished honor of being named salutatorian of the Class of 1939.

I lived in Jones Hall my freshman year; so did my daughter, Treda Sheryl Berry '73. "Ma Mac" was my dorm supervisor. At the time, I was not aware that the dorm assistant and valedictorian of my graduating class, Martha Matheson Baker, and I would become life-long friends after beginning our post-college teaching assignments in the same town.

"Ma Mac"

Bennett College had a wonderful president and fantastic instructors. Dr. David Dallas Jones was the president when I was a student there, and he loved his "girls." Dr. Jones constantly traveled to raise funds for the college and the Bennett College Quartet, a singing ensemble, accompanied him frequently. I always enjoyed listening to them when they performed at our vespers in the chapel which, at that time, was not far from Steele Hall.

I will always remember Dr. Flemmie P. Kittrell, Dean of Students, who was also the

Dr. Flemmie P. Kittrell

home economics department chair. She was a role model and source of encouragement for me as a leading educator in her area. Inspired by her, I continued my education by seeking an advanced degree in education, and I later received a Masters Degree from North Carolina College in Durham, North Carolina.

After graduating from Bennett, I began my teaching career at Friendship High School in Fremont, North Carolina in the fall of 1939. Subsequent to my marriage to the late Hammond Berry and the birth of future Bennett Belle Treda (1952), I taught in Grifton, North Carolina at the "separate but equal" consolidated K-12 school, Savannah High School. After the achievement of racial desegregation, Savannah was closed in 1970 and the teachers transferred to North Lenoir High School.

Through the years, Bennett College's positive impact on my life and career continued to motivate me to involve students in organizations, such as Future Homemakers of America, that encouraged personal growth, practical skills, and leadership. At the time I retired, students dedicated a rose garden in my honor.

I will continue to recommend Bennett College for Women as a wonderful place to learn and grow intellectually as well as personally. During my tenure as president of the Kinston Alumnae Chapter, I encouraged our association to hold its own White Breakfast for the purpose of exposing middle as well as high school scholars to the many benefits of an education at our esteemed alma mater. Several young ladies, including my daughter and my niece, Desretta Veronica McAllister-Harper '62, made Bennett their college of choice at my suggestion and are outstanding examples of Bennett College's legacy of graduating women who are leaders and achievers in all walks of life.

"That's why, dear Bennett ... that's why I love you."

L-R LaVerne Edwards McAllis, niece; Lisbeth, Treda Berry '73, daughter Desretta V. McAllister '62, niece at 90th birthday celebration

Golden Class of 1939

<u>Seated l.-r.</u>: **Elsie Leach Bookhart, Martha Matthewson Baker, Louise Wilson Swift, Olmessa Dunston, Genevive Hall Scott, Sankie Everette Floyd**
<u>Standing l.-r.</u>: **Bennie May Young, Julia Wilson, Frances Lucas Enzlow, Phyllis Shelton, Lisbeth Ellen Edwards Berry**

IN MEMORIAM

Frances Lucas Enzlow '39
(1916-2011)

Submitted by her daughter
Modgie Enzlow Williams

A 1970 BENNETT BELLE LOVINGLY REMEMBERS HER MOTHER,
A BENNETT BELLE IN THE CLASS OF 1939

Frances Lucas Enslow '39

My mother cherished her life as a student at Bennett College. Many of her shared lessons were from her life as a student at Bennett College. The teachers and administration of the 1930's truly helped to make her life what it was. Music and her participation in the Bennett College Choir under Dr. R. Nathaniel Dett offered her priceless memory gifts most of her life. Music and her spiritual life were essential elements of her life always. Mother's love and respect for her training at Bennett College inspired me to attend Bennett College.

My mother was born to teach. If she had not been a classroom teacher by profession, she would have still been remembered as a teacher. My mother, Frances Lucas Enzlow passed away May 29, 2011, just two weeks before her 92nd birthday. Many of her former students shared loving messages about her as a teacher. Some of her church friends did the same thing.

Frances Lucas Enzlow was my mother and my very dear friend. She shared a lot of advice and lessons with me. I am sharing some of the words of advice and lessons.

The greatest advice my mother gave me was the following, in her own words:

"Each of us on God's earth is a worthwhile person. We all have something that we do well. Some of us play musical instruments, others draw well, and still others smile pleasantly. Regardless of how great or small our talents are, we must learn to like and appreciate ourselves as we are. It is through this love and appreciation of one's self that we are able to reach out to others with love and understanding."

As a young black person growing up during the racial problems of the sixties, I found these words to be a guiding light for me through a time of much darkness. When some forces of society pushed me back or aside because I was Black and my feelings got hurt, I always recovered successfully. I knew then, as I know now, I am a worthwhile person, thanks to mother's advice.

Mother shared other lessons that I named the "L,M,N Alphabet Philosophy." Mother was a stately lady and a giant in character. All of my life she was an example of her "L,M,N Alphabet Philosophy."

"L" is for learning and loving. She was a retired teacher of the Guilford County school system. She taught me that learning is a lifelong process. She returned to school at NC A&T State University in 1997 for computer classes in their Continuing Education Program. She was a person who found a way to love everyone with the help of her spiritual life. Mom's spiritual life was the "center of her being."

Because of her strong spiritual beliefs, she naturally shared love with everyone she met. She and my late father, Comey, were married for almost 52 years when he passed in November 1994. Their relationship was a working picture of love in action.

"M" is for mentor. My mother always believed that everyone has a special talent or knowledge that we can share with others. In sharing, we mentor and enhance the lives of others.

"N" is for nurturing. My mother taught me that nurturing is a two-way street. We must be nurtured, and we must nurture others. During the summer of 1993, my mother and I truly learned to nurture each other. We both lost sons that summer. My youngest brother died of a heart attack on June 5, 1993, and my own son was killed in an automobile accident on August 19, 1993.

Even though that summer was very painful, two mothers learned, loved, mentored and nurtured each other through the pain. We both became stronger women through the experience.

During mother's final weeks of life, she developed the "PPG Alphabet Philosophy." Mother was a resident at Adams Farm Living and Rehabilitation Center during the last ten weeks of her life. She _praised_ her Lord several times a day. She _prayed_ daily and often repeated the 23rd Psalm.

Gratitude to the center staff, her biological family and extended church and community families were shared until she took her last breath.

What a wonderful mother, teacher, friend and Bennett sister. I will always love and cherish in memory! My mother's friendship was a priceless gift that continues to bless my life.

ALL THROUGH THE NIGHT [26]

Sleep, my child and peace attend thee
All through the night;
Guardian angels God will send thee;
All through the night,
Soft the drowsy hours are creeping,
Hill and vale in slumber sleeping,
I, my loving vigil keeping
All through the night.

While the moon her watch is keeping
All through the night;
While the weary world is sleeping
All through the night.
O'er thy spirit gently stealing,
Visions of delight revealing,
Breathes a pure and holy feeling,
All through the night.

BENNETT COLLEGE AWARDS AND HONORS
Commencement 1938-1939

SENIOR HONORS
Valedictorian, Maxine Davis, Uniontown, Pa.   *Salutatorian*, Frances Estelle Jones, Greensboro, N. C.

HARRIET G. BROCK PRIZE
Awarded to the member of the Freshman Class making greatest general improvement
Edna Gray Taylor, 1942, Wilson, N. C.

R. B. McCRARY PRIZE
Awarded to the member of the Freshman Class making greatest improvement in English
Mary Frances Harvey, 1942, Athens, Ga.

CLASS OF 1921 PRIZE
For Excellence in Science
Celeste Pamelia Dennis, 1942, Charlotte, N. C.   Edna Marie Webster, 1942, St. Joseph, Mo.

BELLE TOBIAS CURTIS SCHOLARSHIP
Awarded to a member of the Sophomore Class for superior scholarship and promise
Miriam Mitchell Richards, 1941, Asheville, N. C.

BROOK'S MEMORIAL CHURCH PRIZE
Awarded to the student making the most significant contribution to the religious life of the College
Helen Louise Wiggins, 1939, Wilmington, Del.

ELECTIONS TO THE ALPHA EPSILON HONOR SOCIETY
Elected to membership at the end of Junior year
Maxine Davis   Frances Estelle Jones

Elected as of the Class of 1938
Gwendolyn Margarette Davidson   Mildred Irene Dickens
Thelma Cornelia Davidson   Naomi Beatrice Flowe

ASSISTANTSHIPS
Assistant in Biology .... Jennie Cathryn Williams, 1941, New York City
Assistant in Chemistry .... Mildred Virginia Florance, 1941, Carmel, N. Y.
Assistant in Office of Dean of Instruction .... Evelyn Jenkins Floyd, 1942, Danville, Va.
Assistant in Office of Dean of Students .... Gloria Wynetta Bostic, 1941, Goldsboro, N. C.
Assistants in Office of Registrar .... Sibyl Elizabeth Payne, 1941, Jacksonville, Fla.
                                                         Evelyn Louise Love, 1941, Jefferson, S. C.

CANDIDATES FOR THE DEGREE OF BACHELOR OF ARTS

Roxanna Mildred Alston	Mary Genevieve Hall	Mary Evelyn Porter
Maeceon Dianne Bemery	Ella Mervelle Hannon	Frances Randall
Vivian Foard Christian	Virginia Alberta Harris	Ernestine Tolliver Roberts
Bettie Ardene Crump	Sarah Catherine Hawkins	Julia Elizabeth Ross
Maxine Davis	Georgia Mae Hilary	Phyllis Ailene Shelton
Doris Elizabeth Dennis	Mary Juanita Johnson	Pearl Margaret Tate
Ruth Mae Dixon	Frances Estelle Jones	Elvah Marcia Waters
Dorothy Owens Dula	Bertha Elizabeth Joyner	Gwendolyn Maude Watson
Agnes Omesa Dunston	Juanita Jureatha Kirkpatrick	Beatrice Louise Wilson
Sankie Mae Everette	Elsie Louise Leach	Julia Saxton Wilson
Celeste Nadine Fearrington	Frances Pauline Lucas	Vivian Luella Wright
Myrtle Fitzgerald	Martha Elizabeth Matthewson	Bennie Mae Young
Minnie Gilmer	Emma Gill McKoy	

CANDIDATES FOR THE DEGREE OF BACHELOR OF SCIENCE

Elizabeth Ellen Edwards	Lulu Juanita Lyles	Evelyn Dolores Stewart
Helen Louise Hinton	Dorothy Elizabeth Moore	Helen Louise Wiggins
Alice Ruth Jackson	Lillie Mae Scales	Ethel Cavell Williams

COMMENCEMENT 1939

1940s

In Memoriam

Alice Patterson Patience '40

(1916-2001)

World War II WAC

From *Bittersweet Memories of Home* [27]

"The first time I heard the Bennett College choir sing, I was almost moved to tears. Those young women with their trained voices sang beautifully. When they sang, "Go down Moses, way down in Egypt-land and tell ole Pharoah, let my people go," I felt an exhilaration I had not felt anywhere else before. And I also was feeling a sadness because for us, our Moses had not yet appeared on the scene. It would be many years before our Moses (Dr. Martin Luther King, Jr.) was to go down and rescue his people.

Bennett gave me another gift. A love of history. It was here that I first got an accurate knowledge of Negro history. What I knew about the subject until this time was not necessarily correct since in Wilkes-Barre, Pa., we had received information only from black newspapers and from travelers passing through. And they frequently did not know any more than I did.

Carter G. Woodson was the person to open my eyes to my black legacy. In his history book he showed us where we had descended from, where we originated. And it all had started in Africa. He brought us up to what then was the present time. He was the first historian I ever had knowledge of and although there are great ones now, I still have a fondness for this man who let me know that like whites, I, too, had a history.

Bennett College students came from all types of homes, all types of areas and with all types of backgrounds. One thing that Dr. Jones was determined to do was to make us all into ladies, the type that he knew from the South and the type that went to Vassar College. Some of it was interesting and some of it was hilarious.

When we had a date we could not sit in the parlor of our dormitories to wait. We had to stay on the floor above and then sweep gracefully down the staircase. It looked like a scene from <u>Gone With the Wind</u> played by darker characters.

Our table manners were equally outrageous. We didn't know how to set a proper table. We didn't know what the correct utensils should be. We were not part of the current century, so we were told.

I admit that most of what I was being shown was foreign to me. In that little wooden house in Pennsylvania we ate with a knife, fork, and a spoon. That was all that was needed, evidently. But that was not so at Bennett. We were shown how to set a proper table including dessert spoons, forks for seafood, and small knives for bread and butter plates. At the time I thought I would never have need for this knowledge, being unaware that much later in my life when I would be travelling with my husband, I would need a knowledge of these things. So Dr. Jones was right.

Shopping for clothing was hard in Greensboro. There were so many taboos for us. You could not try on a hat. If you did, you bought it. You could buy shoes only behind a curtain that was in the back of the store. No one could see you there and at least you could try them on. I don't remember what we did about dresses and skirts. I guess we bought them without trying them on.

It was at Bennett that I developed my love for the theater. I couldn't draw, even though later I was to marry an artist. And I definitely couldn't sing. So it only left the theater for me.

We were heavy on Shakespeare. My senior play was "A Midsummer Night's Dream." I played Puck. I don't know how well I played him, but I do agree with him. "All the world's a stage, its men and women merely players." At least so it seems to me. We change our parts as necessary, but we keep on playing.

There were no televisions at Bennett. Television belonged to the future. At the time I was a student there was a lounge on every floor and in the lounges were radios. This is where I heard about the abdication of King Edward VIII of Britain.

We were young then. We clearly understood how you would give up a throne for love. Whatever we were to think later in life of the man who was to become the future Duke of Windsor, at that time we were cheering him even though no longer would he be a king. Romanticists as we were, we understood his action.

The words to us were fantastic and believable when he declared he could not continue to serve his country if he could not have the woman he loved by his side. We agreed. At our age we understood giving up everything for love."

Alice Marie Patterson

<u>Class of 1940</u>

Unidentified Belles in the Photograph Album
of Alice Patterson Patience '39/'40

Golden Class of 1942 With Dr. Gloria R. Scott in 1992

Ola Parker Willoughby '42
2404 First Rd., Arlington, VA 22204
703-979-2429

When I graduated from Gary District High School in Gary, West Virginia, the principal, Mr. Joel E. Height, was instrumental in getting a scholarship for me to Morristown Junior College in Morristown, Tennessee. After completion of two years there, the president, Dr. John W. Haywood, secured a scholarship for me to attend Bennett College.

Upon arriving at Bennett in 1940 and viewing the beautifully manicured campus, I knew it was where I wanted to be, I was assigned to Pfeiffer Hall with a sophisticated senior from New York City, Dorothy Steele as my roommate and "big sister." I lived in Pfeiffer for two years under the watchful eyes of our strict dorm mother, Mrs Mamie MacLaurin, whom we affectionately referred to as "Ma Mac." My friend from high school, Helen Horton (Holley) enrolled in the freshman class of 1944.

With a friend from home and family members in nearby Reidsville, North Carolina, I adjusted easily to the new environment, reveling in the warm sisterly spirit which enveloped me at Bennett. I was amazed at the congenial and nurturing demeanor of the instructors and staff. Mrs. Blanche Raiford, my French instructor, gave invaluable assistance to me in my pursuit of a major in English and minor in French.

As a work scholarship recipient, I was assigned several different jobs, one of which was bell ringer, This job was not a good fit for me and I was successful in getting reassigned., My favorite job was checking attendance at the required chapel and vesper services, I liked the vesper services which were usually informative and inspirational, although it was sometimes challenging to stay awake and alert. I remember one service in particular when "Prexy" (Dr. David D Jones) summoned us to chapel after learning of our complaints about the food. Being the prudent intellectual that he was, he related a parable about a man who had complained because he had no shoes until he met a man who had no feet. I have never forgotten that lesson.

As a transfer student, I spent a lot of time studying. However, I found time to play cards with dorm mates in our rooms or in the well-appointed parlor where we received our gentleman visitors.

There were several high points during my two years at Bennett. I was elected to present a replica of the Annie Merner Pfeiffer Chapel to Mrs. Henry Pfeiffer (Trustee/Donor).

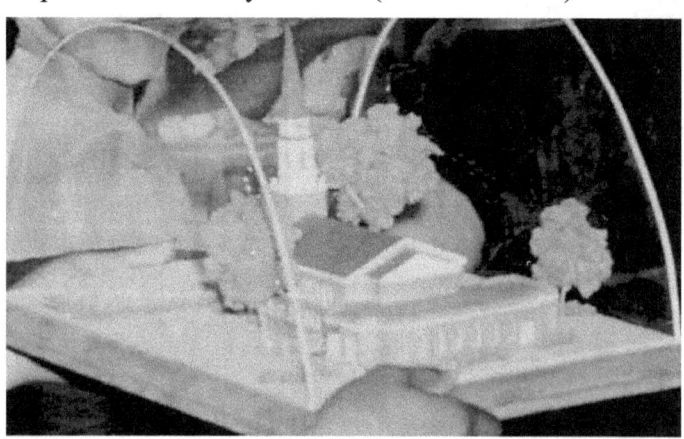

Ola Parker Willoughby & Mrs. Henry Pfeiffer

During my senior year, I was the editor of the Bennett Banner, but not because I wanted to be. I protested, but Dr. Jones ignored my protests and whatever he said I was to do, I did. Considerable help came from Valena Welch Williams (Class of 1945) who became the Banner editor in her senior year.

I took drama class under Mrs. Ernestine Coles and I played "Mrs. Frazier" in a production of "Craig's Wife." The play was so well accepted that I felt like a celebrity for about 24 hours. During that time I was being asked for my autograph. Interestingly, many years later, I was involved with the same play at my church in Arlington, Virginia.

After Dr. Jones gave my degree at graduation, I shed tears "at the thought of leaving dear friends and my beloved sisters of Bennett. It brought me great joy to return to the 45th and 50th year reunions of my class.

I am proud to be a Bennett Belle. The life-long lessons I acquired broadened my perspective and empowered me to become a committed and contributing member of society. I have been privileged to render service in numerous capacities in my church, community service organizations and in the country in which I reside.

Doris Evangeline Boyd Rice
40 Years Secretary to Bennett College Presidents

Around 1942-43 before the majority of students had returned, an oil truck might have exploded at any minute near the corner of Gorrell and Bennett Streets. Mrs. Theophile C. Taylor was still Secretary of Bennett College for Women. She had told Miss DuDonna Tate '39 (a student or graduate in charge of the bookstore in the Student Union Building) and me (a secretary in the Records Office), that she would not come to the campus the next day and would use it as a day of rest that was due her as a vacation day.

I had just come up on the campus to my office and had gone down to the bookstore on business. At the beginning of the arousal, DuDonna telephoned Mrs. Taylor and at first could not connect with her. She was able to talk with her the second time she tried and told her to dress quickly and we would come to take her out of her house and remain with her—much too dangerous to stay in there.

DuDonna locked the bookstore and then she and I ran all the way, hardly stopping to breathe properly. We both loved God and we both loved Mrs. Taylor or anyone in her situation and nothing was too good to try to save Mrs. Taylor. I called my office to let them know my whereabouts. This was not the first time oil trucks had trouble trying to climb that hill, but in a few hours everything was under control and Mrs. Taylor was thankful of our watchfulness of her. May God be praised, for the people living on both sides of the block were excited for a large part of the day until notified that the oil truck was now safe and was departing.

65ᵗʰ REUNION OF THE CLASS OF 1945

Alumnae Weekend 2010
Irene Powell Carter and Vivian Hargrave
(Photo courtesy of Reba Burruss-Barnes)

Dr. Glendora McIllwain Putnam and Roberta Favors Cottman
(Photo courtesy of Reba Burruss-Barnes)

In Memoriam

Mable Vivian Hargrave '45
(1924-2011)

Submitted by Irene Powell Carter '45

Vivian Hargrove '45

My dear friend and classmate, Vivian, went to be with the Lord on July 15, 2011, due to injuries sustained from an automobile accident in Chicago, Illinois. Born in Charlotte, N.C., at age 87 she was the last living member of her family of six children.

Since her graduation from Bennett College, she remained loyal to her Alma Mater and received the Bennett College "Unsung Heroine" Award as a member of the Chicago Alumnae Chapter. She furthered her education by receiving a Master's of Social Work from Clark/Atlanta University of Social Work in 1947, after which time she worked in Minneapolis, Minn., Milwaukee, Wisconsin, and Chicago, Illinois. Her work was mainly with foster care and adoptions.

After retirement, she volunteered in programs such as adult literacy. An active member of the YMCA, she was concerned with wellness and fitness, commencing each day with swimming and walking.

A world traveler, a friend to all, a mentor to her family, a philanthropist, a staunch Christian, she will be remembered as an optimist who never complained. Her closing farewell on telephone calls to her family was, *"God loves you and so does Aunt Vivian."* And we, your Bennett sisters will always love you.

Dorothy Walker Smith '45
169 Hamilton Rd., Teaneck, NJ 7666
201-837-0479   dwws169h@aol.com

"With Founder's Day at hand, Mary Ella Drake, left, senior from White Plains, N.Y., gives Dorothy W. Walker, freshman from Wilkes-Barre, Pa., a historical background of Bennett College. They are observing the marker of one of the many magnolia trees dedicated to the memory of outstanding personalities and planted by various graduating classes." [28]

A strange twist of events led me to Bennett. The journey started in Wilkes-Barre, a small, sleepy anthracite coal mining town in northeastern Pennsylvania. The year was 1941 and I was a high school senior, the only African American girl in a class of 499 students. College was going to be my way out of that economically depressed area, and so I worked hard all through school and graduated near the top of my class.

In those days most students couldn't afford to go college-shopping as students do today, and I was no exception. Rather, we depended a lot on the principal and faculty members to shop around for scholarships for us. College representatives would then come to our school to interview prospective students, as well as to recruit additional ones. Based on my grades and a strong recommendation from the principal, I was in line for a four-year-scholarship to Wilson College, a very prestigious Presbyterian college for women. You can imagine my excitement at the prospect of attending such a fine school and I anxiously awaited the day of my interview.

That day finally came and it was all downhill from that point on. The rep was definitely not prepared to meet a colored girl, as we were called back then. The expression on her face said it all, but she quickly regained her composure and proceeded to tell me how impressed she was with my grades and my participation in the extra-curricular activities of the school and how much she'd love to have me on campus, but that she was afraid it just wouldn't work out. ("Who would be your roommate? The students are housed in suites of rooms and since many of the girls are from the South, it would be difficult to find a roommate for you. You would probably be more comfortable at another school.") And with that I was dismissed. Case closed.

The next option was to go to Bucknell Junior College, a ten-minute bicycle ride from my house and I was accepted for the fall semester with no problem. Three months later with the bombing of Pearl Harbor and the entry of the U.S. into WWII, Uncle Sam was looking for workers to take the place of young men and women who had gone off to service. By the end of the year I left Bucknell Junior and went to work for Uncle Sam in D.C.

After a year of working, I realized I wanted more out of life than earning $17.50 weekly, from which I had to eat, pay trolley fare, and room rent at Stowe Hall. I had never given up on going to college so I decided to give Wilson another try. Even though I was applying from D.C., the same rep was still on the job. The same rep, the same response! "Sorry, our policy still holds."

In the late 1960s I finally got a chance to go to Wilson, not as a student, but as a guest invited to address the annual Synodical Meeting that was being held on the campus. As I look back on that experience, my anger was misplaced. It shouldn't have been with the rep, but with the institution she represented. Had I applied to a

Black Presbyterian related college, I would have had no problem. This leaves me questioning our long history of involvement with minority education. Schools in the South by law had to be segregated in those days, but what was the excuse for segregation in Pennsylvania?

Back in 1941 depending on others finding a college for me didn't work out. I needed to start exploring options of my own. Bennett came to mind because my "babysitter," Alice Patterson Patience '40 had gone to Bennett. Also, during my high school years, I had heard Bennett's choir when it was in Wilkes-Barre while on its annual spring tour to raise funds for the school.

Because I loved music, I was very impressed by the choir. So I applied to Bennett and, lo and behold, two years after my journey began, I was accepted for the fall 1943 semester. I moved into Kent Hall, Room 4. Kat Randolph, Lucille Brown (both now deceased), Rose Hogan'47, Marchita Whitfield Hamlin'45, Jenny Lawrence Moss'45, and Jocelyn Tate Booker'45 were some of the first people I met and we remain friends to this day.

Sixty-eight years have passed since my days on campus, but certain events remain fresh in my mind such as when Jocelyn Tate invited me to spend Easter weekend at her home in Charlotte, N.C., and to attend the Kappa Dawn Dance at Johnson C. Smith University. The following day Jo, our escorts from A&T, and I were at the bus station waiting to return to Greensboro when several policemen approached Jocelyn to ask why she was in "the colored waiting room."

"I'm with my friends," she said. The grilling continued and finally one of them asked, "And what's your name?"

"Jocelyn Tate."

"Oh," And with that the policeman went on their way. Despite Jocelyn's blonde hair and blue eyes, the Tates were a well-known African American family in Charlotte.

Jo's date, shaken by the whole episode, said to her, "The next time we go somewhere, I'll meet you there. This is as close as I've ever come to being strung up, foolin' with you."

Remember---this was in the early 40s. Jo and I are dear friends and we still laugh about that weekend!

Dorothy Walker's Report Cards
Willa B. Player, Registrar

President Franklin D. Roosevelt died in April of 1945 and the train bearing his body from Warm Springs, Georgia, to Washington, D.C., passed through Greensboro some time near midnight. Students, accompanied by chaperones, were allowed to go to the train station where we were joined by other mourners to view the funeral train. It was a solemn and moving experience which I will never forget.

Imagine the thrill I had of being accepted as a member of the very choir that had made such an impression on me during my high school days! The choir participated at vesper services and nearly all programs when guest speakers were on campus. What a privilege it was to sing for and listen to so many esteemed speakers, including Dr. Benjamin Mays, Dr. Mary McCleod Bethune, and Dr. John Hope Franklin.

War-time gas rationing prevented the choir from long-distance travel, so we were only able to travel to cities in North Carolina and also to perform for the soldiers at Fort Bragg. Only the quartet (my voice wasn't one of them) did long-distance traveling during the war years.

Thanksgiving dinner provided the requisite turkey and dressing, but with something additional. A lady bug beetle, not squashed, was in my serving of dressing. I just moved it over and ate my dinner. In those days, it was three meals a day—no vending machines or going off campus for late night snacks. Either eat dinner or wait until breakfast the next day.

Pfeiffer Hall and Ma Mac's inspections after Saturday cleaning were notorious. She was a tough task-master, but loveable.

I think it was the Junior Prom. My date from A&T pawned his coat to buy me an orchid. I though this was wonderful!! Young men's summer jobs were working as Pullman porters. Well, Boyfriend said that perhaps he could stop in Wilkes-Barre to see me on one of his runs to Buffalo. When I told my mother, she wasn't the least bit impressed. Her comment, "Anyone fool enough to pawn his coat to buy a flower, I don't ever want to meet." Case closed. No visit.

Despite the passage of time, I still get "teary" when I hear *Were You There When They Crucified My Lord?* and Dr. R. Nathaniel Dett's *When I Survey the Wondrous Cross*. The tears really flow whenever I hear *Listen to the Lambs*. What memories I have of singing second alto in the choir with Olga Singleton as the soloist and Orrin Clayton Sutherland, II as the organist and choir director.

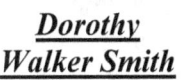

Dorothy Walker Smith

Although I was only a student at Bennett, the "Black Vassar," for two years, the exposure among students and faculty helped shape me for the rest of my life. Prexy exacted nothing less than perfection in decorum and manners. This developed in me the desire to be the best I could be, values I have passed on to my family of four children, ten grandchildren, and fifteen great grands.

Bennett gave me self-confidence to assume positions of leadership in my community and church. Following my marriage, election to the Board of Directors of Planned Parenthood in the 1940s marked the beginning of my participation in civic, religious and cultural organizations in the Scranton, Pa. area.

These included, among others, the YWCA, Visiting Nurse Association, League of Women Voters, Everhart Museum, and the Junior Century Club of Scranton. I had a full time job with attending to the needs of the fast growing Smith family, as well as its extended family since at various periods throughout the years we had two foster children, Rotary exchange students from Argentina and Sweden, and various foreign students from local colleges.

For fourteen years I was an instructor in the school of Chemical Engineering for the International Correspondence Schools of Scranton. My election to the Commission of Ecumenical Mission and Relations (C.O.E.M.A.R) of the United Presbyterian Church in 1966 opened the way to serve on the national and international levels. I succeeded Dr. Charles Forman of the Divinity School of Yale.

In 1971 I was elected as the chairperson, becoming the first woman, the first Black, and the first non-clergy person to head one of the denomination's national Boards. I visited a number of mission fields in Africa, the Caribbean, and South America.

In 1972 I was the first woman elected to serve on the Board of Directors of Blue Cross/Blue Shield of Northeastern Pennsylvania. Interestingly, my "babysitter," another Bennett Belle, Alice Patterson Patience'40, had been the first Black manager in 1954.

After the family's move to Teaneck, N.J. in 1973, I became very active in church affairs there, too. My "love affair" with Bennett was renewed when one year my classmate Jo Tate Booker came from Ohio to Bennett's White Breakfast in White Plains, NY. President Dr. Johnnetta Cole was the speaker.

Although I have not been back to campus for alumnae activities, I did have the opportunity to drive through the campus to behold its distinctive beauty.

In Memoriam
Edith Taylor Sheppard '46

1991 Susie W. Jones Awardee [29]

"An ardent supporter and loyal alumna, Edith Taylor Sheppard devoted many years of service to Bennett College through her membership in the Metro-D.C. Alumnae Chapter and the National Alumnae Association.

At the local chapter level, her services spanned more than 45 years, serving as president, vice president, recruitment chairwoman, as well as a member of numerous committees. At the national level she chaired the National Nominating Committee, served as a member of the original Alumnae House Committee, and because of her outstanding accomplishments in recruiting, served as chair of national recruitment.

Edith Shepard was a successful educator for 21 years before retiring from Frank W. Ballou Senior High School in Washington, D.C. While at Ballou, she was named Volleyball Coach of the Year (1987) and her team participated in a film used for CPR training by the American Red Cross and CPR/health education teachers across the nation. Her work as an educator was recognized by the Washington, D.C. Inter-Alumni Council of the United Negro College Fund and the Morehouse Alumni Association Region IV.

She was an active member of the McKendree United Methodist Church and was the first chairwoman of its trustee board. Another interest was serving on the Anacostia Museum,-Smithsonian Board of Directors and served as the vice-president."

Virginia Jeffries Brown '48
Chapel Hill, N.C. 27517

Remembrance of Bennett Past

When the class of 1948 entered Bennett College in the fall of 1944, World War II was nearing its merciful end, spurred by Allied victories in Europe and the Pacific. At the end of our freshman year, we learned of the death of Franklin Delano Roosevelt, then in his fourth term as U.S. president.

Our president, David D. Jones, made sure that Bennett women were exposed to progressive ideas through distinguished African-American and liberal white visitors and speakers of that period of our history.

Of the many prominent speakers at vespers on Sunday afternoons, I remember vividly Benjamin Mays, president of Morehouse College, fiery and brilliant orator, who attracted a large audience from the city. I recall Mordecai Johnson, president of Howard University, a tall man whose distinction and dignity were reflected in his carefully rendered speech. Frank Porter Graham, president of the University of North Carolina, also addressed students at vespers. He was a gentle man, slight in stature, yet a lonely giant of North Carolina progressiveness. We believe that "Prexy" was equally proud to expose distinguished visitors to Bennett women.

Most of all, I remember Paul Robeson who appeared in concert, spoke to us in Chapel and mingled with us on campus. Attendance in Chapel was required. Selected students, marshals, acted as ushers and sat with diagrams in the balcony to mark our presence or absence in our assigned seats. And oh, those marshals! We envied their poise, neatness and carriage.

When Paul Robeson rose to the podium, and said, "Good morning, ladies", his deep baritone reverberated throughout the chamber, and a spontaneous murmur rose in unison from all the students. I will never forget that response. Except to sing hymns, once seated, it was understood that no one utters a sound in Chapel. In his address to us, Paul Robeson emphasized the injustice of segregation and the exploitation of Africans by the colonial powers of Great Britain, France, Belgium, and Portugal. I believe that he wanted us to grow uncomfortable in our segregated niche.

<u>Paul Robeson's Visit (ca. 1948)</u> [30]

I remember Eleanor Roosevelt, statuesque, her speech distinguished by her broad patrician vowels and clipped consonants. She may have visited Bennett more than once. I know she visited several black colleges beginning in the 1930's. At one of her speeches given in chapel in the evening she wore a brocade jacket that was a present from Madame Chiang Kai-shek.

She visited all over the campus. Some juniors and seniors flaunted their fame offering us their hands to shake as the hand that shook the hand of the great First Lady.

*Mrs. Eleanor Roosevelt &
Dr. David D. Jones* [31]

    Mary McLeod Bethune, president of Bethune-Cookman College, visited Bennett on several occasions. A forceful woman of great presence, she did not have a demure bone in her body. She and Mrs. Roosevelt were good friends, through whom she gained the attention of the President. Sometimes students joked about these two grand ladies' similar lack of beauty.

    Then, there was Helen Gahagan Douglas, liberal member of Congress from California and wife of Melvin Douglas, the movie actor. As I remember, there was a reception for her in the parlor of Merner Hall. She wore scarlet lipstick and a black dress, cut low. When she placed a cigarette to her lips, there was a scramble to find a non-existent ash tray. Later, she ran for an open seat in the Senate against Richard Nixon. He won and in winning used "red scare" tactics to smear her. Postwar America was rife with the "red scare." Anyone publicly supporting unions, minority rights and equality, risked being labeled "fellow traveler" or worse.

They could land on the infamous "Attorney General's List" as a possible subversive.

As part of commencement week, a Greek drama was presented on the quad in front of the chapel. Who can forget Yvonne Peeler's great performance as *Antigone* or was it *Medea*? Not to slight the Little Theater, others may remember Constance Collier in Lillian Hellman's *Little Foxes.* Better than Bette Davis.

Members of our class who entered during WWII brought with them photographs of high school sweethearts in uniform. The U.S. Army established a military base near the A&T campus known as BT (basic training) 10. And the few soldiers who came calling were enthralled by the distinctive specialness of Bennett women.

As I write this, I am reminded once more of the richness of our experience as students of Bennett College during that time. I hope someone else will describe their memories of the separate visits of the Morehouse and Lincoln University choirs. To house them, students vacated the entire second floor of Pfeiffer Hall. With Mom Mac in residence, they were sure to behave themselves.

PFEIFFER HALL

Audrose Mackel Banks '49
121 Smith Street Box 45, Mumford, NY 14511
585-538-4808   audrosebanks@yahoo.com

Four Mackel Sisters in 1965 [32]
l.-r.: Gwendolyn Mackel Rice '61, Dr. Lyvonne Mackel Washington '53, Marilyn. Mackel, JD '65
Audrose Mackel Banks '49

One question that I hear over and over is, "Why did you decide to go to Bennett College?"

(It is proof that teenagers are influenced by the adults in their life.) Since I had never heard of or seen Bennett, it was the Gilbert Academy faculty that introduced me. Miriam Moriniere and Marian Thacker taught at Gilbert; Jimmie Hayes and Gwendolyn Scavella were the dormitory directors. ALL were from Bennett.

Gilbert was a Methodist high school in New Orleans, Louisiana. The school closed in 1949. Hearing about Bennett for three years had made me curious, so I applied. (My sister Lyvonne also attended Gilbert, but since it closed before her senior year, she was able to enroll in Bennett after successful admissions testing.)

Our brother attended Palmer Memorial Institute in Sedalia, N.C., (10 miles from Bennett). This helped with the travel arrangements and it would be nice to have family nearby. All the pieces were in place and I went to Bennett. It was love at first sight and the rest is history. I did enjoy going to a college no one had heard of at the time.

Where were we Mackel sisters from? We moved from Louisiana to Nachez, Mississippi in 1939 after Aunt Cille moved to Illinois. Dad wanted to take care of his mother and did not let her live alone. So we lived with our paternal grandmother. Of course, we did not mind because our maternal grandmother was nearby, also.

Maybe we moved in 1938. What I do know is that we went to the World's Fair in '39 in NY. I can not imagine we moved to Natchez and went to Fair in same year!!!!

Our parents were thrifty and SAVED for education. Our father worked very hard 6-7 days a week. I remember when he was paid with farm meat and veggies, etc. I am amazed at how 4 of us were in school at the same time and never missed a beat!!! God is Great!!

Part of the answer to the questions about the strong education value in the South flows from the education of Black principals, etc. at University of Indiana, University of Wisconsin, etc. For us personally it was Daddy's intent to have no paper on us from MS Separate Colored Schools (his words to me). Dad did not approve of Mississippi schools. Mississippi paid my tuition to go to the University of Wisconsin because I could not go to Ole Miss.

I went to Rochester, N.Y. in 1965 after the Riots of '64, to work with the War on Poverty. I can not find the legislation to be more specific. The OEO (Office of Economic Opportunity) program included Homemaking Programs (similar to WPA). The Homemaking Programs from OEO are now in Social Service Agencies and Visiting Nurses have Home Health Aides, Home Care Corp. etc. That is one Poverty program that has grown and provided a lot of work for people. I did the same thing in Buffalo, N.Y. before retiring and moving to Mumford, N.Y.

In Memoriam

Sylvia Juanita Rock Greene '49
(1927-1997)
Submitted by her daughter
Stephanie J. Greene-Hunley, Tucson, Arizona

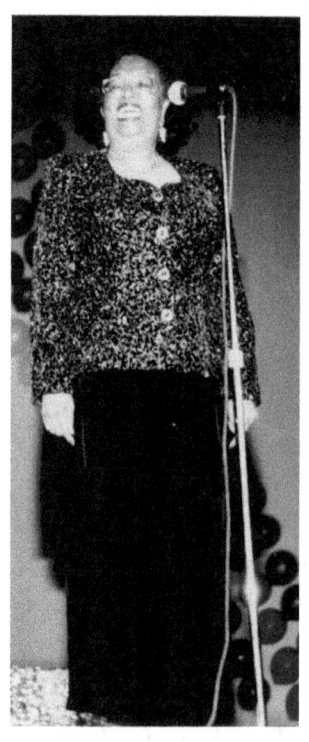

Sylvia Juanita Rock Greene was the pride of her hard-working newly middle-class family. Born in Harlem during the Renaissance period and moved at an early age to the lush suburbs of Montclair, New Jersey, Sylvia represented the hopes and dreams of her multi-generational extended family that believed, scrimped, and saved to send the only child, grandchild, cousin, niece to college-the first of her family. Despite the institutional racism of the times, Sylvia succeeded in graduating from Montclair High School and moved on to bigger challenges.

Sylvia chose Bennett College, a small all-Black, all-female campus where she ultimately came into her own. "Girlfriend" shone at that institution! There, she joined the choir, drama, French Club, and met many life-long friends while graduating *cum laude* with a degree in English and a minor in French. Bennett College instilled and nurtured in young Sylvia an air of confidence that became her lifetime mantra: *"To Thine Own Self Be True."*

She became one of the first African-Americans to go to graduate school at the University of Iowa; the first African American French translator for the Red Cross (in Japan, no less); the first African-American contracted teacher in her hometown of Montclair, New Jersey; the first African-American English teacher at her old alma-mater, Montclair High School; and interestingly enough, the first African-American Ms. Senior Arizona Beauty pageant winner. (She had style, and an inner and outer beauty.)

My mom, Sylvia Juanita Rock Greene, has always been an inspiration to me and to others, and Bennett College helped make her the powerful, confident woman she was. She was unique, intelligent, and unafraid to speak out. I am sure she would be thrilled to have a small part in the legacy of Bennett College through inclusion in this book.

Betty Marie Walker '49
7736 St. Lawrence Ave.,Chicago, IL 60619
773-723-6105

"Some fond memories from my Bennett days: The sisterly spirit I experienced during Freshman Orientation, September 1945. This spirit still continues with many of the Belles today.

A faculty and staff dedicated to helping you become a "Bennett Ideal." They were committed to the development of one's educational, emotional, spiritual, and cultural growth. Ma Mac's motherly concern for her Belles.

Inspirational and spiritual Sunday Vesper Services starting with the choir.

Outstanding speakers, ending with President Jones' "Beloved."

An opportunity to participate in the Commencement at my 50-year Class Reunion.

After leaving Bennett I taught "Homemaking Arts" for five years in the state of Kentucky. In 1955 I joined the Chicago Public School System. I was an Upper Grade Home Economics teacher and eleven year before retiring in 1993, a Parent Resource Teacher.

Over 52 years ago, I was one of the founding members of the Chicago Chapter of the Bennett College National Alumnae Association. I have been consistently active in the Chapter and served in many capacities.

I am a member of the NAA, have served on the NAA Alumnae Awards Committee, and am a Charter member of the 1926 Society. At the 2009 All-Bennett Banquet during the Alumnae Weekend, I was one of the recipients awarded the "2009 Unsung Heroine Award."

During the All-Bennett Banquet of the National Alumnae Association 2010, I was one of the first to get a special presentation of a beautiful crystal Bennett Bell for consistently traveling from Chicago to attend Alumnae Weekends at the College." [33]

<u>Some Members of the Class of 1949 in 2009</u>
<u>60th Reunion</u> [34]

l.-r.:1st. row: *Annie Mae Smith Thompson, Altamese Lester Harbin, Mary Dulin Gaither, Lillie Mosby Brown, Elsie Griffin Foy*
l.-r.:2nd row: *Geraldine Kimber Raiford, Rosa Womble Bowden, Betty Sue McConnaughey McLaurin*

1950s

Claudia Wells Hunt Hamilton '50
50441 Drakes Bay Dr. Novi, MI 48374
248-348-0282 edmond468@aol.com

During my junior year I eloped a week following my 18th birthday. My father was a popular local minister who had established a friendly relationship with Prexy. (That's what we called Dr. Jones.)

When the news was spread about my marriage, my father was summoned to Prexy's office and several demands were made. First, I had to have a physician's statement that I was not pregnant, second my father had to have a formal announcement of the marriage professionally printed to be posted on the bulletin board in the Administration Building, and last when it became time to live the required semester in the dormitory, I could not visit my husband on the weekends in our home unless he sent a written invitation to "Ma Mac" for me to come home. The written invitation had to be in "Ma Mac's" office by Wednesday of each week. (I was not excused from the required Sunday vesper.) Naturally, I was required to wear a hat and gloves when I went home.

Thirteen months later during my senior year, I gave birth to my son. I still had to receive an invitation to spend the weekend with my husband and son or special permission for them to visit me on campus in the parlor of Pfeiffer Hall.

Would you believe that I wear a hat and gloves to church every Sunday, and that my over three hundred hats have been featured in a local Detroit newspaper on several occasion? I credit my love for hats to Bennett.

I have traveled quite extensively. Most recently as February, 2011, my husband and I made our fourth trip to Hong Kong, China. In the past six years we have been to Tokyo, Japan; London, England three times; Bangkok, Thailand; Singapore; Nice, France; Rome, Italy three times; Madrid, Spain, and several major cities in the United

I work extensively with my church, the Church of God in Christ, and am presently a district missionary *emerita*. Wells Temple, located across the street from Bennett, is named in memory of my father, Bishop Wyoming Wells, who founded the church.

I collect hats. I have a room with over three hundred (300). Several newspaper articles, including one two page spread last Easter, have covered me in my hats. My husband built me a 9'x 12' hat room in our new home. I began liking hats when I was a student at Bennett. I am seldom without one on; in fact I am sitting at the computer now sending you a message in a hat.

Claudia Wells Hunt
Hamilton'50

I also wear gloves every Sunday. I have them in most colors: blue, yellow, pink, tan, orange, royal blue, lavender, purple, turquoise, green, black and white. I am a true Bennett Belle.
I buy my hats in London and Paris. In fact, I recently bought one at Harrod's similar to what Kate Middleton wears.

I am a happy, blessed "survivor."

Jeanne Martin Brayboy '51
1608 Patton Ave., Charlotte, NC 28216
704-333-2932 jmbraybo@bellsouth.net

Jeanne Martin Brayboy '51
Presented flowers after her senior piano recital by freshman Arden Buckner Sheldon

A Member of the May Day Court 1949

2nd from right: Jeanne Martin Brayboy

In Memoriam
Alberta Copeland Lewis '51
Submitted by Mildred Copeland Simms '54

55th Wedding Anniversary
Gia Simms; Eugene Simms, MD; Mildred Copeland Simms '54,
Gina Simms, Esq.

A Tribute to My Biological Bennett Sister
ALBERTA

A Bennett Belle residing in Merner Hall,
Was determined to never let her grade average fall;
Oh! Just for pride, one might say,
No, also to show little "Sis" the way.
She accomplished this without dropping the ball.

Her goal for her class was graduating at the top,
My goal is to never let the Bennett memory of her drop;
Because of her dedicated life of caring,
I learned the joy of giving and sharing,
One can make a difference as a fiscal prop.

She was a marshal dressed in white,
Marching in formation can be a beautiful sight;
Yes, walking and standing tall,
This has been my vivid recall.
Serving as a marshal was every Belle's delight.

Bennett was a college for aspiring to be great,
This was possible if one did not procrastinate.
Springtime for dating made it hard,
Watching for "Prexy" kept you on guard.
Many have come close as the records indicate.

CAREER PROFILE OF ALBERTA COPELAND LEWIS '51
EDUCATION AND EXPERIENCE

Alberta Copeland Lewis and Dr. David D. Jones

Bennett College, B.A., Co-Valedictorian	1951
Hunter College, M.S.W.	1969
Social Worker: Montgomery County Children Services, Dayton, Ohio	

AWARDS AND ACCOLADES

Distinguished service award City of Dayton, Ohio	1983
Social Worker of the Year	1988
Lifetime Achievement Award	1996
After 28 years of service, she retired as an Associate Director, Montgomery County Children Services, Dayton, Ohio	1996

Portrait unveiling and dedication of the Alberta Copeland Lewis Conference Room, Montgomery County Children Services   2002

~ IN MEMORIAM ~
March 12, 1928 - February 5, 2002

ALBERTA COPELAND LEWIS' 51
HUNTER COLLEGE, MSW
ASSOCIATE EXECUTIVE DIRECTOR
MONTGOMERY COUNTY CHILDREN'S SERVICES; DAYTON, OHIO

THIS PORTRAIT HANGS IN THE
ALBERTA COPELAND LEWIS CONFERENCE ROOM

Clara Whitmore Burnette '51
6400 Elliott place, Hyattsville, MD 20784
301-270-8631   claraburnette@comcast.net

Clara Whitmore Burmette'51

I graduated from Graham High School in May 1947. My English teacher, Miss Spencer Thomas, encouraged me to go to Bennett College. I began to wonder how my parents could afford to send me to college. I wrote to Bennett for an application. I watched the mailman every day looking for the application. I did not want my siblings to get the mail because they said Dad could not afford to send me to college. Well, I got the application in a few days and I filled it out and secretly sent it back after I found three pennies to put in the mailbox for the mailman to put a stamp on it. The application was received and I was accepted to Bennett. "HAPPY DAY."

My father drove me to Bennett College in September 1947. Financial aid was not available. He paid my tuition in two installments. I was assigned to Jones Hall, Room 29, with two roommates, Jean Martin and Queen Johnson. I was homesick for a few weeks, but I soon became adjusted to being away from home.

As a freshman I was initiated. The initiation required a freshman to wear her dress on the wrong side and 15 braids in her hair, and a sign pinned on her back saying "I am a 'green dog'." I wore a low heel shoe and a high heel shoe, carried a suitcase along with an umbrella with me to class, Vesper service, dining hall, and in fact everywhere I went, and this we had to endure for six weeks. We also had "beauty work," which was cleaning woodwork, polishing brass door knobs, etc.

Oh, yes! The "beauty naps," from 1:00 p.m. to 2:00 p.m., whether we took them or not, no one was seen on the campus at that time of the day. One knew better than to be seen out of your dorm. I appreciated the naps.

During those days at Bennett College the rules and regulations were very strict. Our parents had to send in written excuses for us to go off campus. The dress code was strictly enforced. In going shopping or just walking off campus we had to sign out when we left and sign in when we returned. We were always chaperoned when going off campus. We were always required to wear our hats and gloves when going off campus. The community would always know a "Bennett Girl" by the way she dressed and carried herself with dignity.

We are proud Bennett Belles of Yesterday, Today, and Tomorrow.

BENNETT BELLES FOREVER

<u>Robert E. Jones Hall</u> [35]
<u>Freshman Dorm</u>

Shirley Ann Cundiff Bethea '52
(May 15, 1931-September 19, 1992)
&
Bishop Joseph Benjamin Bethea
(September 9, 1932-March 12, 1995)

Submitted by their daughter Josefa Bethea Wall '87

My mother, Shirley Ann Cundiff Bethea, born in Boonville, N.C., was a second generation Cundiff who attended Bennett College. She followed her mother, Hallie B. Cundiff, and a male cousin who had been students when Bennett was still co-ed.

After college graduation, my mother taught in the public schools of Scotland County, Reidsville, Greensboro, Rockingham, and Raleigh, N.C.; and in Richmond, Virginia. She retired from teaching to become a full-time volunteer in a variety of ministries of the United Methodist Church and participated with the United Methodist Women of the local church, district, and conference levels. Unselfishly giving of her time, talent, and resources, she also was involved with numerous community organizations and served on numerous boards and agencies.

When my father, Joseph Benjamin Bethea, passed away, he was the bishop of the Columbia, S.C. Area of the United Methodist Church. He was the first Black bishop in South Carolina.

Born in Dillon, S.C., he was the son of a Methodist minister, graduate of Claflin College and Gammon Theological Seminary, as well as having studied at Union Theological

Seminary. He received four honorary degrees. He served as District Superintendent of the Virginia District of North Carolina-Virginia Conference of the Central Jurisdiction until it was abolished due to the merger between the Methodist Church and the Evangelical United Brethren Church to become the United Methodist Church. The merger resulted in my father leaving his role as District Superintendent to become the pastor of St. Matthews United Methodist Church in Greensboro.

During my father's tenure as pastor commencing in 1968, Bennett College served as a home for the congregation while the new edifice was under construction. Dr. Isaac Miller gladly welcomed Bennett's founding congregation to worship in the Annie Merner Pfeiffer Chapel. President and Mrs. Miller also welcomed our family into their home.

Student Union Building
l.-r.: Dr. Isaac Miller, Jr., Mrs. Effie Miller,
Shirley Ann Cundiff Bethea, Bishop Joseph Bethea

Gwendolyn Harris Blount '52
(1932-2010)
Submitted by her daughters
Sherri Blount Gray, Esq. and Gwendolyn Blount Adolph

Gwendolyn "Gwen" Harris Blount was born on February 9, 1932, in Henderson, North Carolina. The only child of educators Carl and Anna Harris, she was raised in the neighboring town of Louisburg. Her parents stressed the value of education and Gwen excelled academically. Among her many distinctions, she was the valedictorian of her high school class, as well as captain of the school's basketball team. A young beauty with a captivating smile, Gwen was also the Queen of her Debutante Ball.

In 1948 Gwen enrolled at Bennett College in Greensboro. This was the beginning of her lifelong devotion to the institution. A proud "Bennett Belle," Gwen was the very first resident of Reynolds Hall. She often reminisced about her beloved Bennett days, including mandatory chapel and attire requirements. She was an active alumna.

After graduating in 1952, she moved back to Franklin County and taught high school courses in home economics. She later worked with the North Carolina Extension Service (4-H) in Raleigh, traveling throughout the state. Her work with 4-H led to a brief period as the hostess of a television program in Wilson. Gwen subsequently returned to Greensboro to continue her work with the Extension Service.

During this period, she met and married Alvin V. Blount, Jr., a local physician. Together, they began a life in Greensboro in which she will be remembered as a devoted wife, mother, mentor, community volunteer, activist, and friend. Throughout her life, Gwen tirelessly served others. Her calendar remained filled with PTA meetings, church activities, food and clothing drives, board meetings, carpools, school programs, and political events. At one time, she held the Greensboro record for concurrent membership in the most PTAs! She was a member of numerous civic and social organizations, including The Links, Inc., The Girl Friends, Inc., Jack and Jill of America, Inc., and Delta Sigma Theta Sorority, Inc. She held leadership positions in most organizations she joined.

Gwendolyn Harris Blount '52

Gwen was appointed to several civic boards and commissions, including the Board of Trustees of the University of North Carolina at Greensboro and the N Care Commission. During her tenure on the Greensboro One Commission, Gwen contributed to the development of significant areas of the city. Among her many civic projects, she was especially dedicated to the Children's Voting Program, which taught youngsters the importance and process of voting.

She was a devout member of the Episcopal Church of the Redeemer and served the church in many capacities, including Senior Warden.

An avid sports fan, Gwen was particularly fond of collegiate basketball. She enjoyed tennis and bowling. Her other hobbies included bridge and travel. Gwen relished national and local politics and stayed abreast of current events. She loved fashion.

One of her trademarks was her knowledge of etiquette and protocol. She was a popular community wedding directress and woe be unto the bride who did not start on time! Gwen never minced words in this or any other regard. Extremely forthright and loyal, there was no better person to have on your side. She championed the causes of many.

"Aunt Gwen," "Ma Blount," and "Mrs. B." reveled in being the mother of seven children plus countless others she considered her own. She adored her grandchildren. Her greatest satisfaction and joy in life came from time spent with her family.

A Gift to Alma Mater in 2009 [36]
Seated: **Gwendolyn Harris Blount**
Standing: **Mary Ann Scarlette '54, Honorable Yvonne Johnson '64, President Julianne Malveaux**

In March 2009, Gwendolyn Harris Blount contributed $25,000.00 to Bennett College for Women to be used for scholarships. Through the years she has given much of her time, talent, and treasure to her Alma Mater. Eight months later she succumbed to a massive stroke at Moses Cone Memorial Hospital and passed peacefully surrounded by her children. The celebration of her life took place on Wednesday, November 25, 2009, at the Annie Merner Pfeiffer Chapel.

The Gwendolyn Harris Blount Scholarship fund has been established by her family. She is survived by her husband, Alvin Blount, Jr. and their children: Terrance Blount (Patricia), of Dumfries, Virginia; Carol Jean Robinson (Dennis), of Columbia, Maryland; Toni Harvey of Memphis, Tenn.; Sherri Gray (Edward), of Chevy Chase, Maryland; Gwendolyn Adolph (Gerald), of New Rochelle, N.Y.; Gaye Holmes (Robert), of McKinney, Texas; and Alvin Blount, III, of Cary, N.C.; nine grandchildren; and a host of extended family.

WHITE BREAKFASTS
1"Preference Song" led by Juanita Wells '37 in 1990
2 Angela West Thompson '81, Joy Scott 2003 in 2010
3 <u>Chesapeake Chapter</u>: Guila Cooper '79, Kisha Dodson Evans '98, Margaret Bailey Urquhart '61, Carolyn Maddox McKie '66
4 Helen Newberry McDowell '24, Dr. Margaret Dean Freeman '30
5 Peggy Hall James '54, Janice Dejoie '54, Juanita Patience Moss '54, Mildred Copeland Simms '54, Judith Jackson Adams '54
6. Remembering deceased members of the Golden Class of 1960

<u>Metro-DC White Breakfast 2008 [37]</u>
<u>Seated 2nd from left</u>: Juanita Page Cooke'52
Editor

"One of the earliest, and certainly the most everlasting traditions to be institutionalized after 1930, when Dr. David Dallas Jones accepted the challenge of the presidency of the newly restructured Bennett College for Women, was the "White Breakfast." He and his wife, Mrs. Susie Jones, were determined to establish some lasting values and traditions.

The tradition of the White Breakfast was in place in 1932 and occurred at Thanksgiving time. Dr. Jones felt that since the "girls," (this word was used affectionately by the Joneses to refer to the young ladies attending the College), would be on campus at Thanksgiving, it would be nice to have an entire day of activities devoted to sharing the blessings of Thanksgiving.

The day would begin with the girls rising early and hiking to the Country Home on Market Street, about four or five miles from the campus, bearing gifts for the elderly residents. Afterward, the girls would return to the campus, dress in their finery and go to Wilbur Steele Hall, now the Fine Arts Building for breakfast.

This scenario depicts how the White Breakfast and the day of Thanksgiving was observed through 1937. Some variations occurred during the next ten years. In 1947, the Morehouse Choir gave its first annual Thanksgiving concert at Bennett at the White Breakfast. During the 1965-66 academic year, Bennett scheduled a vacation over the Thanksgiving weekend and the White Breakfast and all activities associated with the weekend ceased. The White Breakfast was reinstituted as an Alumnae Weekend activity in 1976 during the Golden Anniversary of Bennett College as a School for Women.[30]

BCNAA White Breakfast May 2010
(Photo courtesy of Reba Burruss-Barnes)

Northern Virginia Belles at the 2011 BCNAA White Breakfast.
<u>Seated:</u> Pamela Blackman (Associate Member),
Brenda Morgan Nicholson '68
<u>Standing:</u> Juanita Patience Moss '54, Vernelle Clements Boykin '71

BENNETT BELL HISTORY

The BELL RINGER 1951-1952
Alma Fitzgerald Fowlkes '54

The BELL TOWER

The BENNETT BELL was a gift from Lyman Bennett.[38]

Interview in the "Bennett Banner" December 1952 [39]
Mr. Cooper,
"In the theory classes, there are a number of potential composers. There is to be a project which will center around writing college songs. There has been a combining of the arts. Have you noticed modern music and modern art? Isn't it similar? Did you know that the Bennett Bell is truly a good bell? Listen sometimes and you will hear an interval of a tenth. Hear ye, hear ye!"

Bettye J. Washington Campbell '53
9428 S. Michigan Ave., Chicago, IL 60619
773-264-0126

"The Bennett College connection has proven to be an enduring benefit for me starting as a Freshman when Dr. Player personally guided my course of study. This was to continue for four years and occurred prior to her presidency.

Before graduation, the College offered me the opportunity to apply for the United Negro College Fund's FLORINA LASKER FELLOWSHIP that covered all expenses leading to the graduate degree and a career in information sciences. Changes and challenges in this field have been encountered and, even in retirement, skills and experience continue to provide meaningful volunteer service for students, friends and community.

The role played by the UNCF has been remembered and has led to participation in UNCF'S Chicago and National Inter-Alumni Councils. Bennett friendships have continued and taken on new meaning. It is awesome to be a member of the class of '53! A few years after graduation three of us (from different classes) organized the Chicago Bennett College Alumnae. We met regularly; in the 1960's turkey dinners and Christmas fruitcakes were sold to raise money. Today this has changed.

National Association meetings, Alumnae/Commencement Weekends, and gathering of returning graduates provide annual opportunities to revisit the Campus. Consequently, for the distance travelled to make the trips, I was surprised with a special award at the All-Bennett Banquet, Alumnae Weekend, 2010. For me this crystal ball is the symbol of the lasting value of the Bennett College experience." [40]

The Golden Class of 1953
1st row: *6th from the left*: Betty J. Washington Campbell
2nd row: *1st from right*: Ellease Randall Colston

In Memoriam [41]
Ellease Randall Browning Colston '53
(1930-2008)

Ellease Randall Browning Colston served her Alma Mater well, having been employed by Bennett College For Women for forty-two years. A 1953 graduate, she recruited students, chaperoned the choir on tours, helped with the newsletter, organized chapters, and raised funds.

In September 1970, President Dr. Isaac Miller, Jr. appointed her as the first full time Director of Alumnae Affairs. Beginning with three active chapters and the Loyalty Fund of approximately $7,000.00, her leadership, influence, love, and encouragement increased the annual giving to more than $300,000 at the time of her retirement.

The Ellease Randall Colston Service Award has been established in her honor by the NAA. Also, the Ellease Randall Scholarship has been established by her family.

A Tribute to Our Sister Dr. Lyvonne Mackel Washington '53
Submitted by Audrose Mackel Banks '49, Gwendolyn Mackel Rice '61, Marilyn Hortense Mackel '65

Phenomenal Woman Award 2001
Marilyn Mackel JD, Gwendolyn Mackel Rice.
Lyvonne Mackel Washington, D.D.S., Michelle Brower,

A Letter of Nomination for 2001 Phenomenal Bennett Woman Award

We are indeed pleased to nominate our sister, Lyvonne Mackel Washington, DDS, FACD, for a Phenomenal Bennett Woman Award under the Professional Achievement Category and more specifically for the Dr. J. Henry Sayles Outstanding Woman in the Sciences Award. Because Lyvonne was a student of Dr. Sayles and very much influenced and encouraged by him, this would be a particularly fitting honor.

As our statement describing her accomplishments, we submit a letter written by her former employer, Dr. Virginia Caine, M.D., Director of the Marion County Health Department, that nominated Lyvonne for the Center for Leadership Development (CLD) 2000 Neighborhood and Community Service Award. Lyvonne received one of the top honors at the Awards dinner as a result of Dr. Caine's nomination: the Mme. C. J. Walker Outstanding Woman of the Year

Award. Dr. Caine's letter describes Lyvonne's professional accomplishments quite vividly and factually. As Lyvonne's employer, she knew well her professional accomplishments far better than we could ever know or express.

Her resume lists some of her awards received prior to her retirement. However, on the occasion of her retirement celebration, she received the following awards in recognition of her services to the residents of Marion County, Indiana as well as for the dental profession:

Sagamore of the Wabash, the Governor of Indiana's highest City of Indianapolis Outstanding Service Award from the Mayor

State Health Commissioners Award for Excellence in Public Health

Marion County Health Department (MCHD) Award for 35 years of Extraordinary and Dedicated Service to the MCHD

Distinguished Service Award from the Indiana Public Health Association

President's Citation Award from the President of the Indiana Dental Association

Indianapolis Component of the National Dental Association Appreciation Award For Dedicated Service to the Community and the Association

The Mme. C. J. Walker Outstanding Woman of the Year Award was received at a separate event on that evening.

While we knew all along that Lyvonne was a phenomenal woman, there was so much we had not previously known about her exemplary work, particularly her health advocacy efforts for the disadvantaged as Director of Operations for the Marion County Health Department Dental Services. We are quite proud of our Bennett Sister and our sibling.

<u>Dr. Lyvonne Mackel Washington '53</u>

Rosa Fargas '54
749 Baisley Trail, The Villages, FL 32162
352-633-0543

Rather than returning home to Puerto Rico after graduation from Bennett College in 1954, I would work almost two decades for the Mellon Bank in Pittsburgh, Pennsylvania. While living there I became a missionary under the auspices of the Assemblies of God and spread the Word of God everywhere I could.

My enthusiasm took me to such places as Jamaica where I preached the Word to hundreds of people. That is what I refer to as my first missionary trip. The Jamaican people are very sweet and hungry for the Word. Every night many people would come to church and accepted Jesus Christ as their personal Savior. What an experience! All that was done at my own expense.

Rosa Fargas
On The Way To
Sunday Vespers

The second missionary trip was to Peru in South America. There the descendants of the Inca Indians were also interested in accepting Jesus as their Savior. I visited Peru twice because I fell in love with the Incas. They are very short in statues. To them I was very tall (although I am only 5'4" tall). Even the public buses are low from floor to ceiling.

While in Peru I visited the Inca ruins in Cusco, called Machupichu. This area is composed of huge stones that the Incas carried on their backs to build this monument to the sun. Hence it is referred to as the Sun City. The Incas must have been very ingenious to place each stone without mortar, on top of the other in perfect precision, as much so that after so many centuries of wear and tear, earthquakes and pillages of weather, the monument is still in perfect shape. They worship the Sun God. Their gold is inexpensive to them. One could buy 18 karat gold pieces for as much as one can buy inexpensive gold plated jewelry her in the USA.

The church services were held every night and twice on Sunday. Some of these Incas had never heard of the Bible and when I quoted a scripture verse, they wanted to know if that was in the book. Their language is not Spanish, although they understand it. They speak Quechuan. So everywhere I went I had to have a chaperone to interpret to me what they were saying to me, if they spoke in their own Quechuan language.

I shall cherish these experiences and keep them in my heart for as Long as I live.

Que bendicion al ver la gente recivir a CRISTO como su Salvador, el verlos ser renacidos!

(WHAT A BLESSING TO SEE PEOPLE ACCEPTING JESUS AS THEIR SAVIOR! TO SEE THEM BEING REBORN!)

Golden Class of 1954 [42]
2ⁿᵈ row-second from left: Rosa Fargas
(Photo Courtesy of Robert Bell)

In Memoriam
Peggy Jeffries Foman '54
(1934-2001)
Submitted by Dorothy Dixon Morrow '54

My cousin Peggy Jeffries Foman and I graduated together from Pleasant Grove High School in Burlington, N.C., on May 30, 1950. She was the salutatorian of the class. Peggy's intentions had always been to enroll at Bennett College, but I did not make that decision until later.

After arriving on campus, we were met with a great disappointment because Peggy was assigned to Kent Hall and I to Jones Hall. Of course both of us cried because we wanted to be together. We had been together for most of our lives. Peggy had lived with us for a while so she could attend school there until her parents could move into the district. We had been in the same classes from the sixth grade through high school. Our mothers were sisters and our fathers were first cousins, and so Peggy was like a sister to us.

Peggy stayed in Kent Hall with Nurse Alsie Trammell whom we all loved and even spent some summers working at the college. Many times Nurse Trammell and Mr. and Mrs. Robert Jones would bring Peggy home to Burlington just for the day.

1954 Class Poem Read by Peggy Jeffries

Dear Class of '54, let's always keep our promise
Four years ago, we made within these walls.
To bring great honor to our Alma Mater—
To do our best to climb and never fall.
We came today to say farewell to classmates,
To friends we have known—to teachers kind and dear,
Our hearts are sad and filled with countless memories,
Of college days which swiftly disappear.

We go our ways and face life's many problems,
To carry service ever far and wide
With cherished hopes of eager anticipation,
From Bennett where always our love shall abide.
                            Peggy Jeffries and Dorothy Dixon

After graduation in 1954, Peggy and I worked together at the Double Oaks Elementary School in Charlotte, N.C. I would remain there until I married William Grant Morrow on August 20, 1955 and moved to Mebane, my husband's hometown. Later Peggy married and moved to Mebane, too. Again Peggy and I would teach together. This time at the Melville Elementary School.

Believe it or not, later Peggy moved to Durham after I had moved there and we lived in the same housing development, reared our children together and again we taught at the same school until Peggy moved to Maryland.

Unfortunately, Peggy died of cancer on Easter Sunday morning ten years ago. She was such a positive person and talked to many people about cancer. After I retired, I would leave Durham to carry Peggy for treatments in Burlington. We spent many hours of her last days together.

Truly a "Bennett Ideal," she was so kindhearted, generous, loveable, and loved everyone. I never remember having a disagreement with her in all our years together. (That was because of Peggy's personality.) We were like sisters all of our lives. She became a wonderful first grade teacher and many of her students still talk about her.

Dorothy Dixon Morrow '54
427 Denton St., Durham, NC 27713
919-544-3830 dotmorr427@yahoo.com

So much has happened since May 30, 1950, which was the date not only of my graduation from Pleasant Grove High School in Burlington, N.C., but also my 18th birthday. I realized I was about to leave a nurturing environment with devoted parents and teachers who had guided me for many years and I was about to enter a new world where many important decisions had to be made that would affect me for life.

I had graduated as valedictorian and my cousin Peggy Jeffries Foman '54 as salutatorian. Our teachers wanted to suggest where we should go to college. Peggy was sure that she was going to Bennett, but I was determined to go to North Carolina College in Durham N.C. (now North Carolina Central University).

I was familiar with Bennett because many young ladies and cousins from my community and from Greensboro had attended Bennett. My brother was a student at A&T State University and I had been on Bennett's campus many times. However, my mind was made up that I was going to college in Durham. I had an uncle and an aunt who lived there, a few blocks from North Carolina College, and I had spent many weekends with them. During this time I had made many friends in Durham and also another close cousin was going to attend there. I had also met a young man from Durham who was enrolling.

I was the second oldest in a family of ten children who lived on our farm in Alamance County. Our parents had always told us to choose the college we wanted to attend, but **we were**

going to college. Subsequently, all ten of us finished college and beyond.

Along with the other reasons I gave for wanting to go to North Carolina College, I felt if I went to a state college this would help my parents since my brother was in college and my sister, Pauline Dixon Jeffries '57 would be attending college in a few years and my other sisters and brothers would follow every two to three years. Most of the time, three of us were in college at the same time. Six of my siblings went to A&T, two of us to Bennett and the other two chose colleges away from Greensboro.

I remember once when a man asked Daddy where he went to college and Daddy said, "I went to A&T and to Bennett College."

The man replied, "Mr. Dixon, you must be mistaken because Bennett is an all girls' school."

Daddy answered very proudly, "As many times as I went in and out of the business offices at A&T and Bennett to pay the bills, don't tell me that I did not go there."

Even though Daddy and Mother did not go to college, they were well read and always helped us with our homework. Daddy could give us the correct answers to our math problems, but we had to figure out the method he used to solve them.

Mother loved poetry and she could recite many poems from her school days. Mother's favorite poem was "Abou Ben Adhem" by James Leigh Hunt which she encouraged each of us to learn at an early age. My mother has been dead for 39 years and I get comfort when I recite the poem. I encourage my siblings to honor Mother's memory by at least acquainting their children and grandchildren with "Abou Ben Adhem." I think I was inspired to write poetry because of Mother. I have had several poems published.

Bennett College was highly thought of in my community since Dr. David D. Jones had some cousins there and we often heard talk about him. Being a cousin of Arneida Jones Jeffries, he often visited with the family of her daughter Gilberta Jeffries Mitchell '38.

Gilberta Jeffries Mitchell
'38

    She was born in our community, had attended and taught at the school which went from grade one through high school. Mrs. Mitchell had been influential in persuading many young ladies from our high school, as well as girls who lived in neighboring communities to attend Bennett and she was not giving up on me. Every day, near the end of the school year, Mrs. Mitchell would approach me to complete an application for Bennett, but I turned her a deaf ear.

    I was accepted at North Carolina College and I was not going to apply to Bennett. One day without my knowledge, Mrs. Mitchell and her husband who taught me many science courses, went to Bennett with my transcript in hand and met with Dr. Player. They told her the story of my family, how close Peggy and I were, and asked for a scholarship for me. Dr. Player knew the other girls who had attended Bennett because of Mrs. Mitchell. Dr. Player said to the Mitchells, "Bring Dorothy on and we will take care of her." This was two weeks before I had to report with the freshman class. I had to complete an application several weeks after I arrived.

    There was a rule at Bennett that no one was allowed to go home until after Thanksgiving, but I was so homesick until my mother got special permission from Mrs. Smith to let me come home one Saturday with my brother who was at A&T. After staying at home all day, I returned to Bennett and I was not as homesick. I was still homesick, though, but I did not want to leave Bennett.

1950 Bennett College Freshmen Tour Campus [43]
l-r: Peggy Jeffries, Louise Hinson, Ercell Burton, Mildred Copeland, Dorothy Dixon, Frances Allison, Barbara Crutchfield

    After my freshman year, I became the assistant in biology because I thought I wanted to major in biology. Later I became the assistant dormitory director in Pfeiffer Hall for the remainder of my college days. I felt that Pfeiffer Hall was the greatest dorm of all.
    During my senior year, my sister Pauline enrolled in Bennett and stayed in Kent Hall where Peggy was the assistant director. However, this did not keep Pauline from being homesick. She often came too me crying that she wanted to go home. I told her in no uncertain terms that she knew she was not going home and she must get adjusted. Peggy was the assistant dorm director and Pauline stayed in her room so much until Nurse Trammell just let her stay with Peggy. Finally, Pauline got over being homesick and she also loved Bennett.
    Pauline was assigned to work on the switchboard. President Jones called her, "My little Paula," and he liked for her to make his

long distance calls. I think this is why Pauline named her daughter "Paula."

I cannot remember being reprimanded but one time at Bennett. One day I was on duty at the desk in Pfeiffer Hall when I took off my shoes. I did not think anything about it until Dr. Player appeared and said, *"Dorothy, a Bennett young lady keeps her shoes on while on duty."*

Of course, I stood up when Dr. Player approached the desk and I did not have time to slip on my shoes. This hurt my feelings very much to know I had done something displeasing to Dr. Player. To this day, I still think of Dr. Player when I slip my shoes off when I am in a place where I should not do that. (I just can't break the habit.)

Dr. Jones was president of Bennett when I was there. I was aware of all of the rules and regulations before I enrolled and they never bothered me. We looked forward to the annual college parties.

Dorothy Dixon Morrow '54

President and Mrs. David B. Jones
request the honor of your presence
at the
Annual College Party
Friday, January 26, 1951
Student Union Building
Bennett College
Greensboro, North Carolina
Nine until One
Please present invitation at the door

My four years were great years. To this day, I still wear a hat to church. I love all the Bennett songs. I cherish the association with many of my classmates from the 1954 class who often return to graduation and other activities.

Judith Jackson Adams keeps us informed about the latest happenings with classmates. Mildred Copeland Simms, Mary Ann Rogers Scarlette, Hazel Carter Moore, Eugenia Duncan Johnson, Mildred Harris Young, Juanita Patience Moss, Doris Drummond

Gupple, Sydney Roberts, Peggy Hall James and several others stay in touch with me by sending birthday cards, talking on the telephone, attending alumnae weekends, etc.

Dr. Hobart Jarrett [44]

I was so fortunate to have had Dr. Hobart Jarrett as my freshman advisor and my sophomore English teacher. My advisory period with Dr. Jarrett was once a week just before lunch. At this time he would walk with me to the dining hall and we would have lunch together. I enjoyed this time with him, but I was glad when we did not have spaghetti because I was so self-conscious about eating it properly.

I attribute much of my success at Bennett to Dr. Jarrett and to Mrs. Mary T. Coleman, as well as to many other teachers. Dr. Jarrett and Mrs. Coleman encouraged me throughout my four years. They were there to see if I had any problems. Dr. Jarrett would call me to his office to see how things were going even after he was not my advisor.

Valedictorian Speech From Bennett College
Dorothy Dixon Morrow '54

I graduated as valedictorian from Bennett with a B.A. degree in Elementary Education.

I was offered a scholarship to Howard University, but I would not accept it because I knew there would be other expenses for my parents. I wanted to go to work to help my parents with my other sisters and brothers who were going to college. I had several job offers, but then a Bennett graduate, Gwendolyn Cunningham who was a principal in Charlotte, came to Bennett to interview some seniors.

She offered Mary Ann Rogers, Peggy Jeffries, and me jobs at the Double Oaks Elementary School and we accepted. Of course it was great to stay near Peggy. We were not allowed to live in an apartment, so Belle Cunningham put us with Mr. and Mrs. James Lathom on Oakland Avenue and most of the time we walked to school.

I remained in Charlotte until I married William Grant Morrow on August 20, 1955, and moved to Mebane. During that time I earned a M.A. degree from North Carolina College (NCCU). Then after moving to Durham, I did further study at the University of Chapel Hill and at Duke for my reading and administration degrees.

Some of my fond memoirs of Bennett were "beauty work," vespers, May Day, wearing hats and gloves, football games at A&T where I could ride with my brother, rest periods, room inspections, signing in and out, and President Jones' *"What is your purpose?"*

A life member of the National Alumnae Association, I am very active in the Durham Alumnae Chapter which I spearheaded the initial effort to organize in 1969 at the request of Mrs. Mary Mayfield Eady. I will always support my chapter and work tirelessly to assure that all chapter functions are a success, especially the White Breakfast and this year will be our 21st.

During my lifetime I have been the recipient of numerous awards, but one of my proudest moments was when I received the Susie Jones Award in 2001. I had loved and admired Mrs. Jones during my four years at Bennett and receiving this award was a great honor.

2001 SUSIE W. JONES AWARD
l.-r.: Carolyn Walker, William G. Morrow, Dorothy Dixon Morrow, Dr. Marian Lee Bell

Grant and I have three adult sons and three adult grandchildren. I retired in 1992 after a very successful teacher/administrator career in the Durham City Schools.

1954

Class Colors: Green and White

Class Flower: Magnolia

Class Motto:

"In the nature of things, we cannot be wrong with man and right with God."
Some 1954 Belles

Seated l-r: Marian Samuels, Elizabeth Nathaniel, Dorothy Dixon, Mary Ann Rogers, Charlotte Alston, Barbara Crutchfield
Standing l-r: Darnell King, Marietta Harris, Carmen Cora
(Photo courtesy of Dorothy Dixon Morrow)

Mary Ann Rogers Scarlette, H.L.D. '54
1216 Eastside Dr., Greensboro, NC 27406
336-273-4667   maryscarlette@msn.com

I, **Mary Ann Rogers Scarlette,** was the only child born to Lawrence and Clara Rogers. Following my birth in Hampton Virginia, my father, nicknamed "Chief" by Prexy's boys, moved my mother and me into housing for faculty and staff on Bennett's campus.

He qualified for this type

Lawrence Rogers

of housing because he had been employed by President David D. Jones in 1929 as Bennett's first superintendent of building and grounds. My father remained in this position until September 1970. I continued to live in campus housing until the fall of 1970.

I am the original "campus brat," having been raised on the campus, enrolling as a student the fall of 1950, graduating in 1954, returning as a faculty member August 1961, and retiring as Academic Dean in June 2001. I grew up under Dr. Jones, worked under the leadership of Dr. Willa B. Player, Dr. Isaac H. Miller, Jr. and Dr. Gloria R. Scott.

It is hard to believe that I have seen every structure on campus erected (and some demolished) since Pfeiffer Hall in 1934.

My mother, Clara Rogers, served in several capacities on campus. Her longest tenure was that of Dietitian in the Steele Hall Dining Room where students (and faculty) ate three (3) sit down meals on white table cloths every day. Some meals were family style while others were served by student waitresses.

Clara Rogers

Many believe that my tenure at Bennett as my only work experience. As a student, I worked as a domestic for a family in the affluent section of Greensboro. During the summers, I worked as a director of child care centers for the children of migrant workers in New York state and Pennsylvania. After graduating as an elementary education major, I taught in Charlotte, N.C. for seven (7) years. My return to Greensboro and Bennett was prompted by a commitment I had made as the first recipient of the Danforth Alumnae Scholarship to teach on the college level for one (1) year. That year became forty (40). The Danforth Scholarship enabled me to earn a Master's degree at Cornell University.

While at Bennett, I experienced changes, challenges, happiness, sorrow, love, personal and professional growth and numerous opportunities to "give back" to the college community. I held many positions from instructor and assistant professor of elementary education to assistant director of teacher education; supervisor of elementary level student teachers; Interim Director of the Division of Education; supervisor of the Children's House; Chair of the Curriculum Committee, Chair of Ceremonial and Special Events; Chief Protocol Officer, director of many summer programs for incoming first year students; Director of numerous self-studies and finally, Academic Dean in the Office of Academic Affairs.

I taught and developed more courses than I can recall but most of all, I was blessed with the opportunity to learn from, listen to and guide so many prospective educators, administrators, community activists ("movers and shakers"), wives, mothers, change agents, entrepreneurs and dynamic leaders. These were my "Elements," my advisees, mentees, my students, and my friends. Every class I taught was a love affair with learning; every student who visited my office, stopped in for Jolly Ranchers, or sat in the "pink chair" presented an opportunity for me to serve.

Over the years, I had the best colleagues and support team one could ever want. Additionally, I had the privilege of working with my high school and college classmate–Dr. Charlotte L. Alston '54, VP for Academic Affairs/Provost.

Not only did Bennett educate me, but The Bennett Family and my Bennett Sisters were a source of strength and support during the "rough times" in my life.

I married J. J. Scarlette (the college business manager for thirty-eight years) in 1967.

Mr. and Mrs. James Scarlette (1967)

We were blessed with four (4) children: James Lawrence (Jimmy), deceased; Barbara Ann; and the twins – Frances and Mamie. Yes, it is true, I did tape my class lectures, provided all assignments, prepared class materials and graded papers during my child birth absences. Just ask the students whom I taught Spring 1971 and Fall of 1973.

The Scarlettes
l.-r.: Frances, Mamie, "J.J.," Barbara,
Mary Ann (1989)

The Bennett Family was there for me for my mother's death (1965), my son's death (1970), my father's death (1972), and my husband's death (1993).

Carrie Barge Chapel [45]

Bennett gave me a tremendous cultural base. From as early as I can remember, even programs in the old Carrie Barge Chapel, I was exposed to

notable speakers, Greek and Shakespearean plays,
the Living Madonna productions, music by Dr. R. Nathaniel Dett, outstanding choral works, opera singers, stage and screen actors, politicians, presidential candidates, activists, first ladies of our country, international leaders, dynamic theologians, and the men from Lincoln and Morehouse.

The traditions such as the College Christmas Party, Christmas Sister Week, birthday dinners, vespers, campus illumination, the President's Ball, Homemaking Institutes, hikes to the county home at Thanksgiving, junior/senior prom (remember the year we "imported" an entire battalion from Ft. Bragg so everyone could dance?) and the Freshman Choir (Mr. Whiteman's 6:00 a.m. rehearsals). We sang college songs that strengthened the bond of sisterhood and always traveled in groups – even to events at A & T.

Experiences in service to others were nurtured at Bennett – beauty work, waiting tables, Victory gardens, raking leaves and of course – polishing the Pfeiffer Hall brass.

It has been over fifty-five years since Prexy presented my class with their diplomas. Little did we know that we would be the last class to have that distinction.

My classmates, my Bennett Sisters are special to me. We stay in touch, remember birthdays and special events. I sat next to Sydney Roberts for four (4) years and I still stay in touch with my senior year roommate, Allene Dudley Bundy. We are looking forward to our sixty (60) year reunion in 2014.

Since my retirement from Bennett in 2001, I frequently visit the campus. Every time I set foot on the quadrangle or enter a building – especially the Chapel, I am overwhelmed with memories of my life as a child, student, faculty member, and administrator. When I look at the older magnolia trees that my father planted and smell the subtle fragrance of the beautiful blossoms in late spring, my heart and very being are warmed with thoughts of my Bennett Connection. I raised my children on the campus; thus, Bennett

has become a part of their lives, also.

My relationship with Bennett is unique. The many walks on campus with my father while growing up allowed me to gain a perspective of Bennett few people have.

I have been blessed with an experience that will never be replicated. The "Spirit of Bennett" lives within me and will forever remain.

"Bennett Alma Mater, Fairest,
Ever have you stood.
For the gifts of friendship rarest,
Loving sisterhood.
May we catch your holy vision,
Closely to it cling.
Bennett Alma Mater, Fairest,
Loyalty we bring.
CHORUS
Hearts are lifting, spirits singing,
Great thy praises be.
Bennett Alma Mater, Fairest,
Hail, all hail to thee.

Words from "Fairest Bennett" written by Mrs. Guy Lambert (music by R. Nathaniel Dett) 1940.

In Memoriam
Joye Stanley McLean Bridges '54

Submitted by her daughter Rev. Dr. Natalie McLean '80

December 24, 1954
Marriage to Nathaniel Jessup
Dr. David and Mrs. Susie Jones are in attendance

   Joye Christeve Stanley entered Bennett College in the fall of 1950. Even though her mother's desire was for her to major in English, Mom experienced a different calling. She was passionate about music and education and at the tender age of thirteen, Mother became the choir director and minister of music at St. Stephens UCC (where she remained for over thirty years). As a matter of fact, with the money she earned, Mother visited Mr. Bailey each week to make tuition payments, which was $600.00. Though the fee is extremely reasonable by our standards, in Mom's day, tuition was not always easily acquired.

   While at Bennett, Mother was actively involved in campus life as the director for a quartet. They had the opportunity to represent the college in various settings, bringing increased visibility to Bennett and broadening their personal horizons. Mom often talked about completing "beauty work" on Saturday mornings which was the only time students could wear pants on campus and she smiled as she recalled the occasions when the men of Morehouse came to visit. Mother fondly remembered the friends she made while at Bennett; one of her dearest friends was Elizabeth Nathaniel, whose oldest daughter became Mother's goddaughter. Many of the bonds formed at Bennett lasted a lifetime. During Mother's memorial service in August 1999, a woman who came to offer condolences said, "Your mother was my big sister at Bennett."

As student, Mother built on the foundation laid by her parents, the church, community and the school system. The College supported that continuity of care which afforded holistic development and a well-rounded experience for Mom. Bennett College allowed Mother to grow as a woman and nurtured her quiet and gentle spirit.

Mommie spent countless hours preparing herself for every occasion. She commented she played for teas, weddings, recitals, pageants, and worship services – two services on Sunday because in that era, many churches hosted morning and "night" worship. With each ministry opportunity, Mother's gift and confidence blossomed.

Her love for Bennett led her to be a faithful contributor and frequent fundraiser to support the efforts of our alma mater. She loved the mission and the spirit of the college and believed in the possibilities of what Bennett could become.

Mommie was the consummate professional in the varied facets of her life. She completed the Bachelor of Arts in Music Education at Bennett and earned the Master of Social Work at the University of North Carolina at Chapel Hill. She received additional training at the Babcock School of Management, Wake Forest University. The wealth of her experiences was utilized in the North Carolina Department of Human Resources Division of Social Services. She supervised Directors, Program Administrators/Managers and Supervisors in sixteen North Carolina County Department of Social Services for over twenty-five years of distinguished service.

The impact of her life was also felt within the community. Mother was very active with Church Women United; Beta Iota Omega Chapter of Alpha Kappa Alpha Sorority, Inc.; the American Guild of Organists; the E. Logan Penn Choral Society Director; North Carolina Social Services Association; Bennett College Alumnae Association; and Black Child Development Institute, to name a few. She simply loved people!

In 1982, Mother was featured in an organ concert at Providence Baptist Church where she served as musician for twenty-two years. It was wonderful! For fifty-two years, Mother offered devoted service at the piano and organ.

Because of my mother's influence, I have a deep appreciation for various types of music, especially classical and hymns. They still my spirit in times of stress and uneasiness. For me, Mommie's gift of music gave me a glimpse of heaven's melodies. I miss her more than words can express.

I miss my mom's smile and her laughter; I miss her cooking and her counsel; I will never forget the ways in which she could make something most memorable and extraordinary out of the simple and uneventful.

Of all that I miss about my mom, her music has left a void not easily filled. God spoke to me as she played and used her to soothe my spirit as her fingers gently caressed the keys of the piano or organ. How she honored God with His gift! My uncle believes "everyone needs an altar, that place where you commune with God." I have come to know Mother's altars were the piano and organ. There she sat at Jesus' feet, was filled with His Spirit and experienced the commission to "feed the flock of God."

I will ever be grateful to God for choosing Joye Stanley McLean to be my mom. I pray my life is in some way a reflection of the love Mommie shared with so many and that I live up to the meaning of her beautiful, descriptively appropriate and lyrical name – *Joye*!

THE LAST CLASS ON WHICH PRESIDENT DAVID DALLAS JONES CONFERRED DEGREES

Eighty-First Commencement

Monday, May 31, 1954 at 10:30 O'Clock

In The Annie Merner Pfeiffer Chapel

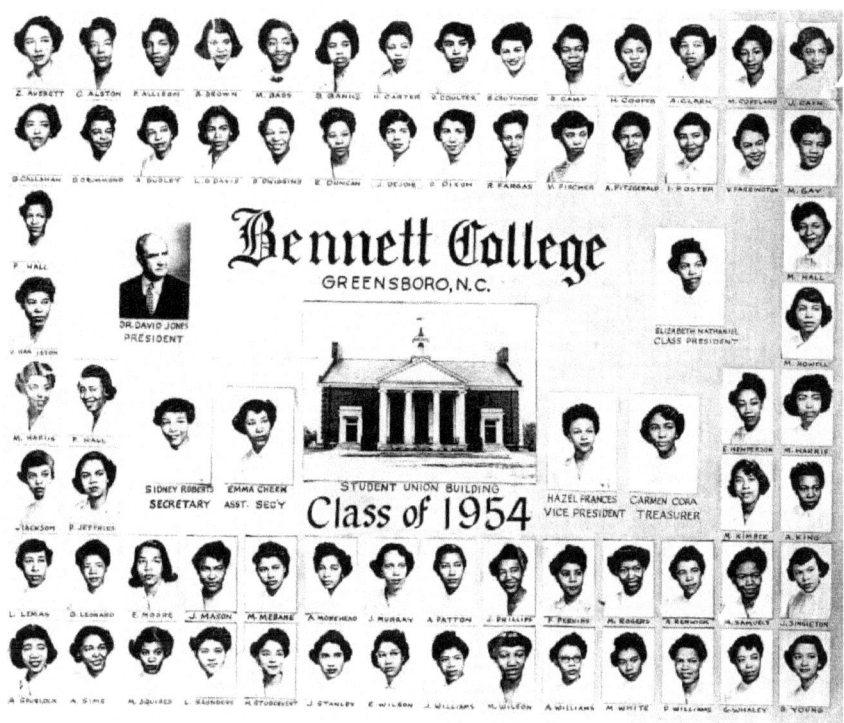

CLASS OF 1954

AWARDS AND HONORS

SENIOR HONORS

VALEDICTORIAN: DOROTHY M. DIXON
SALUTATORIAN: BERTHA OLIVIA BROWN

FULBRIGHT AWARD TO STUDY AT THE UNIVERSITY OF LYON,
LYON, FRANCE, 1954-55
BERTHA OLIVIA BROWN, '54, Asheville, North Carolina

BELLE TOBIAS SCHOLARSHIP
BETTY SUE BRAGG, '57, Greensboro, North Carolina

LULA DONNELL PRIZE
WILLIE LEE HARRISON, '57, Greensboro, North Carolina

CLASS OF 1921 PRIZE
MILDRED EARLE COPELAND, '54, Brooklyn, New York

IRMA GRAHAM PRIZE
MARIETTA JEAN HARRIS, '54, Kansas City, Missouri

GOODE PRIZE FOR HOME ECONOMICS
JUANITA CYNTHIA WRIGHT, '55, Lumberton, North Carolina

OMICRON ETA CHI AWARD
ANN MARIE COOPER, '57, Glendale, Ohio

CANDIDATES FOR THE DEGREE OF BACHELOR OF ARTS

Charlotte LeNora Alston
Bertha Vanessa Banks
Marion E. Bass
Bertha Olivia Brown
Janet Carolyn Cain
Beatrice Virginia Callahan
Doris Althea Camp
Geraldine Wiley Campt
Anita June Clark
Barbara Effie Crutchfield
Janice Lynn Dejoie
Dorothy M. Dixon
Doris Milton Drummond
Frances Allene Dudley
Eugenia Marie Duncan
Delores S. Dwiggins
Rosa Victoria Fargas
Velma Jean Jones Farrington
Velma Fischer
Alma Sidel Fitzgerald
Vera Aileen Hairston
Peggy Louise Hall
Mildred Evelyn Harris
Sylane Brazil Ivey
Judith Claye Jackson
Peggy Joan Jeffries
Doris Alvina Jones
Mary Marie Lamb
Lillian Alice McKay Lemos
Gwendolyn Bernice Leonard
Jennie R. Mason
Mary Ruth McCrimmon
Margaret Leo Mebane
Earline Moore
Almetta Morehead
Elizabeth Nathaniel
Cleo B. Nimmons
Barbara Winona Parks
Annetta Jo Patton
Flossie Perkins
Ellease Randall
Ruth Amanda Renwick
Sydney Junia Roberts
Mary Ann Rogers
Marion Frances Samuels
LaMara Elizabeth B. Saunders
Jacqueline Joyce Singleton
Joyce C. Stanley
Margaret Catherine Studevent
Grace Marie Whaley
Annie Mae Williams
Dorothy Allene Williams
Edna Joan Williams
Eloise Rose Wilson
Mary Gretta Wilson
Nannie Elizabeth Young

CANDIDATES FOR THE DEGREE OF BACHELOR OF SCIENCE

Frances Louise Allison
Hazel Araminta Carter
Emma Marie Cheek
Mildred Earle Copeland
Vada Dean Coulter
Stella Ann Ferguson
Irene Foster
Hazel Lee Frances
Mamie Grey Hall
Marietta Jean Harris
Effie Jeanette Henderson
Mable Lee Howell
Marilyn Louise Kimber
Alice Darnell King
Ina Elnora McCarther
Julia Bernice Moore
June Edwadine Murray
Barbara Jeanne Phillips
Mae Yvonne Squires
Mable Beatrice White
Barbara J. Young

In Memoriam
Dr. David Dallas Jones [46]
(1889-1955)

When **Dr. David D. Jones** became the 9th president of Bennett College in 1926, the campus looked like a corn-and-turnip patch. There were ten students and three buildings.[47] A Greensboro native and Y.M.C.A. secretary with no experience in education, he was chosen by the Methodist Church to run a college that would be for women only.

Indeed, the right man was chosen, for he was a visionary with a purpose. Consider how he was grooming Dr. Willa B. Player for the presidency without her even being aware of his purpose. Consider how he allowed students to organize and to carry out the "Boycott of 1937."

He gave and demanded excellence, his favorite question to his "girls" being, *"Young lady, what is your purpose?"* And he would expect to receive a satisfactory answer.

His philosophy, along with that of such personalities as Eleanor Roosevelt, Herbert Hoover, Helen Keller, and Pearl S. Buck appeared in *This I Believe,* a book produced by Edward R. Murrow. [48]

His persona is remembered vividly by every Belle whose president he was. "Prexy's" greatest legacy is the love he had for his *beloved* **daughters** *of God* as indicated in the following articles:

THE BENNETT BANNER
JUNE 1940

President Jones Addresses Seniors On Class Day

"Using as his theme the quotation, *'He required so little, he gave so much,'* President Jones in delivering his traditional address on Senior Class Day, said in part:

"*'This ceremonial is a mere symbol that someday you will have something to give.'* He advised the seniors to be self-forgetful, grateful, and diligent to the task that they set for themselves."[49]

THE BENNETT BANNER
DECEMBER 1952

"*'We hardly realize,'* Dr. Jones said in the book, This I Believe, edited by Edward R. Murrow, *'the sense of glow, the sense of achievement which can come from doing a job well. Just working at a thing with enthusiasm and with a belief that the job may be accomplished, however uncertain the outcome, lends zest to life.'*

"And well might this man in his maturing sixties know, for through his efforts at the college he now heads, Bennett has grown from ten students to nearly 500 per year in the past 25 years. Three campus buildings have mushroomed into 31.

This year leading Methodist educators hailed this zestful man to the nation's capitol to pay tribute to his outstanding work as an educator in the South. The Christian Education Magazine, Methodists' official publication conferred high honors on Dr. Jones for his 25 years of service at Bennett." [50]

Joyce Evelyn Martin Dixon '56/ '81
503 Waycross Drive   Greensboro, NC 27410
336-294-0221   jdixon39@triad.rr.com

(1981)
<u>Receiving Diploma from Dr. Isaac Miller, Jr.</u>

The tour down Martin's Memory Lane took me to our "Happy Home," "Support Street," "Party Place" (we loved to entertain), stopped briefly at "Tearful Towers," and ended on "Amazing Grace Avenue."

The time has come to tell my story. First of all, I did not want to attend an all-girls' school. A big lesson was in store for me: some of life's roads have detours (especially when a mother and college president are the traffic directors). I went to Bennett against my will and graduated with tons of gratitude for the manipulators.

I was a non-resident student, yet required to abide by the same rules and regulations as resident students. My voice with others was raised about off-campus attire, attending vesper services after worshiping at our own churches, and the requirement of being in assigned seats at inconvenient times. You have probably guessed the complaints fell on deaf ears. A room was provided for non-resident students in the Student Union Building and I served one term as the president of the group. Reminiscing moments include activities, dynamic speakers, and faculty members, especially Mrs. Streat and Miss Gilbert.

Rather than share further details about my days as a student, welcome to "Life away from and return to Greensboro."

Janice Gail Dixon

Love, marriage and baby carriage roles were accepted with the intensity of most 1950's wives. I married Jacob "Jake" Dixon, Jr., my childhood sweetheart and graduate of the first Air Force ROTC class at NCA&T. We had the perfect family: a boy and a girl. All of us enjoyed the traveling that was synonymous with military life: Paris, Rome, Amsterdam, Venice, Frankfurt, Athens, and most of the United States. You get the picture.

Then, more detours! Janice, our fun-loving and energetic prima ballerina was diagnosed with leukemia and an incurable kidney disease at the age of four. That was before dialysis and transplants. She passed away six months later.

Jacob, III, Duke graduate, followed in his Dad's footsteps and became a military instructor pilot for NATO Forces. He was piloting a plane one summer afternoon in Wichita Falls, Texas, when it gave out of power and crashed. He at age twenty-seven and the passenger were killed. Devout faith in God, along with the support of family and friends plus demanding work schedules, sustained Jake and me through the losses. A scholarship is given in our son's memory every year and I began a program fifteen years ago that addresses organ, tissue, and bone marrow donation awareness.

Jacob Dixon III

The road straightened and a dream was realized in 1988 when Jake and I opened the doors to Creative Management Technology, Inc. (CMT), a government services contracting firm. The company grew from the two of us to over 550 employees at Kennedy Space Center and installations from North Dakota to Arizona. Performance awards were received at the White House, NASA, Johnson Controls, McDonnell Douglas, the Small Business Association, and other organizations.

Sixteen years later, another major detour! Jake received a blood transfusion shortly after he had joined the armed forces that affected the liver and several years later attacked the kidneys. He began dialysis treatments in February 2004 and passed away three months later. The emotional journey that accompanied being left totally alone would require a book of its own.

Joyce and Jake Dixon

I moved back to Greensboro in 2006. A short time later, an invitation to dinner with Dr. Johnnetta Cole, then President of Bennett College, was accompanied by an offer for the position of Volunteer Corporate Fundraiser. The reply was, "That is not one of my talents; however, a niece said the parlors in residence halls are in deplorable condition and I would welcome the opportunity to join a redecorating committee." Dr. Cole was ecstatic.

Before we finished the meal I was Chair of the Bennett College Parlor Renovation Committee and had names of three alums to assist with the task. During conversations the next couple of weeks, seven Belles and one instructor volunteered to serve on the committee. Their alumnae chapters and/or classmates provided funds for specific parlors and two members were interior designers. Those eight angels I refer to as "The Dream Team" are: Joyce Dunn Garrett '65, Rosa McDaniel Hill '50, Iris Jeffries Morton '61, Alma Pulley Stokes '64, Mischelle Simone Thompson'70, Ava Taylor Williams '69, Betty Brown Wilson '81, and Rita Lamb.

The above paragraph could have ended with: "*And the rest is history,*" but "Bennett's Needs List" continues to grow. With prayerful gratitude for the success of CMT, funds were made available for the Fitness Center in Player Hall, the Bennett Boutique, assistance with paving Union Drive and naming of the Martin-Dixon Intergenerational Center. *"To whom much is given, much is required."*

Dr. Julianne Malveaux, Bennett's current President, graciously presented me with the Woman of Substance Award in 2007 and the Board of Trustees and Faculty joined her three years later to confer the degree Doctor of Humane Letters *Honoris Causa,* and for both I am humbled and most appreciative. Obedience really does have its rewards.

Commencement 2010 on the Quad

Dr. Joyce Martin Dixon '56
Doctorate of Humane Letters, Honoris Causa
1st row: 2nd from left
(Photo courtesy of Reba Burruss-Barnes)

AWARDS AND HONORS

SENIOR HONORS

VALEDICTORIAN
BARBARA RAYMOND BROWN, '56, Akron, Ohio

SALUTATORIAN
CHARLIE REA HARVEY, '56, Columbus, Georgia

* * * *

FULBRIGHT FELLOWSHIP, UNIVERSITY OF BORDEAUX
Bordeaux, France, 1956-57
BARBARA RAYMOND BROWN, '56, Akron, Ohio

FULBRIGHT ASSISTANTSHIP, RANKE SCHULE — FREE UNIVERSITY
Berlin, Germany, 1956-57
RUTH LOUISE REESE, '56, Darlington, South Carolina

BELLE TOBIAS SCHOLARSHIP
MARY JANE WILLIAMS, '59, Winston-Salem, North Carolina

LULA DONNELL PRIZE
JOSEPHINE ANNE RAIFORD, '59, Greensboro, North Carolina

CLASS OF 1921 PRIZE
DORIS JEAN HUMPHREY, '56, Dallas, North Carolina

IRMA GRAHAM PRIZE
RUTH LOUISE REESE, '56, Darlington, South Carolina

GOODE PRIZE FOR HOME ECONOMICS
ANN MARIE COOPER, '57, Glendale, Ohio

OMICRON ETA CHI AWARD
ANECE D. FAISON, '59, Dudley, North Carolina

W. W. CHARTERS LEADERSHIP AWARD
QUEEN E. FARRISH, '57, Roxboro, North Carolina

FACULTY SCHOLARSHIP AWARD
DORIS A. LANIER, '57, Bath, North Carolina

CANDIDATES FOR THE DEGREE OF BACHELOR OF ARTS

Harriett Ann Anderson
Barbara Ann Babbs
Lila Mae Barber
Lannie Dalores Barnes
Marion Jacqueline Bowman
Barbara Raymond Brown
Charlotte Annette Brown
M. Naomi Brown
Betty Ann Burgin
Helen Cumbo Cooke
Delores Patella Cox
Betty Gwyn Davidson
Joyce Fifimae Dobson
Dolores Elizabeth Douglass
E. Lea Dunston
Pearl Floydelia Farrish
Alice Ann Foster
Loretta L. Free
Elizabeth Garrett

Sarah Lee George
Queen Idell Ghee
Maxine Igatha Gilchrist
Gertrude Odell Gill
Grace C. Grant
Ruby Louise Grant
Margaret Hall
Adelia Anetrice Lorraine Hammond
Charlie Rea Harvey
Marie Mavis Hawkins
Edna Earle Jeffries
Ida Mae Johnson
Evelyn Marian King
Estella Bernice Lowe
Lorraine Vivian Marshall
Juanita Antonio Martin
Ruth Edna McNair
Gertrude Jacqueline Millner
*Jean Anderson Moreland

Christine Evangeline Oliver
Clara M. Perry
Ellen Marie Perry
Nannie Pinnix
Geneva Virginia Porter
Elestine Drayton Powell
Shirley G. Reamey
Seneith Elizabeth Reynolds
Beatrice Sanders
Dorothy Elizbeath Sanders
Madie Joyce Skeens
Della Augusta Thomas
Felishia Dorothea Thornton
Mary E. Tillery
Nurry Ann Turner
Joyce Ward
Katie Wilhelmina Webb
Bernadine Naomi Wheeler
Ruby Jeanne Wright

CANDIDATES FOR THE DEGREE OF BACHELOR OF SCIENCE

Dorothy Jean Anderson
Henrietta Brevard
Mary Odessa Brincefield
Mary Elizabeth Brown
Fannie B. Crosby

Mary Elizabeth Graham
Doris Jean Humphrey
Ellen Josephine Hunter
Lois Ingram
Cornelia McCoy

Emily Jean Montgomery
Robbie Jean Morgan
Ruth Louise Reese
Dorothy Lorraine Robinson
Irene Green Russell

*Graduate of the Class of 1955.

COMMENCEMENT 1956

Ida Johnson Martin '56
2203 Church Street, Georgetown, SC 29440
843-546-2345

In the fall of 1952 I left Georgetown, S.C., to attend Bennett College in Greensboro, N.C. My sister Earline Conley, now deceased, was a graduate of Shaw University and became a librarian in New York City. Because of her I was able to attend college. She wanted me to attend an all-girls' school and the choices were Spelman and Bennett. For some reason which I do not remember now, I chose Bennett.

I really enjoyed my years there, especially attending the football games and other exciting events at A&T University. On the serious side, I especially remember how much I enjoyed a religion class taught by Rev. John Bryant. He was very persuasive and challenged us to think for ourselves. When I left his class I was always wondering about something.

For instance, he talked about what we have been taught about the world being destroyed by water. Was it the whole world or just an area? I had never thought about it that way before.

He told us to look in the Bible to see exactly how the stories are told. One of his questions to us was, "Is it true because it is in the Bible or is it in the Bible because it is true?"

Dr. Rose Karfoil

Another favorite professor was Dr. Rose Karfiol who had escaped from Nazi-Germany. She taught Economics and Political Science 123. I really enjoyed her classes. After graduating from Bennett, I returned to my hometown and began my teaching career in Georgetown and Marlboro Counties where I would remain for thirty-one years and six months. I became the care-provider for my elderly parents, Levi and Janie Johnson, who are now deceased.

Presently, I sing in the choir of my church, Bethesda Missionary Baptist Church in Georgetown, S.C., where I serve as the secretary of the choir. In addition, I was the correspondence secretary of the Howard High School Class of 1952 class reunions.

Volunteer activities include Boots & Booties Day Care Center, Georgetown, S.C., and Holy Cross Faith Memorial School, Pawleys Island, S.C.

I am employed as a part-time associate, "People-Greeter" at Wal-Mart, in Georgetown. Recently I received an award "in recognition of her exceptional service, performance and dedication."

My hobbies include creating programs, cards, signs, and banners of all kind. Also, I am a videographer for all occasions.

I am blessed with two sons, Larry and Dwayne Martin, four granddaughters and one great granddaughter.

Ida Johnson Martin '56 and Granddaughter Brittany Nicole Martin

Josephine Hunter Robbins '56
73 Ruspin Ave., Buffalo, NY
716-838-3631   jorobb@verizon.net

I was reared in Raleigh, N.C., by my grandmother, Mrs. Lucy Hunter. I went to Bennett College because I received a $100.00 scholarship upon my high school graduation.

I was fortunate to live in Kent Hall with special friends Charlotte Alston '54 and Alma Fitzgerald '54 (Counselors}, Barbara Brown Tazewell, Naomi Brown, Betty Burgin Jackson, and Sarah George. Other close friends were Doris Humphrey Ferree, Ruth Reese Fiuczynski,

Kent Hall

Etta Woodfork Marcellus, as well as Nurry Turner Johnson and Sydney Roberts '54 from High School.

Mr. Van S. Allen (biology) was my favorite and most supportive professor. My most memorable events were receiving the Belle Tobias Scholarship for the most outstanding progress during my freshman year and being selected as the speaker for Senior Vespers.

September 1956 was the beginning of a forty-year career in the field of education. I was a junior high science teacher in the Raleigh Public School System for three years before studying for a year at Brown University in Providence, Rhode Island.

While I was going to visit Barbara in Akron during spring break, I stopped in Buffalo to see Constance Eve (Miss Bowles, instructor-Little Theater.) I applied for a teaching position while there and was hired. Until 1966 I taught seventh grade science at the Junior High School. The summer of 1966, I was asked to direct a summer program for pregnant and parenting teens. At that time any student who became pregnant had been excluded from school. This was a Board of Education school which provided a very successful program through 1996. I started as Teacher-in-Charge, later becoming Project Administrator, then Principal. The school included grades 6-12. I retired in 1995 and then served as a consultant to the Board of Education, working with pregnant and parenting teens throughout the district.

I was married for ten wonderful years to James Edward Robbins who died from lung cancer in June of 1998. I have two stepchildren and I also played a major role in rearing two children whose mother died when they were very young.

In the early '60s I left the Baptist denomination to become a member of the St. Philip's Episcopal Church where I was confirmed in 1964. My participation has included serving on the Vestry for more than twenty years, as Warden at least eight different terms, as Sunday School Superintendent, and as advisor to the Youth Group. Currently, I am a Eucharistic Minister, Visitor, and Worship Leader. Beyond the Parish level, I have been a member of Diocesan Council, Deanery Youth Advisor, Board of Directors-Episcopal Charities, Church Home and St. Philip's Community Center. Currently I serve on the Commission on Ministries and Bishop Brent School.

In the community, I serve on many committees, as well as being a member of a number of professional organizations. In 1962, I became a member of Alpha Kappa Alpha Sorority, Inc., of which I am a life member and remain very actively involved.

My travels have taken me to many places primarily in the United States, from Alaska to Puerto Rico with a number of Caribbean trips. Photography and rubber stamping are the two hobbies I truly enjoy. The organization of pictures is not a strong point and so I have boxes of pictures in addition to the few albums

I have completed. For the past four years, most of the holiday cards I have sent were made by me because I do enjoy it very much during my retirement. I have enjoyed every second of it because there is just so much to do.

Josephine Hunter Robbins

Hideko Tamura Snider '56
1402 Andrew Drive, Medford, OR 97501
541-734-8525   h.tamura@charter.net

Hideko Tamura Snider '56

A Letter to the Golden Class of 1956

February 18, 2006

It looks like that fate has determined that I cannot come to the 50th, although I've been really looking forward to finally seeing all of you.

I never thought that a life in retirement would be this hectic, that I have to stay up every night way past like Ms. Grier's nightly "Lights-Out" time in Jones Hall. Remember how I used to sneak out to the bathroom so I could work on my homework until she caught me one night and I got busted? Well, I'm still behind in my work, but I can stay up as late as I have to and I'm in the middle of a gigantic project. My lifelong appeal for collective healing from war wounds in celebration of Life resonated among the members of the Rogue Valley Peace Choir here in southern Oregon and I'm taking them on a Peace Journey, concertizing in Kyoto, Kobe, and Hiroshima. We'll be singing in the Peace Park in Hiroshima on the 61st memorial of the A-bomb before the 10, 000 lanterns float.

I met you when I was eighteen, just seven years before that, having lost my entire universe and really struggling when I arrived. You probably remember me looking pretty cheerful and running all over the place. Thank you ever so much for giving me your warmth, company, and friendship to this uninformed and mischievous foreign student. You were my Ellis Island, my very first introduction to the only alternative I had for the lost and decimated world I left behind. You didn't intrude in, but simply accepted ne as I was and gave me the space I needed. I had a lot to catch up to understand all that you were experiencing. Today, I consider those days I spent with you as your great gift. I've moved around and lived within many groups since, but I was never to capture the warmth of a community as I felt with you at Bennett ever again.

As for the life after Bennett in education and work life, I finished BA at Wooster College and an MA from the University of Chicago, School of Social Work. I also completed a four year graduate program at the McCormick Theological Seminary. I did adoption and foster care for the Chicago Child Care Society, supervised in the Adult Psychiatry Clinic at Northwestern University Medical School and ran social work programs for the Department of Radiation Oncology at the University of Chicago Hospitals. I also kept a private practice in the western suburbs of Chicago in business and therapeutic consultations. I've lectured at universities in the U.S. and the U.K extensively in the last 20 plus years.

I wrote a book, *One Sunny Day*,[51] by Open Court Publisher in 1996, "Hiroshima Memories" for Bulletin of the Atomic Scientists, May 1995, Hiroshima's Shadow, Bird, Kai, Pamphleteers

Press, 1997, and "Hiroshima Remembrances" for Asian Weekly, August 1996. Interview articles in Good War, 1985 and in "Will the Circle be Unbroken?" in 2001 by Studs Terkel.

Since retirement in 2003, I moved to Oregon where I serve on the Multicultural Commission of the City of Medford as a commissioner responsible for annual multicultural fair and other multicultural forums. I sing in the Rogue Valley Peace Choir, enjoy Japanese cooking, tea ceremony, flower arranging, and dancing.

I have two adult children from my first marriage: a daughter and a son. A romantic story about my second marriage is in my book.

Remembering Hiroshima and Nagasaki | Hideko Tamura Snider, 77, speaks Sunday during the "How Can We Create a Nuclear-Free World?" event to remember the U.S. bombing of two Japanese cities during World War II. The Medford woman, who was 11 on Aug. 6, 1945, tells a crowd gathered at the Japanese American Historical Plaza at Tom McCall Waterfront Park about watching family members die or disappear in the Hiroshima blast.

I chair O.S. D. (One Sunny Day) Initiatives with emphasis on anti-nuclear proliferation and peace education (www.osdinitiatives.com) so that we may work towards a future free of nuclear weapons use.

Adelia Hammond Williams, Ph.D '56
6006 Riggs Road, Hyattsville, MD 20783
301-434-5191 ahwilliams@sprintmail.com

When I arrived on the campus of Bennett College for Women in the fall of 1952, I became part of a population that was smaller than the population of my entire high school graduating class in Baltimore City. Upperclassmen, faculty, and school staff were so welcoming and cordial that I felt very comfortable right away. My mind was blown away when "Prexy" met me as we were walking on campus and called me by my first name. No other head of any other school I had ever attended recognized me and called me by name as he greeted me. Two of my classmates from Douglass High School (Baltimore, Maryland), Felicia Thornton, and Carolyn German came to Bennett at the same time as I.

I will hold dear in my memory two Bennett faculty members during my matriculation at the college: Dr. Hobart Jarrett and Dr. George Breathett. Each one played a significant role in my development at Bennett and in shaping the decisions and choices I have made in my career.

Dr. Jarrett was the primary professor in my first major, English, and Dr. Breathett was the primary professor in my second major, social studies. They both are remembered for their knowledge of the subject content and their encouragement.

Three years after graduation, on May 9, 1959 I married the love of my life, Thomas "Tommy" S. Williams. We have two sons and six grandchildren

Mr. and Mrs. Thomas Williams on their wedding day and riding "happily ever after" 52 years later.

Following graduation from Bennett in May 1956. I got my first teaching job at PS 49 in Baltimore City. I remained in the Baltimore City public school system until 1966. I left Baltimore to work closer to my family in Prince Georges County (Maryland) where my older child was starting school.

In 1973, I took a leave of absence from my teaching job to complete requirements for a Masters Degree in Education from the American University in Washington, D.C. Years later I received a Doctor of Philosophy Degree from the same university.

My career in the field of education has taken me to many different settings, such as federal government offices, Howard University and American University classrooms, and United Methodist Churches. In these places I have facilitated or instructed courses in English, reading, psychology, sociology, English as a Second Language, and Bible study.

In addition to my career, I have been president of the American University Chapter of Phi Delta Kappa (Educators' fraternal organization), president of the Baltimore Washington Conference Educators' Guild, and, currently, president of the Wesleyan Choir of my church, Asbury United Methodist Church Washington, D.C.

I have enjoyed being an active part of the Metropolitan Washington D.C. Alumnae Chapter. I have served the chapter as president, hostess of chapter meetings, and facilitator of the presentation of the college choir at Asbury United Methodist church.

Dr. Adelia Hammonds Williams '56

"*Alma Mater, now we sing...*"

<u>*Alice Hayes Scipio '57*</u>
3330 N. Leisure World Blvd. Apt. 5-308
Silver Spring, MD 20906
301-598-9261   aandrsc@aol.com

I had not visited Bennett before arriving on its campus. But, I had imagined what its campus would look like, listening to the conversations of three of my high school teachers, who encouraged me to attend Bennett. And, the spouse of one was a Bennett graduate. Among those three was my homeroom teacher; she assisted me in getting a scholarship to Bennett.

The day before I arrived on Bennett's campus, my excitement hardly permitted me to contain myself. My first day arrival on campus was a bright, beautiful, sunny morning in early September 1953. An aunt and family friend drove me to Bennett from Whiteville, a small, southeastern North Carolina town; my mother was unable to take leave from work. Once on campus, we parked next to Jones Hall. As I stepped out of the car, the first and only person I saw was a tall, lanky girl standing by the entrance to Jones Hall. I walked over to her and introduced myself; she, in turn, did the same. Thus, the first person I met would be my classmate, dorm mate, roommate, and long-time friend Doris Striggles Porter. Doris had arrived earlier from Brooklyn, N.Y. via train. Having registered already, she directed my aunt and me to the Administration Building. There, we met Ms. Mayfield, Records Office, and then Mr. Scarlette, Business Office. Mr. Scarlette taught me statistics later. I had been a good math student in high school, but statistics would be my hardest subject at Bennett.

Once my trunk had been lugged to my room, my aunt kissed me goodbye, then she and her friend returned home. Unexpectedly, her friend gave me five dollars; I thought that was a lot of money at the time. Now, Doris and I could get acquainted somewhat before our roommates arrived. Doris' roommate Lena Wood Tillman came from Washington, D.C. Although Lena stayed only one semester at Bennett, she, Doris, and I became friends and remain so.

My roommate arrived that afternoon; I think it best that her name and hometown remain anonymous. Upon her arrival in our room, we exchanged pleasantries. We had gotten along fine until one day in October, at the time of A&T's homecoming; I borrowed one of her sweaters to wear to the game. After the game, I washed the sweater before returning it. There were no care instructions inside the sweater, but it did not appear to be made of wool. Behold what was once an adult sweater would now fit a toddler perfectly! Hindsight tells me that I should have asked her for care instructions. I was extremely sorry and upset to the point of tears. I apologized and asked if I could repay her for the sweater; I got no response. From that day forward, my freshman roommate and I had a most uncomfortable relationship. Henceforth, I only changed clothes and slept in my room. My free time, including beauty rest, was spent in Doris and Lena's room. I think at some point, my big sister Dr. Jacquelyn (Jackie) Lightsey Collier-Pembroke wondered why I was never in my room when she visited. However, she couldn't believe my "why" once she was told. My roommate did not return to Bennett our sophomore year. And, I have often wondered why?

When Doris' second semester roommate Sarah Taylor of Sumter, S.C., arrived, as we became acquainted, we liked each other. Again, I could comfortably spend most of my time in their room. Sarah's aunt had raised her; she invited Doris and me to come home with Sarah one weekend. Later, we obtained parental permission, went to Sumter on a Friday evening, and returned to Bennett Sunday afternoon. Sarah's aunt owned a small restaurant/juke joint. Doris and I enjoyed her good food and her kindness. Also, we had big time fun, especially after meeting some young, handsome marines stationed in Beaufort, S.C. Like Lena, Sarah, too, left Bennett after one semester. For a while, we heard from her, but that ceased. Many years later, Sarah appeared at one of our class reunions, as she had a daughter graduating from Bennett the same year. During that time, Sarah located Doris and me; the three of us had a short and joyous mini reunion.

Less than a week at Bennett, more than half of our class (mostly Jones Hall residents) decided to venture off campus to The Blue Lantern in Sedalia. We began as a naughty and daring group! How such a large group managed to sneak off and back on campus remains a mystery to me. Had the one person who was expelled not drank too much, gone to her room without vomiting and being loud in the hall, we may have been able to have this coup to boast of. To this day, I believe that there was a snitch in the dormitory. Otherwise, Miss Smith, our dormitory matron, would not have known what had happened that night. By morning, we could have cleaned the hall and that person could have slept enough that night to be sober the next morning.

Once the news spread and reached President Jones, he summoned us individually to his office. Thus, during my first week's stay at Bennett, I had an untimely meeting with "Prexy." We weren't able to prepare for such, as he randomly summoned us. He forbade us to discuss our conversation with him, following a meeting. Only one person was sent home from a group of approximately 50 or more. I think others were disciplined, according to their defense. I was grounded for a month, and I think Doris was also.

Doris and I became roommates during our sophomore year, moving into Barge Hall, together with a third roommate Ethel Maddox Bowen. But a fourth person, Jamescina (Cina) Johnson, spent most of her time in our room also. Cina left during her sophomore year to marry Wade Degraffenreidt, an Aggie. She and Ethel loved to play cards and would invite Mildred (Millie) Battiste Blue, Dorothy (Dottie) Carr McKennie from Kent Hall, and others most nights to play cards. Doris and I did not play; after we enjoyed the available snacks, we went to bed. When one of us received a care package, the contents were shared among us, as we were not overly fond of dining hall food. At dinner, Doris, Dottie, Ethel, Millie, Cina, and I always ate together. One of us would get to the dining room early to claim a table. Dottie, Ethel, and Millie are now deceased.

Following our freshman year probationary period, Doris and I walked the straight and narrow. However, we did manage to sneak to a few off campus parties successfully. During my senior year, I decided to have my hair tinted. I wanted my hair to be dark brown; but instead it became slightly blondish (lack of beautician experience). This precipitated a call from Dr. Player to meet with her. My meeting with her was quite short; she asked me whether I planned to graduate, and I said "yes." Then, she said "Miss Hayes, I expect you to have your hair back to its natural color when I see you again," and I did!

I loved my four years at Bennett -- the Sunday vespers, especially when such renowned persons as Drs. Mordecai Johnson and Benjamin Mays graced our chapel; the daily chapel services that I learned to appreciate; the lyceum programs; the required dining hall duty; and the beauty rest and work. My teachers were great and accommodating. The only sadness I experienced while at Bennett was the day that our beloved "Prexy" died in January 1956.

I feel lucky to have attended Bennett during the administrations of Drs. Jones and Player, and to be a Bennett Belle and graduate!

NO TIME FOR TEARS but commencement day at Bennett College in Greensboro, N.C., brought tears of joy to this graduate, Miss Mildred Battiste, center, of Kingstree, S.C. She is being consoled by Misses Alice Hayes, left, of Whiteville, N.C., and Gwendolyn Harris of Greensboro, N.C.

NO TIME FOR TEARS [52]
Alice Hayes, Mildred Battiste, Gwendolyn Harris

30th Reunion in 1987
Alice Hayes Scipio, Doris Striggles Porter, Cecily Baxter Johnson

---

Fannie Lillian Bellamy '58
9637 Courthouse Road, Vienna, VA 22181
703-938-0661

At Bennett College, a Methodist school, all students were required to attend chapel four times each week—Mondays, Wednesday, and Friday mornings and Sunday afternoon. However we were free to attend churches of our choice Sunday mornings.

Each Sunday at the end of chapel, Dr. Jones, President of Bennett College and after his death, Dr. Player would use as the Benediction verses 2&3 from the first epistle of John.

"Beloved, now are we the sons of God, and it doth not yet appear what we shall be; but we know that, when He shall appear, we shall be like Him; for we shall see Him as He is.

And every man that hath his hope in him purifieth himself, even as He is pure."

Even though Bennett is supported by the Methodist Church, we had many great speakers from all walks of life—

President of colleges and universities, entertainers, and even Martin Luther King, Jr. however, each Sunday I took with me the words of Dr. Jones and Dr. Player.

Another great thinker and scientist whose philosophy I often recall is Rene' Decartes. It is called the wager (Le Pari-the bet). That is, that you can bet or not bet there is a God. Descartes says that he will always bet that there is a God.

My hope is that one day I will see my father and mother and all the people I hold dear, and we all will see the face of God.

How could the majority of people on this earth believe that there is a God if there were not God. He may be called by different names, but the fact is, most people on this earth believe that there is something much greater than mankind.

As for me, I firmly believe there is a God. There is also good and evil, But GOOD out numbers EVIL by a very wide margin.

I felt that I had a special calling in life. It was teaching! This journey began in my French I class at Central High School, Charlotte Court House, Virginia. French was the only foreign language that was taught, and all students who aspired to go to college took French. My French teacher was Miss Triplet, a perfect name for her. She was teacher, confidant, and guidance counselor. I wanted to be just like her so I knew what my major would be when I entered the gates of Bennett College. However, I also took all of the English courses that would give me a double major. As a teacher I would hand out my rules of conduct on the first day of school. My students always followed these rules with very few exceptions.

One day I took my French I class on a field trip. I left my Introductory to Foreign Languages Class behind. The lady in charge of substitutes didn't realize that the sub had not shown up. Janet Dovall, one of the secretaries in the main office sent a pass for one of my students who had a dental appointment. The office helper returned with the student and informed her that there was no teacher in the trailer. The class was being conducted by a student known as a troublemaker in most of his classes—but not in his French class. On another occasion a substitute left a note stating that a small group of student had been very rude. Of course they got a good scolding. They tried to explain that the sub was giving the wrong answers, and would not take their corrections. I replied that was no excuse ever for being rude to a guest teacher. I believe that was the only bad experience a substitute had in all the years I taught middle and high school.

For a short period of time Fairfax County had "Pay for Performance." At that time I was teaching French I and Introduction to Foreign Language which meant that I was being evaluated by the principal, vice principal, and a supervisor of foreign languages. At the end of the evaluation I was called into Leslie Kent's office along with one of the vice principals. Needless to say, I was pretty nervous.

Fannie Miles' French Club

Ms. Kent said, "Please relax." The only comment she had was her visit to the Introductory to Foreign Languages when students were given reports on French speaking countries in

English. She said she didn't understand what they were saying. I explained that many of the students in this class were also taking English as a second language. I understood what they were saying and so did the other students.

The other evaluators who visited my class had no complaints—even the foreign language supervisor who visited my class when I was teaching Latin. I had never studied Latin. I used tapes to learn basic Latin word and expressions. My students kept reminding me that, "Latin is a dead language."

"That is true, but there are so many English words that are derived from Latin."

To make a long story short, I met the criteria for an exceptional teacher, and received a hike in pay as long as the "Pay for Performance" lasted—which was for only a few years.

There is a habit I am glad I didn't take up as a teacher—smoking. When I came to Luther Jackson a lot of the teachers would go to the teachers' lounge to socialize and smoke. I tried taking up smoking, but I never could get the hang of it. I stopped trying and would return to my classroom. I would always have students who wanted to come and talk or entertain me and other students during the lunch period.

My classroom was always divided into halves so that the students would be facing each other. This would allow for conversation between the two sides when necessary. I never sat at my desk during class so having short rows of two to three students permitted me to keep all of the students in my view.

I also kept a very neat classroom and bulletin boards were updated according to what was being taught. The custodian who cleaned my room said he was happy to do so because there wasn't much for him to do. Students were not allowed to leave papers or any junk in their desk.

I taught for thirty years and substituted for seventeen (17). I really believe I had a special calling to teach.

After retiring I began writing. My most important work is **_My Love Affair with the French_**, *A Personal History.*

*Fannie Lillian Miles Bellamy '58
With Cousin And Mother Sailing To France 1962*

l.-r. Barbara Hickman Wells '57, Fleming Cheek, Ann Cooper Poindexter '57

Barbara Hickman Wells '58
3702 Baskerville Dr., Mitchellville, MD 20721
301-464-2541   bjhickmann@aol.com

My home town is Freeport, in northern Illinois approximately 200 miles north west of Chicago. My father left Louisiana on foot in 1911 and eventually met my Mom. My Mom was born in Missouri and her parents relocated to Illinois about 1915. From that union nine children were born.

My high school, Freeport High was a magnificent learning institution. The curriculum required each student to identify and concentrate on a major. If you know me, I chose Spanish. I had a wonderful teacher from McGill University... ... ...led to Bennett and met another wonderful teacher Mrs. Blanche Raiford.

I had read about Bennett College in the Ebony Magazine and decided it was for me! Of course, there were few funds in the family for higher education, so I stayed home one and a half years and worked in order to enroll at Bennett in January 1954. Yes, I was the only new student that semester.

After graduating from Bennett College, I traveled to New York City and found a job at Yeshiva University. Eventually, I married and relocated to Washington D.C. In Washington I found employment at the Department of Education and stayed about thirty-eight years.

My Bennett experience was wonderful. I enjoyed Chapel, marshaling, the dining room assignments, Sunday Vespers, and Sunday dinner. I am in contact with many of my friends and roommates constantly.

I am proud to be a Bennett Belle and look forward to seeing my roommates and friends whenever the occasion arises.

February 1958

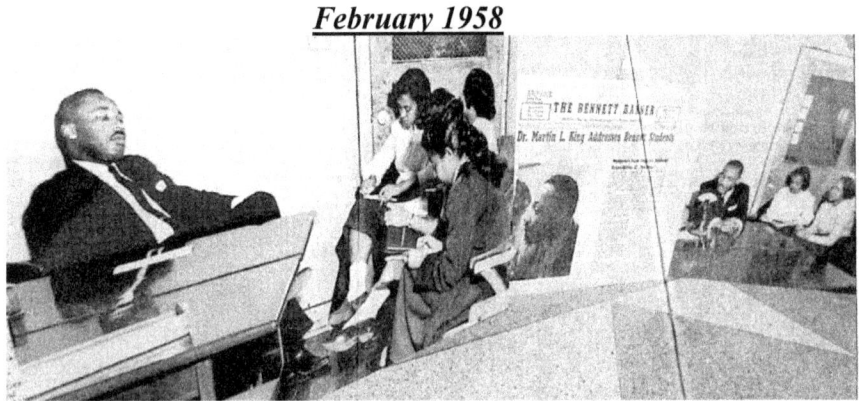

Enlarged Photos of Dr. Martin Luther King, Jr. Displayed at Bennett "Long-Forgotten Tape Brings King's Words Back to Life" [53]

Sculpture of Dr. Martin Luther King, Jr. (Photo courtesy of Wanda Mobley)

1960s

50th YEAR REUNION: CLASS OF 1961
REUNION COMMITTEE:
Class Coordinator: Roslyn Smith,
Joyce Pullum Gray, Laura Plummer Marshall, Iris Jeffries Morton, Barbara Miller Moore, Margaret Bailey Urquhart

Souvenir Journal

The famed and dynamic Class of 1961 celebrated its 50th year of graduation from Bennett College during Alumnae Weekend, May 5-8, 2011. Our bold, classy and full-of-life class presented to the college $153,650.61 at the All Bennett Banquet on Saturday, May 7, 2011, exceeding our goal of $150,000.00. **This amount represented the largest honor class donation in the college's history.**

In addition this committed and audacious class added to its earlier amount, and by June 30, 2011, **$165,000.00 was the final total!** When we met at our 45th reunion, we had agreed that each classmate would be asked to give $5,000.00 in 2011. A revised request of "What You Can Give" was decided in early 2011 due to the economy, stock market, health and family challenges. WE CHALLENGE OTHER HONOR CLASSES IN THE FUTURE TO EXCEED THE CLASS OF 1961 CONTRIBUTION.

We decided to publish a journal with ads and personal pages to supplement our personal contribution. Classmates were asked to submit a theme. The final selection was "AN AMAZING

JOURNEY OF FIFTY YEAR" submitted by Karen Leach Wilson. Our amazing journey began in September 1957 with 166 freshmen (the largest entry class up to that time). 102 graduated on June 6, 1961. 37 classmates are deceased. Eight (8) have lost contact with us and the college.

Thirty-four classmates, including several who did not complete their undergraduate studies with us and/or completed their studies elsewhere, returned to celebrate THIS ONE TIME MILESTONE IN OUR LIVES. There were nine (9) spouses and/or significant others, friend and family in attendance. Bennett College prepared and fostered SISTERHOOD, along with academics, activism and responsibility. Our class embraced them all and continue to do so to this day. We use every opportunity to add to our life experiences and to assist ALMA MATER and others! SOME MEMBERS WERE A PART OF THE INITIAL ORGANIZING COMMITTEE TO PLAN AND STRATEGIZE FOR THE FAMED WOOLWORTH SIT-INS AND "OPERTION DOORKNOCK" which we helped surrounding residents in voter registration. Our cultural life was enhanced by the Lyceum programs, senior voice and piano recitals, our dance team and the Little Theatre performers. We still embrace SISTERHOOD AND ARE ARTWORKS IN PROGRESS!

WE HAVE NOT AND WILL NOT EVER FORGET WHAT BENNETT COLLEGE, OUR ALMA MATER, MEANS TO US AND WILL ALWAYS SUPPORT HER AS LONG AS WE LIVE!

IN ATTENDANCE: Nettie Baldwin, Doris Neely Blake, Idajeanne Robinson Brown, Linda Brown, Eleanor Lotson Canty, Dorothy Grove Chambers, Barbara Rice Chapman, Elizabeth Daise, Jacqueline Daise Lee, Marva Lucas Douglas, Carolyn Brown Edwards, Dolores Finger-Wright, Doris Luck Fullwood, Shirley Dismuke Graham, Joyce Pullum Gray, Minnie Sims Holmes, Von Moore Kersey, Patricia Hargrove Lockett, Elishama Madison-Withers, Helena Howell McCorkle, Daisy Robinson McIlveen, Shirley Degraffenreidt McQueen, Barbara Miller Moore, Constance Colston Oliphant, Johanna Polanen Hattie Green Price, Valaida Wynn Randolph, Gwendolyn Mackel Rice, Roslyn Smith, LaRita Waters Tanner, Esther Alexander Terry, Ometria Campbell Trimble, Laura Plummer Marshall, Millicent Allen White, Jacqueline Boseman Wilson, Karen Leach Wilson

SOME GOLDEN MEMBERS OF THE CLASS OF 1961 [54]

SOME GOLDEN MEMBERS OF THE

CLASS OF 1961

1	Laura Plummer Webb-Marshall
2	Joyce Pullum Gray
3	Kay Frances Henry
4	Barbara Miller Moore
5	Carolyn Purvis Clarke
6	Johnsie Williams Thomas
7	Elizabeth B. Daise
8	Dr. Linda Beatrice Brown
9	Dr. Nettie N. Baldwin
10	Larita Waters Tanner
11	Patricia Hargrove Lockett
12	Ometria Campbell Trimble
13	Elishama Madison-Withers
14	Marva Lucas Douglas
15	Geraldine Brown Harrison
16	Eleanor Lotson Canty
17	Jacqueline Daise Lee
18	Minnie Sims-Holmes
19	Karen Leach Wilson
20	Daisy Robinson McIlveen
21	Johanna Polonen
22	Dr. Esther Alexander Terry
23	Roslyn Smith
24	Margaret Bailey Urquhart
25	Dr. Dolores Finger-Wright

Joyce Pullum Gray '61
Baltimore, MD 21221
(H) 410-391-6682 © 410-908-6142 doubledigits12@hotmail.com

Joyce Pullum Gray   *Marshal Pin*

Bennett College was the institution that cultivated the seeds as it prepared me to meet the challenges I would face in life. I will be eternally grateful there was a Bennett College for me. Not only was I exposed to the academics, I was given the "tools" that would guide me in my life's journey. I could not have left Bennett College without the education that would stand the test of time.

When I think of Bennett College, I think of: Dr. Clinton Armstrong, Ms. Georgia Lattimer, Dr. Louise Streat, Ms. Joyce Bremby Jones, Mr. Clarence Whiteman, Dr. Hobart Jarrett, Mrs. Mary Eady Mayfield, Mr. John Crawford, Mr. Van Allen, Mr. Young, Ms. Ellease Colston, Mr. James Scarlette, Mr. Zack Browning, Nurse Trammell, and the many others who helped set the stage for my journey. I am grateful for the myriad of experiences I had at this giant of an institution for higher learning. Those faculty members and staff members who gave of themselves; their knowledge and wisdom did more than teach, they helped us establish the foundation for our future. For this we are grateful!

I could not think of Bennett without remembering Thanksgiving and preparing for the Morehouse Choir concerts; being in awe of the stately Dr. Benjamin Mays; hoping to meet a Morehouse MAN and establish a special relationship with (did not happen); wearing my black or white shirtwaist dress, befitting the occasion; waiting for the ringing of the bell and realizing it was 10 PM and I had not begun to study for Mr. Young's test the next day; being a marshal and serving at vespers; trying to "out-smart" Amelita Moore; playing cards when I should have been studying; shining the brass as in "beauty –work"; having family-style dinner in the David Dallas Jones Student Union; going to the campus post office and hoping there was a message from home that included $2 or $3. Even as I think about, and remember my life at Bennett 50 years ago, the nostalgia is consuming me. I pause to say thank you to my parents who made the ultimate sacrifice to give me the Bennett experience. For this, I say thank you again.

Oh yes, I still have my mom who is 97, and has taken that trip to Greensboro and D.C. to share many a White Breakfast with the Bennett Belles.

Could I think of Bennett College and not remember my roommate, Angela Carroll Russell, whose friendship with me began as sophomores and is one of my dearest friends 54 years later? My sister love is overwhelming when I stop to think about how my life has been enriched through my friendship with Laura Plummer Webb-Marshall; Leacy Shipman Pierce; Jackie Boseman Wilson; Shirley Thompson (deceased); Connie Colston Oliphant; Betty Jean Harley; the Daise sisters - Liz and Jackie; Doris "Lokie" Cox Pittman (deceased, class of '55) with whom I lived when I worked in Charlotte, my first teaching assignment; Gladys Merritt '59, Maggie Bailey Urquhart, Carolyn James Johnson, whom we affectionately still call "Lag"; Jean Gerst Stewart; Gwen Mackel Rice; Esther Alexander Terry; Barbara Rice Chapman; Roslyn Smith; Elishama Madison "Shama" Withers; Angela Carroll Russell; Dolores Finger Wright; Iris Jeffries Morton, to name ONLY A FEW!

More recently I am happy to share a friendship with Juanita Patience Moss '54 and Marion Lee Bell '53. Space does not permit

Dr. Marion Lee Bell '53

me to list the name of each Bennett Belle whose life, then and now, has intersected with mine. Please know that I have captured something from each of you which has given me a moment to remember. Thanks for helping to make my life more complete. May the presence of God surround you from this day forward. *I love you*!

thankful for the poised, strong, Dr. Willa B. Player, who had expectations of what a Bennett Belle should be, who referred to you by name as you crossed the campus and your path crossed hers. Every girl who attended Bennett during Dr. Player's tenure has to remember her with fondness and love. While I think in some instances we may have feared her, we also revered her. As for me, I remember "DP" with honor, love and respect.

Dr. Willa B. Player

I have not been able to recall all the Bennett professors who were instrumental in molding me into the person I am, I say, "Thanks and hats off to you. For those who are no longer with us, I am certain God had a special place for you as he greeted you with this scripture: '*Well done my good and faithful servant, you have been faithful over a few things, I will make you ruler over many things: enter you into the joy of the Lord.*'"

Words are inadequate to describe the celebration of my fiftieth year as a graduate from our beloved Bennett. Alumnae weekend, May, 2011, was a major highlight of my life. I will savor every moment of that weekend. Thanks to each person who did their extreme best to make certain the class of 1961 would convene at the many events, rejoice at the very sight of each other, laugh or cry, then depart from the weekend with a renewed caring, and love for our alma mater. I extend my thanks and appreciation to each of my classmates who supported our class in order for us to present a gift of $165,037.61 to the college.

"*To whom much is given, much is required.*"

Golden Class of 1961 Led By NAA President Dr. Lisa Johnson '81
Joyce Pullum Gray Directly Behind
(Photo by Valaida Wynn Randolph '62   May 7, 2011)

Bearden Gate [55]
(Photo by Wanda Mobley '83)

Walking through the Bearden Gate on May 7, 2011 with the Golden Class of 1961 was a feeling of excitement and reverence.

I reflected on the book, ***The Long Walk,*** by Dr. Lynda Brown, my classmate. I thought about the many times Dr. Willa B. Player had graced the Bearden Gate in the course of her presidency of Bennett. It was an honor to be following in Dr. Player's footsteps, remembering her walk and the solemnity of this occasion.

I was quietly rejoicing as I made that walk with my classmate, Laura Plummer-Marshall. Laura and I had sat shoulder to shoulder during weekly chapel and Sunday Vesper for four years during our time at Bennett. As we walked, I felt it could not have been more fitting than to take this walk together, shoulder to shoulder, through the impressive gates, *fifty years later.*

l.-r.: Laura Plummer Marshall, Joyce Pullum Gray,
Shirley Dismuke Graham, Dr. Linda Brown
(Photo Courtesy of Valaida Wynn Randolph '62)

I was so proud of being a Bennett woman, holding onto tradition and following the legacy that has been set before me. As I type this I am filled with emotion. I pray that this tradition will outlive time. If God has anything more special than Bennett College, He has not revealed it to me.

I am extremely proud of the institution that played a major role in providing the foundation for my future. I also am reminded of the strong family ties and the magnificent upbringing from my parents; my role model was my mother. I can recall my parents sending me to Bennett by train my freshman year - 1957. We did not have the financial means to have my folks accompany me to college, but my mom's desire was for me, her only daughter, to have a Bennett College education. Unfortunately, Dad passed away during my freshman year, and Mom sacrificed to see her dream materialize. She first saw Bennett when she came to my graduation four years later. The "can do" confidence was obviously instilled in me in my youth; so leaving home for college unaccompanied, was the way this was to be. Thank you Mom and Dad; thank you for your sacrifices and struggles that allowed me to have my Bennett College education.

Without a doubt, Alma Mater Bennett gave me the key that has helped me to open many doors as I have navigated this course over the years. As I reflect on my past, I am grateful. The stage was set and the characters were in place for me to move forward with my life after Bennett.

During these past fifty years, I can truly say that I have wonderful memories. I have memories of a successful career and good and bad memories in my personal life. I have two children of whom I am very proud. I have absolutely enjoyed the role of mother to Joy and Jarrett. Being the mother to my children has been an awesome journey. While my career was excellent, motherhood has been an experience that has allowed me to embrace life completely. Were there struggles? Yes. Were there disappointments? Few. Were there challenges? Yes. Was it a job? Yes. Having said that, I can give testament to the fact that my life has been enhanced because I am the mother of Joy Danielle and Jarrett Daniel. I pause to thank the father (Dan) of my children for being the best parent he could be. Our paths have taken different directions, but I am thankful for the time we shared together.

I could not end this without mentioning my most recent role of being a "Grammy." Joy and Corey (son-in-law) have given me my treasured dream; that of being a grandparent. The two little Prince girls, Catherine Grace and Julia Gray, entered my life four years ago, and "rocked my world." You may have heard me say that Joy and Jarrett enhanced my life; you can only imagine what Catherine and Julia are capable of doing! Not to worry though, Joy is keeping me in control; she is not allowing me to break the bank and spend the retirement savings- laughter. For your viewing pleasure, I am closing this with a photo of Catherine and Julia. Maybe someday they will contribute to their memories of BENNETT COLLEGE for WOMEN as they remember their grandmother who came before them.

"................ *'til the evening shadows fall; 'til we heed our last clear call......................"*

l.-r.: Mother -Grace B. Pullum,
Daughter- Joy Gray Prince,
Belle- Joyce Pullum Gray '61

<u>**Granddaughters**</u>
<u>**l.-r.:**</u> *Catherine Grace and Julia Gray Prince*

COMMENCEMENT 1961

50 YEARS LATER

The Golden Class of 1961 [56]

Carolyn James Johnson '61
70 Palmer St., St. Augustine, FL
904-823-9644   carolyn.johnson@comcast.net

Dedicated to my mother and father: Hazel and Roosevelt James; husband Ernest Johnson-El; daughters: Dr. Mignonne Pollard, Michelle Pippen, M.B.A., and Dr. Sherrie Proctor Brown; grandchildren: Bria Joi, Mariah, and Brendon; sons-in-law: Robert Brown and Gerald Pippen.

Jones Hall
Patricia Hargrove & Carolyn James

My first knowledge of Bennett College was in 1956 at a Career Day in Jacksonville, Florida. The presenter, Ms. Foster, was very impressive. Both my cousin Betty Harley '61 and I decided that we would apply to Bennett. After some anxious months we were accepted.

My parents accompanied me to Bennett via Silver Meteor (train) and my cousin Betty was accompanied by her mother Gertha Motley who worked in Atlantic City, New Jersey. During my trip to Bennett I met a number of girls from Florida on their way to the college, and also Juanita Coglin (Lockley) '61, Barbara Melvin (Jefferson) '61 and a number of other girls.

Upon entering the gates of the college, the beauty of the campus helped to dissolve some of my initial fear. My parents appeared very happy with my choice of Bennett.

During my freshman year in Jones Hall, my roommates were Barbara Hawkins from Rock Hill, S.C., and Anette Hall

(Moore) from Greensboro. I was very homesick during that year. My roommates and some of the other girls in Jones Hall (Dorothy Albritton [Reid], Anne Wright, and Barbara Melvin [Jefferson]) were there for me, reassuring me that I would be over my homesickness soon. In addition, my parents' friends Bill and Fritzell Smith would have me over to their house for dinner and sightseeing around Greensboro.

My first attempt to answer a question in Dr. Edmonds' class was a name changing experience. Dr. Edmonds was lecturing on "cultural lag." I raised my hand and said, "I know it is like my hometown, St. Augustine." From that moment to this day my nickname has been "Lag" among my close Bennett friends and classmates.

l-r: Dorothy Albritton, Carolyn James, Margaret Bailey

Dr. George Breathett's history classes presented a challenge. I remember trying to get a handle on all of the material and studying with Margaret Bailey and Patricia Hargrove. I am thankful to Maggie, Pat and Dr. Breathett.

Dr. Clinton Armstrong was very lively. I can remember him asking a question of the class. If the answer was not to his liking, he would close the door, push his desk behind the door, and say, "I cannot allow this ignorance out of this room." I always thought this was very comical.

During my sophomore year when I was assigned Barge Hall, my roommates were Saundra McBride from Sumter, S.C., and Sylvia Smith from Franklin, Virginia. The three of us remained roommates until graduation. I always enjoyed going to the home of Mrs. Ellease Browning (Colston) with Juanita Coglin on some weekends.

A Sunday trip to Farley's one afternoon turned into a very scary situation. As my cousin Betty and a few other girls were rushing back to campus, a train was blocking the street and not moving anytime soon, it seemed. So we crawled between the rail cars as we prayed that the train would not move. We made it back to the dorm just before the doors were locked.

Voter registration in Greensboro was a very vital part of the community. I had the experience of going from door to door to encourage people to vote. I am still involved in trying to make things better in our community through the power of the vote.

My most traumatic experience at Bennett was being on campus my junior year with just a few girls who did not go home for Easter Holidays. During that time we received word that Lyla Blanding from Sumter, S.C., had been killed in an auto accident. This was a very sad time. My roommate Saundra, her sister Yvonne McBride (Barrett) '60, and Lyla were home-girls.

A very valuable experience for me was serving as the editor of the Bennett Banner during my junior year. Mr. Gibson was my faculty advisor and was very helpful in guiding me through the process of getting the paper in print. This experience allowed me to meet many notable people who came to the campus. I remember Dr. Benjamin Mays, Dr. Howard Thurman, Dr. Frederick Patterson, Dr. John Hope Franklin, Mattiwilda Dobbs, Hon. Patricia Harris, and others. I also had the opportunity to meet Dr. Martin Luther King, Jr. during his visit to our campus. During the summer of 1964, the unrest in St. Augustine, Florida, brought Dr. King here. The rest is history.

My experiences at Bennett were essential in motivating my desire to always act like a lady, to serve in my community, and to exercise morality and compassion. The sisterhood, vesper bells and magnolia trees will forever be a part of my memory of Bennett College.

Snow on One Cold Winter Day
l.-r.: *Carolyn James Johnson, Saundra McBride, Charletta Pickering, Patricia Hargrove Lockett*

Karen Leach Wilson '61
128 Gail Ct., Newport News, VA 23605
757-838-6395

In September of 1957, at the age of 17, I, **Karen Leach**, entered Bennett College as an excited bright-eyed teenager! I had no clue as to what was expected of me as a Bennett Belle or a Bennett Sister. Thus, my freshman year became traumatic for me.

To begin with, I was placed in Kent Hall on the second floor in a room with two older freshmen. From the onset, it was really "all about me!" The word "selfish" was not a part of my vocabulary! Therefore, it was my radio, my clock, my Vaseline which was used on my legs, my chair, or my space. To add insult to injury, I did not have to obey any rules or accept any rules set by the Dormitory Director. Yes! I had a serious attitude!!

Needless to say, I was headed in the wrong direction. Thus, Mrs. Susie Jones, the Director of Admissions, summoned me to her office. Thinking that this "invitation" was for a special recognition, I eagerly entered Mrs. Jones' office unaware that I was in for a shock!! I closed the door behind me as she greeted me with a smile and invited me to sit down. Mrs. Jones first inquired as to how I was doing as a new student. Of course, I told her how wonderful I had been, and how much I was enjoying myself. Well, she was not amused. She calmly told me how disappointed she was in my behavior towards my roommates, and especially my total disrespect for my Dormitory Director. Mrs. Jones further admonished me that though my parents had spoiled me, they did not expect me to behave in such an unacceptable manner! The last thing that she said to me with emphasis and much "clarity" was that if I had to return to her office because of any negative reports, she would put me across her lap and give me a good spanking. Her comments did not fall on deaf ears, therefore making a believer of me. My behavior improved as the year progressed!

However, at the end of my freshman year trauma re-surfaced. My mother died on April 28th. I went home for the funeral which was a week before Mother's Day. I returned to school in time to receive my white rose on Mother's Day as my roommates and other students wore red roses & walked the campus with their mother. Nevertheless, I held my emotions intact. Final exams soon followed, and I completed all of them successfully. Again I was summoned to Mrs. Jones office.

On entering her office, I lacked exuberance and I had matured quite a bit. Mrs. Jones invited me to sit down and wasted no time in praising me for developing and maturing into a young woman of whom she was proud. She also praised me for the manner in which I coped with my Mother's death especially since it was near Mother's Day, and I had also succeeded in taking my final exams, Mrs. Jones concluded our visit by telling me that I had an inner strength and determination that would help me to succeed at Bennett.

Mrs. Jones followed me through the four years that I was at Bennett. During my senior year, she wrote my Dad and told him how proud she was of my participation in the Civil Rights' activities by my writing letters to the Greensboro Record's editorial page which she included in her letter to Daddy.

My freshman year was traumatic at Bennett, but Mrs. Jones took an interest in me and helped to guide me through it. This interest continued through my senior year!

Shirley Degraffenreidt McQueen '61
smq1146@aol.com

Shirley Degraffenreidt McQueen '61

Northern Virginia's Unsung Heroine 2010

A native of Pittsboro, N.C., I earned a BA degree in elementary education and a minor in art from Bennett College. My teaching career began in Pittsboro and then continued in Washington, D.C where I studied administration at the University of the District of Columbia.

Until my retirement in 1996, I was a classroom teacher in D.C. Public Schools. As a Master Teacher, I mentored new teachers entering the profession and served as presenter and consultant for professional development workshops while sharing my expertise in the area of reading.

I was recognized for eight consecutive years by Friendship Educational School with the "Excellence in Teaching" award. Currently I am mentoring new teachers and substituting.

I am a charter member of the Northern Virginia Alumnae Chapter (NOVABC) which was organized in 2003 and presently serve as Vice President. I annually contribute to the College at the 1926 Society level and contribute many hours supporting NOVABC fundraisers and activities. I have assumed the chair responsibility for many of NOVABC's fundraising activities such as shopping tours, theater parties, jazz brunches, fur raffles, casino nights, concerts, and helped with the sales of the first volume of

Bennett Belle memoirs, all of which successfully raised over $240,000.00. In addition, I chair the chapter's Benevolence Committee. In addition, I recruit at Alfred Street Baptist Church's annual HBCU College Fair and am responsible for several students considering attending Bennett College.

The late Rev. Dr. John O. Peterson, Pastor Emeritus, Alfred Street Baptist Church was delighted when he learned that I was involved with my College's alumnae chapter. Rev. Peterson was the Baccalaureate speaker in 2004 and he received the "Friend of Bennett" award in 2005.

I am the proud mother of one son, Burnie Antonio McQueen III, who graduated from Howard University and received his Master's Degree from George Mason University in Northern Virginia.

Bennett Belles
in the Civil Rights
Movement. [57]

Shirley Degraffenreidt
McQueen '61
and Hazel Abron Smith
'61
Lead the Downtown
Greensboro Theater
Boycott

Iris Jeffries Morton, M.S., D.D.S. '61
2712 Unicorn Lane NW   Washington, DC 20015
202-364-1309   ijeff@aol.com

Recipient of 2010 BCNAA Achievement Award

The epilogue of my life can best be told by the people whom I have had the privilege to serve. Thanks to the patients whom I have treated and the students whom I have taught for allowing me to serve you. My sincere thanks to God for giving me the ability to serve. Thanks to Bennett College for preparing me to serve.

I entered Bennett College with a dream of becoming a scientist. I wanted to do research or become a physician. My high school chemistry teacher, R.G. Mitchell, was a very encouraging teacher and promoted my dream.

My first day of class in chemistry at Bennett, I met Dr. J. Henry Sayles. Dr. Sayles introduced the chemistry class by giving a history of outstanding chemistry teachers and the students whom they had taught. He finished each point of his chronology by saying, *"Some of them flunked and some of them passed."* Then he introduced himself and made the same analogy. That was my motivation and my determination to pass.

I was fortunate to become the chemistry lab assistant for Dr. Sayles and Dr. Roy Lee. I was in "chemistry heaven." Preparing for experiments for Dr. Sayles and Dr. Lee not only helped pay my tuition, but helped me to further realize my dream. My first year at Bennett launched my career. Thank you Dr. J. Henry Sayles.

After graduating from Bennett College, I came to Howard University where I received a Masters degree in Biochemistry. While studying for my degree, I worked as a reader and lab instructor for undergraduates. After graduating from Howard, I worked as a biochemist at the National Institutes of Health and at the Department of Defense. Even though I enjoyed my job, I realized I wanted to be in patient care. That is when I went to dental school. In dental school, I taught biochemistry in the Academic Reinforcement Program to students who had been accepted to dental school pending completion of academic requirements.

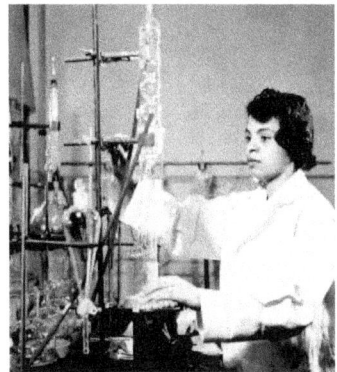

Iris Jeffries in the lab

Dental school has allowed me to serve and provide care and pain relief for many patients. As an associate professor in the College of Dentistry, currently I am training young dental students. This is the highlight of my career.

Thank you Dr. Willa B Player for being an outstanding lady and role model and showing Belles by example how it should be professionally done. Thank you, Mrs. Susie Jones, for sharing your "Tea Times," for being another mother, and teaching me to appreciate the social graces of life.

Thank you, Nurse Trammel, R.E. and Bernadette Jones, for providing the nurturing home away from home haven for me when I needed to break the chain. Thank you, Dr. Sayles and Dr. Lee, for giving me the challenge, encouragement and academic background to persevere.

Thank you, Bennett sisters, for always knowing that you have "a sister." Thank you, Bennett College, for exposing me to the arts, social and political issues and great cultural events. My family and community set the basis of my life; Bennett College enriched it. **Thank you, Bennett College.**

A Woman of Substance Circle Inductee 2011 [58]
Dr. Iris Jeffries Morton '61

Gwendolyn Mackel Rice '61
8600 S. Prairie Ave., Chicago, IL 6619
773-488-590 gmrchi@aol.com

I went to Oakwood Friends School at age 13 to enter my sophomore year of high school. (We all started school early--Mother taught us.) My mother and I traveled by train from Mississippi by way of Chicago to Poughkeepsie, New York.

We arrived on a Saturday evening. That Sunday morning even before putting our feet on the campus, Mother found a black church to attend. We were AMEs and the closest to that denomination was an AMEZ church. We went and the minister or someone introduced us to a family whose children attended Oakwood--turned out the father was a dentist. We went to their home for dinner and every first Sunday after that, they picked me up for church.

I was totally shocked at Oakwood--everyone was so friendly and there were a few other African American students (we were Negro then), several from down South. My mother had been gone for three days before I realized that she had gone, I felt so welcome. She just snuck away and left money for a heavy winter coat with the headmaster's wife. (We couldn't find one heavy enough before she left--or in Chicago--guess it was too early.)

Some of my schoolmates were from celebrity families--such as Lena Horne's daughter, Montague Cobb's daughter, Ralph Bunche's son, and a few others whose names you might recognize. It made no difference.

As a matter of fact, my first roommate was the granddaughter of Conrad Adenaur, then Chancellor of Germany--for about two weeks. I think when they learned that I was Negro--a change was made. They then placed the Headmaster's daughter with her and her roommate was placed with me. She was Deborah Wedgwood, granddaughter or great granddaughter of Josiah Wedgwood (china). We're still friends--don't correspond as much but when its reunion time, she always writes or calls to see if I'm coming. In 1993, one of my classmates (we actually marched together at graduation) became president of the U of Chicago and he invited me to all of his inauguration activities. Had he come the year before, he would have awarded my master's degree.

I was chair of Girls' Council, member of student council, theater guild, captain of basketball team, etc. It was a rich experience but I really and truly missed being in the midst of my culture--especially during my senior year and I had already fallen in love with Bennett so I didn't bother to apply elsewhere. I wanted my older sisters' experiences. Mind you, my grades at Oakwood were awful my first year but before long--I caught up. My parents expected it. Daddy wanted me to apply to Radcliffe, but I wanted no part of it.

I traveled to Bennett alone by train. Actually, it never occurred to me that my parents would take me. I guess I saw my siblings travel back and forth and going to meet them at the train stations--what other way was there--and I was quite used to traveling alone. I think of all the money that parents spend now getting their children to college.

Mind you, Bennett was a challenge and my education at Bennett was the best--even compared to the U of Chicago. Loved Bennett. Felt so at home.

So re: Mount Holyoke--that exchange confirmed my love for Bennett. I had never stayed on a predominantly white college campus. One of my Oakwood classmates was there as well, as a faculty couple (one had taught me math, the other physical ed and was our Girls' Council sponsor).

They loved Dr. Hobart Jarrett who made the journey with us and Roslyn Smith was one of those in our group.

A TRIBUTE TO
Dr. Tressie Wright Muldrow '62

Ellease Randall Colston Service Award [59]
2010

l.-r.: Sandra Walker Johnson, Dr. Julianne Malveaux, Dr. Tressie Wright Muldrow, Dr. Lisa Johnson

Dr. Tressie Wright Muldrow earned the Bachelor of Arts Degree from Bennett College in 1962. She continued her education at Howard University, earning a Master of Science and a Ph.D. degree. Currently, Tressie is a Senior Psychologist in the United States Office of Personnel Management.

Dr. Muldrow has worked unstintingly for her alma mater since 1967. Her work began as local chapter recording secretary and chapter president. Dr. Muldrow served as President of the NAA 1979-1985 which included an unprecedented 3rd term which resulted in cultivating the seed of securing voting positions on the Bennett College Board of Trustees for the SGA and NAA Presidents.

She also served two terms as the NAA's Annual Fund Chair. As chair she was instrumental in implementing strategies *to increase alumnae giving to over $1 million dollars for not only the first time in Bennett's "her-story" but also making history and raising the bar nationally for all HBCU alumni.*

Her accomplishments while serving Bennett include: implemented recognition of the 50th year Classes; instituted student personal loan fund; conceived and executed alumnae phone-a-thon concept; enhanced Alumnae Awards program from one award to four awards; increased NAA presence at UNCF/National Alumnae Council Conferences; served thirteen years on the Bennett College Board of Trustees; and cultivated a Regional Structure and alumnae regional recruitment program.

Tressie is a charter member of the 1926 Society and a Life member of the Bennett College National Alumnae Association."

<u>Sylvia (Tisha) Fish Harris'63</u>
1201 Eleanor Avenue Las Vegas, NV 89106

Alana Chapman Hickman & Tisha Fish Harris

Memories of "dear ole Bennett" are best done sometimes in pictures, so I've included some for " the second volume of Bennett memoirs. The following pictures are moments of my fondest memories of during my years at Bennett.

I remember well things from each of the pictures as if it was yesterday, and it saddens me to know that some of the people in the pictures that were very dear to me are no longer with us. For some odd reason the pictures I have are only from my freshman and senior year and I have no idea why. Could it be I was too busy studying or having fun?

We celebrated each other's birthdays with cake, ice cream and other refreshments. I still have two handmade cards made for my 21st birthday party, one created by Gloria Barnes Bates and signed by Gloria, Carolyn Owens, Carole Collins Leach, Bonita Davis, and Jackie Burkes McElrath. The hand drawn and water colored character pictures are of fish, including starfish (to play on my maiden name). It reads... *"The fish are all gathered ONE by ONE"* - next page *"We're so glad you're 21"* - next page, *"The fish bowl is all aglow; so...let the gin and bourbon flow!!"* Not that we had the gin and bourbon.

I am so grateful to the ladies in these pictures for making my time at Bennett so enjoyable and happy. We laughed and cried together through our four years and I am so glad they have been and still are a part of my life.

Over the past forty-eight years there have been many experiences and a few job changes. From teacher; to housewife; to owner/operator of Airport Travel Services, a travel agency in McCarran International Airport; and to currently Senior Vice President of Unibex Global Corporation (husband is Chairman & CEO. It helps when you know the boss!). And Bennett College for Women is one of the reasons I've been able to accomplish these tasks. ***Lots of Love to all my Sisters***

Merner Hall Gang 1959/60
Gloria Black, Tisha Fish Harris '63, Liz Patterson, Ozietta (Zett) Thompson, Robbie Hamlett Dancy '63, Florence Burnside, Betty Jo Murphy, La Forest Williams, Dorothy Hampton

For the first big snow 1959, some A&T guys came over and helped us build a snowman.
r.-l.: Ezell Blair [60] and friend from Jones Hall, Norman Robinson,
Robbie Hamlett Dancy '63, Zett Thompson (peeking over),
Edwina Coleman Clark, La Forest Williams, Sandra Hann
Belles from l.-r.: Joyce Collins Clarke, Mae Young Cundiff

Freshmen On The Chapel Steps
Front row: ???, Zett Thompson, Alana Chapman Hickman,
Brenda Wilkerson Hoover, Edwina Coleman Clark
Middle row: Mae Joyce Burke Singleton, Gracie Jones, Harriet Upton, Alice Airall-Owens, Doris Bowman, Florence Burnside, Connie Spotts, Delores Coe
Top row: Leslie Doty-Anderson, Rose Jackson-Coleman,
Robbie Hamlett Dancy

"Hey, Mom, we got our letters!! I'm graduatin!"
<u>l-r</u>: *Robbie Hamlett Dancy, Carolyn Wright Black, Agatha Ricks , Yvonne Harris Ashe, Gloria Barnes Bates, Rose Gill Langford (1963)*

Parents of roommates Tish Fish Harris and Robbie Hamlett Dancy finally got to meet each other on graduation day June 3, 1963. Martin Luther King, Jr. was scheduled to be our commencement speaker, but he was in a Birmingham jail, writing his book *Letter From a Birmingham Jail.*

In Memoriam
Audrey Wynn Spence '64
(1942-1992)
Submitted by her sister Valaida Wynn Randolph '62

In 1952 when Juanita Patience married Edward Moss, the eldest of nine siblings, she was blessed with eight new brothers and sisters-in-law, two being eleven year old Audrey and thirteen year old me. Talk about buddies!

We were inseparable, mostly because we lived in a very conservative patriarchal family and one of our Dad's house rules was where one of us went, so did the other. All of us children were and still are very close to our oldest brother and so we spent a lot of time at his apartment. For instance, he had a television. That was something in 1954. So Saturday nights became family nights with Jackie Gleason.

We belonged to the Bethel A.M.E. Church where Juanita taught Sunday School and formed a small teenage choir. Both Audrey and I were members. One Christmas Juanita decided to use one of her Bennett experiences, that of the Living Madonnas. Of course, no one had any idea what she was trying to accomplish. A member of the church built a frame with a curtain. After weeks of practicing, we performed as if we were pros. This was the first introduction Audrey and I had to Bennett College, but it would not be the last time we would hear about it.

As I neared high school graduation and had major decisions to make, Juanita kept encouraging me to attend Bennett College. At least for a year, just to see. I was not enthusiastic.

My excuses were: "Oh, but North Carolina is so far away. I have never been any far distance from home before. I won't be able to come home on the weekend just to sleep in my own bed and eat my mother's cooking as some students had the luxury of doing. I don't know anyone else who is going there."

The whole prospect of leaving home was such a daunting one, but once the decision was made, off to Bennett I went by train to the segregated South. Once I arrived at Bennett, I immediately fit right in as a freshman. Soon it was time to begin encouraging Audrey to make the same decision. By that time Edward and Juanita had moved to New Jersey and were not around to give Audrey the push they gave to me. But being her "big sister," I provided the incentive for Audrey to travel the same path to Bennett College two years later, where she, too, blossomed as she studied for a career in elementary education.

l.-r.: Edwina Coleman Clark,
Audrey Wynn Spence,
Gracie Jones [61]

WILKES-BARRE [62]---*When Audrey W. Spence returned to her hometown in 1984 after being away 25 years, she thought things had changed.*

But they hadn't, she discovered.

As a black woman, Spence still found stumbling blocks in her way for equal opportunity. It was her difficulty in finding an apartment in Wilkes-Barre that caused her to act.

When she died Friday night at age 50, the retired school teacher left behind a legacy to the community that includes a local branch of the National Association for the Advancement of Colored People where one had been dormant for so long.

"If Audrey decided to do something she would stick to it until it got done," said a former NAACP Wilkes-Barre branch vice president.

Her successor as branch president described her as a person of action, willing to attack problems head-on.

A graduate of GAR High School, Spence left Wilkes-Barre in 1959 to pursue a college degree at Bennett College in Greensboro, N.C. After receiving her bachelor's degree, Spence got a job teaching in public schools in Washington, D.C.

She first taught elementary school. Then after earning a master's degree from the University of the District of Columbia, she taught reading in Washington.

Altogether Spence spent 20 years there as a teacher, and in 1984 she opted for early retirement. In an interview published in The Times Leader after she returned to Wilkes-Barre in 1984, Spence said she came back because it was an area she felt she could afford to live in on her retirement. It also was her home.

When she had trouble finding someone who would rent to her, she made noise. She never stopped.

"My feeling was that if I as a native was having problems coming back here trying to just find a place to live, then, of course, there must be other problems that were in the community

and had not surfaced," Spence said in a 1987 interview with The Times Leader.

"The NAACP was reborn because of her drive," said the current president of the local branch. "Her greatest dream was to see things done right.

Another person said, "Her interest was in people who were forgotten about. She always was for the underdog.

But it was her volunteer work with the Job Services Center on East Union Street that won her admirers. Even after she stopped volunteering to help minorities and women with problems on the job, she still got phone calls. For several years she worked on a program that helped young people learn resume writing and job search skills.

She left the legacy of a person of action who looked out for the underdog. She is sorely missed.

The skills Audrey acquired while at Bennett from the "sit-in demonstrations and from "Operation Door Knock" came in handy when she returned home to address the discrimination in housing and employment in our home town of Wilkes-Barre, Pennsylvania.

VALAIDA WYNN RANDOLPH '62

NAA ACHIEVEMENT RECIPIENT '91
EUNICE DUDLEY BUSINESS AWARDEE

Marilyn H. Mackel JD, Commissioner '65
Los Angeles Superior Court
201 Centre Plaza Drive, Department 402
Monterey Park, CA 91754
(323) 526-6402   mmackel@lasuperiorcourt.org

I never knew another school existed but Bennett College. Is there one? I don't even know if I had a choice. I never even questioned it, except as a cantankerous child, "No, I am never going to Bennett, never, no way." I recall meeting Dr. and Mrs. Jones and Dr. Player (DP) as that tetchy child. I never even applied to another school. I don't know, maybe it was legacy instilled without the spoken word. All I knew for sure that I wanted out of Chicago—a city, I call Northern Mississippi, and still have issues with it.

I could count on Audrose coming to homecoming and being the hoot" that she can often be. Everyone except me left home (Audrose before I was born, Lyvonne shortly thereafter) to go to boarding high school. Our parents did not want us to have a high school diploma from Mississippi Separate Colored Schools.

It was my saving grace that I never had to hear Gwen complain about me wearing her clothes at Bennett. None of us had to deal with sibling stuff at Bennett. I had to deal with the academic successes of all three of my sisters, and the often stated belief (which did not last long) that I would do likewise.

I was quite cynical about certain traditions when I attended Bennett - the uniformity, mandatory chapel, the black and white dresses, the rituals, etc. Now I know how important they were to my evolution. I think those traditions are more important to this generation of College students than they ever could have been to students attending Bennett pre *de jure de*segregation.

The three times weekly 30 minutes mandatory chapel where we heard lecturers from around the world, gave a personal exposure to everyone from Benjamin Mays, Mordecai Johnson, and Roy Wilkins, to Constance Baker Motley, and Pauli Murray, two women who have been very significant in my life.

From DP we heard about her travels to Wall Street, how to pack clothes so that they would not wrinkle, and following a service where it seems that everyone had a bad cough, we learned about the necessity to exercise discipline; the need to be continuously mindful—something akin to you cannot scratch every itch. I think if may have been from DP that I first heard the word "mindfulness," a meditation practice that is critical to my existence today.

Just after graduation I served the City of New York (for 6 years) as a Juvenile Probation Officer and as a Foster Care Social Worker for the Bureau of Child Welfare. While in New York, I earned a Masters Degree from the City University of New York, John Jay College of Criminal Justice (1971). I moved to the District of Columbia to teach Criminal Justice at Washington Technical Institute (now the University of the District of Columbia, UDC), and earned my Law Degree from Georgetown University Law Center (1976). I continued teaching at UDC for 17 years, while practicing entertainment law in D.C. for 12 years. In 1988, I moved to Southern California.

Since 1991 I have been a Dependency Court Judicial Officer with the Los Angeles Superior Court, Juvenile Division. I was initially appointed to serve in an as-needed capacity as a Referee, and became a full-time Referee in 1996. In 2002, the Los Angeles Superior Court Judges appointed me Commissioner.

Prior to my work as a Judicial Officer, I was a Professor at Western State University College of Law and at the University of West Los Angeles School of Law. I have been a Senior Associate and of Counsel, at a Newport Beach Business and Real Estate Litigation firm. I am Chair of the Dependency Court's Court Scholars Committee which has brought together all of Los Angeles County's Public Colleges and Universities, various non-profit organizations, the Department of Children and Family Services, and Counsel for Children to assure that foster, probation, and kinship youth are appropriately supported when they seek higher education. I represent the Dependency Court as a member of the County wide Transition Age Youth Partnership. I also serve as co-chair of the Dependency Courts Coordinated Health Care Committee. This committee assures that the medical needs of children in foster care are appropriately met.

I consider myself fortunate to be able to sit in the Dependency Court where I hope I am able to positively impact, in some way, the lives of children and families who have come under the Courts Jurisdiction because of Child Abuse and Neglect.

Wilma Giles Marshall '65
333 Carteret Terr., Orange, NJ 07050
973-673-2789   wilma_marshall@msn.com

I was a student at Bennett from 1961–1965. My high school home *Mrs. Mary Mayfield Eady and Wilma Giles* '51, was influential in my decision to attend Bennett College. She always raved about Bennett and how it was an excellent college for Negro girls, as we were still called in the sixties. Prior to coming to the small rural town to teach, she had worked as a dietitian in New York City.

I had always been fascinated by what makes the human body work, but I decided to major in nutrition rather than pre-med. Further, I felt that my family was too poor to help me go to med school. In fact, I was a work study student who worked for the registrar, Mrs. Mary Mayfield Eady.

These were still the days of social protest. However, I didn't go to jail, although I was among the students picketing McDonald's fast food facility that would not
 permit us to sit and eat on their premises. We were still expected to wear our gloves and hats, do beauty work, and dining hall duty.

Chapel: I attended chapel three times per week for 30 minutes and Sunday Vesper every Sunday at 4:00 p.m. We were exposed to both world leaders and those from the African-American Community who left mostly positive imprints on our young minds. In order to avoid sitting in my assigned seat every Sunday, I became a checker which allowed me to sit in the balcony.

Freshman year: I had two roommates, Regina Carpenter from D.C. and Charlayna Crawford (Gilmer) from Greensboro, North Carolina. I was the last person to arrive so I had the privilege of sleeping on the top bunk bed and sharing whatever closet space that was left.

It was during this time that I met Mary E. Lownes (Rock) who became my best sister-friend. We have continued this relationship for over forty years. My son and her two sons have developed their own relationship. They

<u>**Mary Lownes**</u>

even participated in each others' weddings. Clemontene Watkins (Rountree) and Patricia Corry were also friends who accompanied me to my uncle's house in the city for delicious meals and fellowship. Clemontene's sister attended Saint Paul College in Lawrenceville, Virginia so we hung out with her a weekend for a Mardi Gras. Of course my parents and Clemontene's parents had to write letters of permission.

Faculty: The faculty was diverse, highly qualified and nurturing. Dr. John H. Sayles was our very capable chemistry teacher who seemed brilliant to us. One day, Mary Lownes asked, "Do you think we will ever know chemistry like Dr. Sayles?" I replied, "Probably, after we've taught it for about 20 years."

Mrs. Louise Streat, Clothing/Textile instructor; Director of Family Life Education, could tell the hem of your garment was 1/8 inch off without measuring it. She required excellence from all her students. I remember when I matriculated in the Masters Program at New York University, Dr. Henrietta Fleck, Chairman of the Home Economics Department, commented to me during a conference, "Oh, you're one of Mrs. Streat's students. They're always well prepared."

Reverend James M. Busch taught Religion and Philosophy. His favorite expression was, "Young people, why are you looking so down today? Better days are coming." Through the years, I've often said to myself, "Reverend Busch, I don't know where you are, but I am still in search of those better days."

Physical Education was required for four years. Most of us hated it probably because we didn't realize it was helping to make us physically fit. My only regret was that the new gym which had a swimming pool did not open until the fall of 1965. Thus we were not required to take swimming.

However, my most vivid memory is of my classmate, Jean Bailey (Braxton), running down the field with her field hockey stick up in the air not paying much attention to the proximity of others on the field. Luckily, she didn't injure anyone.

It was very special being Junior Sister to Molly Lisa Spruel (Thompson) from Montclair, New Jersey. Upon graduating in 1965, I relocated to Newark, New Jersey, where our paths crossed again. We both became active members of the Northern New Jersey Chapter of BCNAA and were employed by the Newark Public school system. We maintained this relationship until Mollye retired and she and her husband moved to Hunterville, North Carolina.

My senior year I completed a student teaching practicum at Dudley High School in Greensboro North Carolina under the tutelage of Mrs. Vashti Goodman. She was an experienced teacher who was well organized, liked by her students, open to new strategies / ideas, and demanded good work from her students. I was really impressed with her community Christmas wworkshop during which participants made various ornaments for the holiday season.

Who can forget some of the special occasions that were part of the Bennett tradition? Thanksgiving day we had the annual White Breakfast with the Morehouse men and Dr. Benjamin E. Mays as our special guests. Then, there was the joint concert featuring the Morehouse Glee Club and the Bennett Choir and then one featuring just Morehouse. Both were awesome. The Living Madonnas at Christmas and May Day celebration were other special events.

Graduation Day: May 31, 1965 at 10:30 a.m. in the Annie Merner Pfeiffer Chapel 105 young Belles were awarded their degrees indicating they had been prepared to make their contributions to society. I was privileged to be one of them. I will be forever indebted to Alma Mater "Bennett." Each time I return to the campus as an alumna, I am reminded of my rich heritage and feel a new sense of loyalty and appreciation.

30th Class Reunion in 1985
Regina Carpenter Wade, Wilma Giles Marshall, Charlayna Crawford Gilmer

North Jersey Chapter Alumnae Chapter (circa 1990) [63]
1st from left: Wilma Giles Marshall '65;
4th from left: Mollye Spruel Thompson '57

Wilma Giles Marshall '65 &
Dr. Frances Jones Bonner '39
(Daughter of Dr. David D. Jones)
1998

Beatrice Perry Soublet '65
Beatrice Perry Soublet '65
2104 Crest Ridge Dr., East Point, GA 30344
404-629-9654 Beelady20@bellsouth.net

Mid-week Vesper Committee [64]
Lily So, Rosetta Hayden, Beatrice Perry Stanley

My junior year was spent at Willamette University because on one fateful day during my sophomore year, I had received a brief letter in my mailbox from Dr. Willa B. Player, college president. It read simply "Please see me in my office at your earliest convenience."

Needless to say, I was petrified. I went at once, heart in mouth, expecting some belated reprimand from my civil rights era activities or my complaints about our new sociology professor (another story for another day).

To my great surprise, Dr. Player informed me that I had been recommended by my teachers to represent the college in an exchange program at Willamette University in Salem, Oregon. My entire junior year would be spent away from my comfortable, familiar college home in a place that seemed half a world away.

The long train ride was quite an experience. Although I was traveling alone, I managed to make some "traveling buddies" on the three-day trip. When finally I arrived, representatives from the college met me in a warm and welcoming manner.

My first experience with the students was an overnight retreat for the entire junior class. I had to talk about my participation in the Civil Rights Movement at the retreat. I was so nervous about speaking that I was actually shivering. I remember that a nice guy gave me his jacket. My talk was well received.

Dorm life was memorable. I lived in York House, one of two independent dorms. All of the other dorms were sorority or fraternity dorms, which did not welcome Negroes (as we were called then) or Jews. My roommate greeted me with a warm hug, showed me around the dorm and helped me unpack. Our room had two desks, a chest, closet, and window seat. We slept at the end of the hall on the sleeping porch where the beds for the entire floor were. There was a dining room in the dorm. We were served our breakfast eggs to order. Friday night was steak night with our steaks cooked, of course, to our order.

I was convinced that my class at Willamette would be much more difficult than those at Bennett. Was I wrong!! I had labored under the illusion that "Negro" meant inferior. The academic rigor of the freshmen and sophomore years at Bennett prepared me very well for the junior year at Willamette. I made a 3 point average—all A's and was inducted into two honor societies. One was Psi Chi, the psychology honor society and the other was Mortar Board, a national leadership honorary that recognizes senior women for superior scholarship leadership and service.

Because I felt that I was not just representing Bennett College but representing my entire race, I made every effort to show that I was a well-rounded student. I sang in the choir, danced in the talent show, volunteered for service projects, participated in a religious study group and attended services at First Congregational Church. I was on a mission to show that a Negro girl from a little southern school could excel at a big white school out West.

I recall an event where a fraternity house held a competition for queen. The queen would be chosen from the princesses that would be sent from each dorm. I was selected to represent York House—my dorm. I sang "Star Dust" for my talent and was selected 1st maid of the fraternity court.

Beatrice Alice Perry
Phi Delta Princess
and Escort '64

Although this exchange program was called a race relations program by the local newspaper, as far as race and racism were concerned, the only overt act that I remember is that people would sometimes sniff as I passed them on campus. When I asked the only other Black student about this, she responded that some people thought that we smelled differently. In another incident I told a singer who was performing *Ole Man River* in the talent show not to use the word "darky" because I found it offensive. He didn't use it. I was impressed with the fact he was willing to make that change out of respect for me

Even though few had ever met a black person before, they were As an example, because I was junior year, my roommates and other friends gave me a lovely surprise shower. One of my friends even sent a dozen white orchids from Hawaii for my wedding.

This is a quote from a Salem newspaper dated May, 1964: *"Said Miss Perry, 'I have grown both academically and socially. I've changed---become more extroverted and less inhibited. The faculty has received me quite well and seems interested that we students understand. I thought before I arrived that the professors would lecture too fast and students would be ahead of me, but I will take back the idea that Negro and white education in college is not so much different.'"*

My junior year at Willamette taught me valuable life lessons. It also taught valuable lessons about my people to those for whom such lessons were sorely needed.

Some Activities of the Class of 1965

Barge Hall Dorm Council [65]
l.-r.: Essie Lyons, Pat Murray '65, Janice Norwood, Dorothy Wilkerson—Jones '65, Beatrice Perry Soublet '65, Linda Blackman Jones '65-(President), Mrs. Mary Ball (Residence Hall Counselor)
Back row: Hazel Abron Smith '63, Emma Curry(Junior Counselor),

Senior Marshal Board [66]
l.-r.: Regina Carpenter, Wie Lie So, Lily So, Doris Forney, Winona McDowell, Jothany Williams, Charlotte Tenbrook, Adrian Jackson, Beatrice Perry Stanley, Peggy Largent, Patricia Washington, Elnora Harris, Alice Williams, Edna Smith, Brenda Stallworth, Sandra Vails.

1st row: Mrs. Hoyle, Lily So, Elisapeta Saeula
2nd row: Frances Campbell, Grace Bennett, Beatrice Perry, Yvonne Panell, Sheila Brinkley
3rd row: Mildred Reddick, Alice Williams, Jean Fleshman, Juliana Adjani, Zenora Williams
4th Row: Barbara Washington, Iva Baker, Brenda Reynolds, Charlie Rountree, Carrie Cotton, Carolyn Livisay, Marilyn Livisay, Shirley Watson, Wei So

---

FOLLOW THE TRUTH [68]

Sunlight is gleaming o'er the mountain heights,
Earth's radiant loveliness thrills with her youth,
Moonlight shines over water
And Bennett is calling to follow the truth.

Join now in sisterhood, spreading
The gospel that warfare and discord may cease,
Let us in humble devotion march onward
To follow our Christ, Prince of Peace.

35th Reunion of Class of 1965
*l.-r.: Dr. Jean Bailey Braxton, Beatrice Perry Soublet,
Charlene Sanders Jones, Synora Fogg Wilder*

Receiving the 2010 Susie W. Jones Award [69]
Carolyn Maddox McKie '66
_l-r:_ *Sandra Walker Johnson, Dr. Malveaux , Dr. Lisa Johnson*

Faye Ann McClain Dixon '66
1903 Wintergreen Ave., District Heights, MD 20747

*Winner of Northern Virginia Chapter's
2009 Fur Raffle*

Jewel Merritt Johnson '66
790 Mountain Falls Ct. Apt. 101, Raleigh, NC 27617

My Bennett College experience was very meaningful and rewarding for me. It was my preparation for life. And that it did. I am thrilled to have been a part of this great institution. I give high regards and to my family, friends, and teachers for supporting me and helping me to make this important decision to attend Bennett.

One of my most memorable experiences was participating in the sit-ins and Civil Rights Movement my freshman year in 1963. My group was asked to help integrate the movie theater. At the time, it was a frightening experience because we did not know what was going to happen, but we were ready and able. We were not going to turn around.

We did go into the theater and we sat down front. We were arrested for trespassing. We spent three nights and four days in jail. We were taken away in paddy wagons and finger printed.

The jails were crowded and full because students from A&T, Bennett and the community were participating. Jesse Jackson, Sr., was our leader and Floyd McKissick, Sr. was our attorney. He was able to get all of our cases acquitted and thrown out, We were successful in integrating the movie theater because we were not going to come out of the jails until they changed the law.

We returned to the campus and did not have to take exams because they knew we were exhausted. School closed early that year. The movement had the attention of everybody nationwide. Demonstrations were happening all over the country.

Dr. Player visited us in jail to give us support. She sent our parents telegrams to let them know that we had the college's support and not to worry. That was a relief for us.

I also enjoyed learning while I was at Bennett. One of my greatest inspirations was that of Ms. Mary Ann Rogers Scarlette, Class of 1954 and a Bennett icon. She was the greatest influence on me.

Some of the girls that I met while at Bennett and had fun learning with and had lots of fun with are and have been lifelong friends. My roommates while at Bennett were Katherine Rosemary Williams and Priscilla Brunson Stuckey. We do stay in contact with each other right now. It is a joy.

I have lunch once a month with four Bennett Belle classmates in the Raleigh area. They area: Edna Walker, Doris Forney Frazier, Willa Foster Anurs, and Hattie Plummer Perry. We have lots of fun talking about our Bennett memories. We all graduated in 1966. Our date was 6-6-66.

I became an educator and taught school in Washington, D.C. for thirty one years. I received a Master's of Education from the University of the District of Columbia in 1972. I was a leader in many areas in the education process while there.

I retired and moved back to North Carolina and now live in Raleigh-Durham. My hometown is Durham, N.C. and I am thrilled to be back home after forty-eight years. I am a member of the Durham Alumnae Chapter of Durham, N.C.

Married to Reynold Charles Johnson, I am enjoying my retirement.

I will always love, love, love Bennett College.

Peggy Patrick Eakins '67
8601 Shadymist Drive, Richmond, VA 23235
804-276-4797 ppeakins@verizon.net

I was born into humble beginnings in Kinston, North Carolina – the oldest female and second child in a family of nine children. My beloved and now deceased grandmother, Mrs. Mary Greene, who raised me from an early age, was my staunchest advocate and dedicated provider of love, guidance, and inspiration. Because she highly valued education, she motivated me to seize every opportunity in the pursuit of excellence. Her favorite and most often-stated quote was: "Always do your best, and never rest until your good gets better and your better gets best!" Consequently, I consistently performed at a high level all through elementary and secondary school and exhibited leadership qualities in numerous school, church, and community clubs and activities.

In my senior year of high school, I visited Bennett College with a classmate and her parents. My first impression of the campus was an awe-inspiring and lasting one. I was mesmerized by the beautifully manicured tree-lined lawns, stately brick-columned buildings, and magnificent sweet smell of magnolias. I vividly recall attending a "get acquainted" session where I sat on the floor in a circle with Bennett students and other visitors, like me, who were there to learn what Bennett had to offer. As we all talked, laughed, ate, and sang the alma mater and other Bennett cheer songs, I felt such a strong bond of sisterhood. Finally, when several girls spoke of how much the college had changed their lives, I knew this was where I was meant to be!

At the end of my visit, I left Greensboro with a prayer in my heart that I would somehow be blessed to become a part of the Bennett experience. My prayer was answered in June 1963, when I graduated from Adkin High School with honors and five scholarships. I was so thankful and proud that I would be the first person in my family to attend college.

That fall, as I boarded a bus bound for Greensboro, I had mixed feelings of excitement and anxiety because I knew I was making a journey that would change my life forever. After a tiring trip and arriving in Greensboro after midnight, I learned that my footlocker and suitcase were missing. I naturally assumed they would arrive on the next bus, so when an elderly kind-faced taxi driver approached and offered to drive me to Bennett's campus … I accepted. On the way, after I expressed concern about my luggage, the driver said he would pick it up and deliver it the next morning if I gave him my claims tickets. Because I was young, inexperienced, and naïve, I innocently handed the tickets to him. When I checked into Barge Hall and told the dormitory director why I had no luggage, she shook her head and said I would "probably never see those bags again." Fortunately, I had encountered a man who chose to help a student in need. Through a simple act of grace, when I woke up later that morning as a brand new Bennett Belle, my luggage was sitting in the parlor.

The stress of my travel woes was quickly overshadowed by the excitement of first registering as an English major and library science minor and then meeting other freshwomen arriving at Barge Hall. My "roomie" was the late Carolyn Gardner, a lovely and sociable young woman from Allendale, South Carolina. We bonded quickly and shared many late-night talks while getting to know each other. When I suffered occasional homesickness, Carolyn encouraged me to get out of the dormitory and embrace campus life in a more outgoing manner.

I smile whenever I think about our visits to each other's home, serving as college marshals, rushing to class with pajamas rolled up under our coat when we sometimes overslept, racing to buy Nurse Trammell's chicken and other mouthwatering treats, making a last-minute dash (before curfew) to Sampson's Pharmacy for a Cherry Coke, and going to dances and other events at A&T. Carolyn and I were roommates all four years and continued our friendship after graduation.

l.-r. Peggy Patrick, Veda Patrick, Melba Ollie, Arlene Hanson

My close association with many students from different backgrounds, locations, cultures, and faiths helped me to develop a broader perspective of the world at large as well as an increased appreciation and tolerance for others. As a result, my ability to communicate and interact effectively with a varied range of personalities was significantly enhanced. This skill was of great benefit in my chosen field of education, where both communication and collaboration are essential attributes.

Four of the most important and influential people who made a huge impact on my life were ***teachers*** who provided the academic preparation and life lessons that helped me get where I am today. I owe much gratitude to:

Mrs. Mabel Lenhart, my high school senior Honors English teacher, whose college-level instruction in composition and literature equipped me to handle the most challenging college English assignments with ease;

Dr. Georgia Latimer and **Dr. John Crawford**, who were highly qualified English professors whose instruction was student-centered and encouraged the application of maximum effort to every assignment, presentation, or test. Those two could be tough sometimes, but they ensured that their students obtained the skills to make a smooth transition from college to career. I actually cried during my first class with Dr. Latimer because her stern look and tone scared me so much that no words would come out of my mouth when she called on me. She kept me after class and gave me a quick confidence-building lecture, after which she gradually became one of the best counselors and role models I ever had;

Dr. Myrtle B. Sampson, who was not only a teacher but also a friend and dinner hostess to her library science minors. In her classes, we constantly learned something new and unique about the world of books and libraries. From an early age, I grew up loving books and still treasure memories of weekly trips with my childhood best friend to the Negro library in Kinston – a small shack beside the railroad tracks – where we would sit and flip through pages that took us on voyages we could never physically make. Dr. Sampson's classes reinforced and magnified that love to the extent that I decided to become a teacher-librarian instead of an English teacher.

In June 1967, many members of my family, including freshwoman Veda Patrick, and close friends rejoiced with me as I received the diploma that was my passport to a new beginning. I was sad to leave Bennett College, the oasis that groomed me to be a sophisticated and well-educated young woman with the potential and preparation to become a leader in her profession. However, with a fond look back and a hopeful look forward, I stepped out on faith ... ready to embrace the success that had started with a dream and a prayer.

In the fall of 1967, I began my career as the first Black teacher to integrate the teaching staff of any White school in

Wilson, North Carolina. In 2002, my career ended with honor and distinction when the Chesterfield County School Board voted unanimously to "name the library at Swift Creek Middle School for Mrs. Peggy P. Eakins, retiring librarian." These are only two examples of many proud moments for which my grandmother and Bennett College helped lay the foundation.

Left to Right: Maya, James, Peggy, and Erica Eakins at the CCPS School Board Dedication

Today I am happy, successful, semi-retired, and married to a special Aggie whom I met at a Reynolds Hall dance in 1964. We are blessed with two wonderful daughters and a brilliant, beautiful fifteen-year-old granddaughter. I keep busy as director and designer for Simply Elegant Paperie, a home-based graphics design studio I founded in 2003 that specializes in upscale wedding invitations and small business marketing. Additionally, I am a certified wedding planner and a member of the National Association of Professional Women.

Ralph Waldo Emerson said: "To know that even one life has breathed easier because you have lived ... this is to have succeeded." I am so proud to be a Bennett Belle, one whose success story is **still in progress**. For the 2011-12 school year, I have volunteered my time and use of bibliotherapy as a resource to help motivate a small group of bright inner-city girls whose hopes and dreams are clouded by instability and losses in their lives. My first discussion with them will focus on the Bennett Creed, *"Whatever I can envision, I can achieve."* Wish us luck!

<u>*Mollye Elisa(Lisa) Spruel Thompson '67*</u>
1403 Cold Creek Pl., Huntersville, NC 28078
704-439-2111 Sirrod55@aol.com

I thank God and consider it a blessing whenever I think of dear old Bennett, because if it had not been for Bennett College for Women, I would not be where I am today. I retired in 2004 from a very satisfying thirty-seven yearlong enjoyable career as an elementary school teacher in the Newark, New Jersey, school system. I was blessed to have experienced thirty-six of those years teaching at Hawkins Street School, where I knew the families in the neighborhood, and the parents, teachers and school personal considered themselves to be a big happy family.

Back in August 1963, my mother, Mollye, and my father, Sam, drove me from Montclair, New Jersey to the Bennett College campus in Greensboro, N.C., where my four memorable years began at the college of my choice as a Bennett Belle. In those days my parents, and those of my friends, could not afford to let me visit colleges where I had been accepted, so once I made my choice, there would be no changing my major or college hopping.

My mother informed me that I would be attending a historically Black women's college that was the "Vassar" of the South where I would receive instructions in refined, lady-like mannerisms and behaviors, which would include pouring tea properly and attending the prestigious White Breakfasts. I soon learned that strong refined, lady-like qualities had to have been instilled at home before-hand because as with any on-campus college experience, temptations of every sort awaited my new found freedom far from parental supervision.

I was encouraged to stay focused, "to get my education." If I did not finish at Bennett, I would be on my own financially. I definitely appreciated the fact that my parents had worked hard and sacrificed greatly to pay for my tuition and other necessities. Thank God I did graduate on time, thereby allowing my proud folks to burst their buttons at my 1967 graduation ceremony

I remember thinking during my first days as a freshman in Barge Hall, as my dorm mates and I gazed (hung) out of our dorm windows or walked the grounds, that it looked like a co-ed college since the A & T men had come in droves to check out the "freshman crop". While living at Barge Hall I began to make friendships that have lasted from then until now, lifelong, with Pamela Wimberly Jones from Delaware, Roberta Goode Wilburn from N.J. via Pittsburgh, Barbara Edney from Philly, and others. We Barge Hall residents became a very close-knit group through thick, thin and all experiences in between.

"Man on the hall!" That phrase had to be stated loudly and repeatedly by all workmen who had business beyond the front desk in our dorms. With that warning we had enough time to scurry out of sight into our rooms.

I studied elementary education as my major with art as my minor. I had chosen Bennett College because it was a small women's college, 620 young women, (I had had it with the distracting shenanigans of the boys in high school!), and as I discovered, I was among teachers, professors, and staff who cared about my welfare. Therefore, I was not just a number lost among the crowd as I would have been in a larger student body.

Our supervisor, Miss Mary Ann Rogers and the elementary education teachers prepared us well for our future career. Miss Rogers was adamant about her ladies faithfully attending classes, being on time, striving for excellence, and producing our very best work. If she got wind of someone who had over slept, (as though she could not hear the famous Bennett bell proclaiming the hour!), or decided to sleep in instead of being present, Miss Rogers was known to walk to the dorm, rouse the student and bring her back to class! Now, that was dedication!

Mary Ann Rogers Scarlette '54

She showed us how much she cared about our being responsible, successful young women. I appreciate Miss Mary Ann Rogers '54 (who later became Mrs. Scarlette) to this day as a role model for a woman of fine character excellence, integrity, dedication, and devotion to her elementary education majors. She is a true "Bennett Belle."

I especially liked studying my art minor with Mr. MacMillan, fondly called "Mr. Mack." He was an expert in his field who taught elementary education majors formal art skills along with creative classroom methods. The main thing I liked about Mr. Mack's approach to assigning our projects was how he would give us several at one time, explain what he wanted, set a due date, and then left us alone. He expected us to accomplish our tasks at our own rate of speed, a system that allowed freedom of expression and creativity without undue pressure. As a result, we were inspired to want to get the work done with pride.

When I became a teacher I made his useful technique for cutting letters freehand out of paper a mainstay for decorating my classroom bulletin boards. I even shared my knowledge with other teachers, their students and mine.

I wanted to continue my love of classical music, so soon after I arrived at college, I wanted to play the bassoon in the orchestra as I had in both Montclair High School's symphony orchestra and concert band for all four years. As a matter of fact, I was the only bassoonist in the township of Montclair! Nearby Bloomfield, N.J., had the only other bassoon player in the area.

I was very disappointed that I did not find the building where the orchestra practiced, because there was no organized orchestra or bassoon to play at Bennett. By the time the music department began to consider forming an orchestra, I had moved on to other activities and had lost interest in any further symphonic endeavors.

Most of my fondest memories revolved around the school choirs, because my favorite form of creative expression was singing I remember joining the freshman choir directed by Mr. Low and becoming a member of the Senior Choir directed by Miss Crawford. Being able to sing beautiful hymns in Chapel on Sundays after ironing my surplice and robe was a joy and made the church service more meaningful.

Five of us choir members formed a singing group on our own, apart from the main choir, just for fun and the fact that we liked harmonizing together. It was a convenient arrangement because we lived in the same dorm, Merner Hall, practiced our parts together and were elementary education majors, except for one French major. Our name was "The Elements + 1." Pam Reddick, Pam Wimberly, Jean Williams and I, Lisa Spruel, were The Elements, and Carol Jennings was + 1.

We sang Temptations and Aretha Franklin songs in A&T and Bennett talent shows and gospel songs when the choir toured at Morehouse and other places. We even appeared in a talent show competition on a local TV channel. We sang our best rendition of "Natural Woman" by Aretha, but disappointingly, lost to the Watauga County Squirrel Shooters, a blue grass band. It was a memorable experience for all of us in the contest.

I also was privileged to take part in the Bennett College Choir Tour of the Mid-West during Easter break 1967, my senior year. I will always remember the wonderful, hospitable church families we stayed with, the excitement of being assigned a traveling buddy, meeting new people, viewing gorgeous scenery and traveling by bus to states and cities I had not been to before. What a fantastic experience it was. We visited Morehouse on the way and sang with their choir. We sang in Nashville, Tennessee; St. Louis, Missouri; Dayton and Cincinnati, Ohio; and Pittsburgh, Pennsylvania.

One day while tooling along on an unknown highway, we heard a police siren, but thought little of it until we looked out the back window and realized our bus was being closely followed by "the law." Yes, our bus driver got a speeding ticket, and, No, he did not get another!

Our most exciting experience, however, happened while riding through the state of Kentucky. One morning we awakened to find the bus listing far to the right. After exiting the vehicle, we saw the reason for the strange angle. The narrow country road ahead was flooded and had disappeared! We were stuck in the corner of a flooded corn field! We found out that when our driver was trying to turn the bus around, it got totally bogged down in the mud. So, he eventually walked to a distant house on a hill to call a tow truck which came to our rescue several hours later.

We counted our blessings as we waited. It was a lovely warm, sunny day. We practiced our songs, watched turtles dive into the water and fish wiggle by, walked, talked, and enjoyed the quiet country setting. It was good to be young and alive.

Our class of 1967 was the one that rebelled about wearing dresses, hats, and gloves to town and skirts and dresses to football games. We may have worn them one or two times, no more! We figured such attire was ridiculous since we did not wear dresses when we visited up or down town back home. Not for us!

We also welcomed the coming of President Isaac Miller and his wonderful wife and family. He was so friendly and much more open minded than Dr. Willa Player had been. He actually asked all of us for suggestions for improving the morale among us grown women. One of the first things we asked that he change was the curfew. At that time, freshmen had to be in the dorms by 9:00 p.m., sophomores and juniors, 10:00 p.m., and seniors, 11:00 p.m. including weekends. (I believe these times are accurate, but they might not be.) Now, I ask you, "What kind of curfews were those for women 18- 21 years old who had later hours at home?"

He changed freshman hours to 10:00 p.m., sophomores and juniors and seniors 11:00 p.m., and seniors 12:00 p.m. Saturday. We were elated to say the least! When Dr. Miller arrived, the over-all atmosphere at Bennett became more relaxed and realistic. We gained greater confidence, freedom, and academic achievement, along with trust as young black women under his presidency

I remember that we were always hungry, searching for food, and usually without funds. Our dear Nurse Trammel would make her weekend rounds to the dorms to sell delicious fried chicken sandwiches for 50 cents. I would save my coins for that specialty whenever I was able. If my nose led me to her kitchen before hand while she was frying up her goodies, as it often did, she would give me fried livers as a treat. Yum! She also took good care of me during my sophomore year close to Easter vacation when I had to be in the infirmary with red measles. That was the one and only time I flew home for Easter because my mother and father wanted to get me home as soon as possible. I didn't care if I had to travel by stagecoach, Conestoga wagon, motor cycle, or ox cart as long as I could get home to my comfortable surroundings.

Nurse Trammel was a kindly, doll baby of a lady who made my stay at Bennett a little sweeter experience. My group of friends would send me throughout whichever dorm we were living in to ferret out supplies of snacks. Our plans usually included keeping close tabs on the local Belles who visited their homes on the weekend and returned with home cooked fried chicken, desserts, sandwiches canned goods, and rolls, They must have liked me, because I never returned empty handed.

Since the Thanksgiving holiday was celebrated only one day at Bennett and I could not go to New Jersey, my parents would cook and freeze my Thanksgiving dinner and then send it to me by Greyhound bus. My friends and I would eagerly walk to the Greensboro bus station to carry back one or two good sized boxes, "care packages, as we called them. They would be overflowing with all the holiday trimmings: a small turkey, stuffing, gravy, candied sweet potatoes, a vegetable, cranberry sauce, rice, cake, chocolate chip nut cookies. We would heat and share it with great gratitude to God, and my folks. Whenever any of us got care packages from home we gladly shared our bounty.

Finally, attending Bennett has touched all aspect of my life in positive ways. The academic, social, and cultural opportunities provided for me were tailor made to fit my specific personal requirements. My thorough college education there prepared me to be successful in my career as an elementary school teacher.

Because of Bennett College, I caught the eye of and have been married to Roddy M. Thompson, a fine Southern gentleman, for twenty-five and a half years. My husband is very supportive of all things Bennett, so I call him a "Brother Belle." He often tells me that he also thanks God for Bennett College because if it had not been for Bennett he would not have met and married me. I am blessed to be retired with him and living in Concord, North Carolina, not too far away from my Alma Mater.

North Jersey White Breakfast 2006
Lisa Spruel Thompson '67, Roddy Thompson "Friend of Bennett," Nichelle Gordon-Scott '90
(Photo courtesy of Reba Burruss Barnes)

As I look back at years gone by, I truly value and cherish my time spent at Bennett College for Women. The fine education I received, the beautiful campus, lasting friendships made, Sister Belles, the nurturing, loving atmosphere, and memories, will accompany me in my heart for the rest of my days. It was a joy.
Thank you, dear Bennett. You are still the best.
That's why I love you.

Brenda Morgan Nicholson '69
14006 Tarn Hill Rd., Clifton, VA 20124
703-815-9255 Bmnicker@aol.com

Northern Virginia's 2011 Unsung Heroine [70]

A native of Americus, Georgia, I currently reside in Clifton, Virginia. I graduated from Sumter County High School in 1965 before entering Bennett College for Women.

After receiving the Bachelor of Arts degree in Business Education in 1969, I worked for Southern Bell and WQXI Television Station, both in Atlanta, Georgia. In 1971, I was hired by Delta Air Lines and retired from the company in 2000 while living in Dallas, Texas.

At the present time I devote much of my time in working for organizations within my church, Metropolitan African Methodist Episcopal Church in Washington, D.C.

I joined the Northern Virginia Bennett College Alumnae Chapter in 2003 and have faithfully served since then; at present as Secretary/Treasurer. I act as Co-Chair of Hospitality during NOVA-BC's annual theatre fundraiser at MetroStage in Alexandria, VA. Whatever projects the chapter assumes, I gladly participate and volunteer to perform duties in order to make fundraising efforts successful. I am an annual attendee at The National Alumnae Association meeting in Greensboro and a member of the 1926 Society. Chapter meetings are frequently held at my home.

I am a proud alumna of Bennett and well known at church and in my community for being on fire for Bennett. In addition, I work as a recruiter for Bennett at the annual HBCU College Fair at Alfred Street Baptist Church, Alexandria, Virginia. I proudly tell the students about my Bennett school days and offer advice on selecting the right college.

The Bennett Book of Memoirs, ***Tell Me Why Dear Bennett***, premiered May 2009 during Alumnae Weekend. At that time I assisted in selling the book. I am also a contributor in the first volume with my entry found on pp. 257-259.

Married to T.J. Nicholson, a Morehouse alumnus, I am the mother of one son, Gibron.

Brenda and T.J. Nicholson

40th Reunion [71]
Brenda Morgan Nicholson (Back Row: Second From Left)

THE FIRST SORORITY ON BENNETT'S CAMPUS
Zeta Phi Beta Sorority, Inc.

Submitted by Michelle Thompson '70 and Wendy Neeley '70

1969
Seated: *Marvelyn Fuller, Marsha Dalton*
Standing: *Mischelle Thompson, Modgie Jeffers,*
Constance McLear

Just to set the record straight, **Zeta Phi Beta Sorority, Inc.** was the first sorority on Bennett's campus and here is the reason why. By the time my junior year rolled around, I, **Michelle Thompson,** wanted to pledge Zeta Phi Beta Sorority, Inc., but we did not have sororities on campus. In fact, sororities were not allowed on campus.

I came from a long legacy of Zetas from my Mom, Lallian Stephens Thompson, who has been a Zeta since 1943 (66 years). Her three sisters, my aunts, are also Zetas. You see, I had no choice but to become a Zeta! Along with two other young ladies, we had several appointments with Dr. Isaac Miller, the President at the time, to try to convince him to allow sororities on campus.

Finally, after many, many meetings with Dr. Miller, he reluctantly granted the request in 1969 to allow sororities and, of course, Zeta Phi Beta Sorority, Inc., became the **FIRST** sorority on Bennett College's campus.

I was the Basileus of the first chapter, the Chi Gamma Chapter of Zeta Phi Beta Sorority, Inc. We had five initial members and were provided guidance by the late Mrs. Ruth Gore, a longtime Greensboro Zeta and Mrs. Queenie Bell, another Greensboro Zeta. The following year in 1970 we had seven young ladies on line. All seven fulfilled all requirements and became proud members of **Zeta Phi Beta Sorority, Inc**. [72]

2nd from left: Wendy Ervin Neeley '70

LIFT EVERY VOICE AND SING

Lift every voice and sing,
Till earth and heaven ring.
Ring with the harmonies of Liberty;
Let our rejoicing rise,
High as the listening skies,
Let it resound loud as the rolling sea,
Sing a song full of the faith that the dark past has taught us,
Sing a song full of the hope that the present has brought us;
Facing the rising sun of our new day begun
Let us march on till victory is won.

Stony the road we trod,
Bitter the chastening rod,
Felt in the days when hope unborn had died;
Yet with a steady beat,
Have not our weary feet,
Come to the place for which our fathers sighed?
We have come over a way that with tears has been watered,
We have come, treading our path through the blood of the slaughtered,
Out from the gloomy past,
Till now we stand at last
Where the white gleam of our bright star is cast.

God of our weary years,
God our silent tears,
Thou who has brought us thus far on the way;
Thou who has by Thy might
Led us into the light,
Keep us forever in the path, we pray.
Lest our feet stray from the places, our God, where we met Thee,
Lest our hearts, drunk with the wine of the world, we forget Thee,
Shadowed beneath thy hand,
May we forever stand
True to our God,
True to our native land.

James Weldon Johnson and John Rosamond Johnson

1970s

ADDITIONAL SORORITIES IN 1970 YEARBOOK

ALPHA KAPPA ALPHA SORORITY, INC.

DELTA SIGMA THETA SORORITY, INC.

**Bennett College for Women
Class of 1970 ~ 40th Reunion**

<u>Seated:</u> *l.-r. Rev. Patricia Galloway Landingham, Veda Patrick Cook, Veronica Reddick Bell, Libda Bost Ebron, Tyna Wilson Key, Eddie Sifford Reid, Hattie Carwell, Irma Bivens Jackson, Patricia Harris Thomas*
2nd row: Lynn Henton Lanier, Jackie Brimage Anderson, Jannifer English McAdoo, Vernelle Hudgens-Payne, Alice Baldwin Wilson, Audrey Blaylock Tate, Alese Latham Young, Elizabeth Patterson White, Jocelyn Shaw, Hazel Brown, Winzel (Wendy) Ervin Neely, Cynthia Huntley Crocker, Janice Hill Connor, Carolyn Silvers
3rd row: Dr. Carolyn Burrell Buck, Modgie Enslow Williams, Lillie Garrison Williams, Mischelle Simone Thompson, Sandra Sanders Meacham, Delores Dillary Banks, Gwendolyn Keita, Ann Johnson Lanear, LaVerne Brown Starks, JoAnn Phillips McCrary

---

**<u>Adjunct Professors</u>
<u>2010</u>**

*Elizabeth Patterson White '70, Veda Patrick Cook '70,
Winzell (Wendy) Ervin Neeley '70*

FRESHWOMEN ORIENTATION 100
2010-2011

Orientation 100 is a General Education requirement for graduation. During the first semester of 2010-2011, the orientation for all freshwomen was taught by volunteers who were alumnae of Bennett College for Women. We three Belles, White, Cook, and Neeley, decided to become a team because we each had commitments that would not allow us to be present for each scheduled class.

We started off by sharing some of our wonderful experiences during our four-year stay at Bennett. The students could not believe some of the rules and regulations by which we were governed and to which we had to adhere.

For instance, we were expected to wear hats and gloves downtown and no pants were allowed in the chapel. We were not allowed to walk across the grass or yell across the campus. We were taught that young ladies "should be seen and not heard."

Then the students were asked to share their reasons for choosing Bennett College as the place to continue their education. Included in the orientation course was journal keeping where reflections and Bennett history were to be recorded following each class period. For instance, we had discussions about all of the presidents of Bennett College. We also discussed and learned all the names of the present Trustees at Bennett College. Students looked up biographies of Trustees on the internet. Included was Trustee Andrea Harris who is a member of our class of 1970

The students were taught the favorite songs of Bennett Belle tradition: "Alma Mater," "Preference Song," "The Bennett Ideal," and "Tell Me Why."

ORIENTATION 100 COMPONENTS- FALL 2010

Bennett College for Women History

Culture & Traditions/Campus Tour

College Mission & the Bennett Ideal

Study Skills

Test Taking Skills

Code of Conduct/Student Handbook

Bennett College Songs

Time and Stress Management

Handling personal Finance

Academic Divisions/College Catalogue

Problem Solving & Learning Styles

Social, Dining & Technology Etiquette

The Global Student

College Organizational Chart/Board of Trustees

Leadership Development

Love Letters Exercise

"Amazing Race" Activity

Vernelle Clements Boykin '71
15780 Hunton Lane, Haymarket, VA 20169
703.753.1708   vboykin@aol.com

40th Class Reunion of 1971
<u>Seated l.-r.</u>: *Bernadette Gregory Watts, Jimmie Gravely, Vernelle Clements Boykin, Gladys Ashe Robinson, Katherine (Kathy) Stewart Wilson, Rita Deans Brown*
<u>Standing</u>: *Rose Jewel Jordan, Carolyn Prince, Janise Kyle, Judith (Judy) Brooks Buck, Joyce Jenkins Jordan, Joycelyn Johnson, LaCheata Graves Hall, Florenzia Watson Davis, Christine Fitch, Esther (Peggy) Oliphant, Barbara Martin*

Having just celebrated my fortieth wedding anniversary in August and my fortieth class reunion (1971) in May, I began to reminisce about my four years of matriculation at Bennett College. My journey started when my high school principal invited my parents and me to his home to discuss colleges and recommended I consider Bennett. He sent me home with several colleges' catalogs and applications. After being accepted to several colleges, Bennett became my choice. I discovered that my high school classmate, Joyce Russell, had also accepted the challenge to attend Bennett. Joyce and I became traveling companions throughout our four years as we went back and forth from South Hill, Virginia.

Actually, I began at Bennett in the Humanities Summer Program and met some of the most brilliant, humorous and lovely girls (Linda Silver, Rose Cole [RoCo], Juliet Shepard, Lasenia Smith, Edna Williams [Tiger Lily], to name a few). In the fall, I met more young girls and upperclass women with the same attributes. My "Big Sister" Carolyn Johnson was so kind to me!

After my freshman year, I became a dormitory assistant and loved the job. I was privileged to develop close friendships with students from all classes, such as Kay Patton, Valeria Outen, Raynardo Brown, Brenda Steele, Joyce Jenkins, Florenzia Watson, LaCheata Graves, etc. During the four years at Bennett, we grew and developed from girls into young ladies who were serious about making an impact on the world and we have done so.

Providence Baptist Church provided transportation to its church for many of the Bennett students. A group of us (Jimmie Gravely, Barbara Martin [alias Bam Bam], Evelyn Chapman, and Peggy Oliphant) went together nearly every Sunday. It provided spiritual growth along with our 4:00 p.m. mandatory Chapel Service.

The class of '71 was indeed made up of pioneers, from the infamous campus sit-in to community and academic activists. As mathematics majors, several of us approached Dean Winston to develop a plan for us to student-teach and also take a needed math course instead of taking the class in summer school. He complied and the course was scheduled at 5:00 p.m. We were able to complete the course and our student teaching concurrently. Carolyn Lee, Evelyn Chapman and I were assigned to student-teach at the same school and they were my riding buddies every day. I graduated with a BS in mathematics and several job offers.

My husband, Willie, was introduced to me by a Bennett sister and our wedding included many of my Bennett sisters. My attendants included my first roommates Jimmie Gravely and Dorothine Murphy, my Little Sister Elizabeth Hemingway (Liz), and Barbara Martin. Carolyn Harrison was my soloist. Peggy Oliphant and Kathy Stewart were hostesses. Most of us keep in contact or retreat together annually.

Bennett was the launching board for my successful career, thirst for further education, desire to give back to others, and to travel the world. Working in the Aerospace Industry as a mathematician led me to advance my education by attending CA State and later NCA&T State Universities in Electrical Engineering. Teaching in Fairfax County, Virginia, with the desire to implement more technology into the curriculum, I obtained my MS Degree from The Johns Hopkins University in Technology for Educators. I have been privileged to appear on the cover of the Virginia Journal of Education, to present at the National Council of Teachers of Mathematics and to be featured in a video for teacher training by the Association for Supervision and Curriculum Development. Retirement (2010), from Virginia Fairfax County Public Schools after teaching mathematics for the past twenty-one years, is affording me more time to give back.

As one of the co-founders of the Tutorial Program at church, I have tutored/mentored community students each week for over twenty years. Now I often volunteer to tutor several times weekly and council persons with finances and budgeting. I became a VA Cooperative Extension Master Gardener (2011); I am a volunteer educator who encourages and promotes environmentally sound horticulture practices by providing current, unbiased, research-based, environmental recommendations to county residents.

Just as Bennett kindled my thirst for learning and adventure, so have my travels. My husband and I have traveled to five of the seven continents, experienced their natural beauty and historical treasures and delved into the richness of their cultures.

Reminiscing has brought so many Bennett sisters and happy times to mind. I always look forward to reuniting every five years with all of my sisters who return. This year was a really special one, especially seeing some sisters who were in reunion with us for the first time. Forty years seemed to pass so quickly. The sisterhood and great education I acquired from Bennett taught me to move outside of my comfort zone and reach for and explore new horizons. As the African Proverb says, *"It takes a village to raise a child."* Thanks Bennett and sisters for being my young adulthood village away from home and providing my foundation for making an impact on this vast world.

Dr. Gladys Ashe Robinson '71
Senator, North Carolina Senate, District 28
2107 Hunter's Ridge Drive, Pleasant Garden, NC 27313
336-274-1507   gladysrobi@bellsouth.net

"A Change Agent in an Era of Change – Why I Love Bennett College"

The mid 60's was an era of change in Greensboro, but also for Bennett College. Not just in terms of revolutionary impact the Sit Ins (which involved many Bennett women); but 1967 brought in a new category of revolutionary women –not present during the sit-ins, but affected as teens by Sit-ins across the country. Coming from Columbus, Georgia, a city the size of Greensboro in land mass, but not as populated and further behind in economic and social growth, I was a freshman excited about possibilities of becoming a Bennett Belle, because of an English instructor at Spencer High School, my high school. Mostly comprised of valedictorians and salutatorians or the top 5-10 of their senior class, these women would be known as the "Revolutionary Class" that changed the social culture of Bennett College.

A rather shy, yet confident freshman, and a bit overweight, my freshman year was filled with self-imposed challenges and personal goals. I soon became acquainted with grassroots activist groups in the community as the Greensboro Association of Poor People and SOBU (Student Organization for Black Unity). The "Black and Proud" movement convinced me to shed the perm in my hair for an Afro, lose about 25 pounds, and of course I had never worn makeup which was a taboo. One of the great things about Bennett was its focus on the total woman- mind and body. We had four years of physical education, requiring swimming, ballroom dancing, field hockey, tennis, and so on. The inspiration to lose weight came from Dr. Kinney, our physical education instructor, who said, "Girls, you do not need girdles; your bodies are your girdles – you must tone them." And so I and others in my class participated in daily exercise, ate less and most of us lost 15 or more pounds our freshman year.

Taking on the image of Black pride, I shed many habits and philosophies that exemplified the "white cultural society," and focused on making positive changes in the Black community. Dr. Grandison, my psychology professor and major advisor influenced me and other Belles to get involved in community issues – convincing us that change would only come through change agents – and Bennett Belles had historically been change agents.

I, along with Connie Smith, Lasenia Odom, Beverly Lucas, Carla Friend, and others volunteered at the GAPP office, and helped organize neighborhoods and groups, passing out flyers, talking with people about their jobs and other needs. We were a part of the Garbage Workers Strike, the Cafeteria Workers Strike, protesting the unfair wages (25 and 50 cents an hour) paid to these mostly Black workers.

Quite traditional for Bennett Belles, we worked voter registration drives and canvassed neighborhoods for the "Get Out to Vote" (GOTV) campaign. I remember following community activists such as Lewis Brandon, B. J. Battle, Nelson Johnson, Howard Fuller, Cleveland Sellars in Greensboro and across North Carolina to organize communities and protest injustices. A most vivid memory in participating in the campaign to elect a first Black person to the North Carolina House of Representatives since Reconstruction- although he lost the first race, in the race in which organized communities, Henry E. Frye, Sr. won the seat for N.C. Representative for Guilford County. I am proud to say that the experience was a significant predictor of where I am today: a member of the NC Senate.

Once asked in an interview, "What was a most significant experience that led to your leadership role in the community?" The answer: "Bennett College." Although I attribute a lot of my passion for people to my grandmother, Mrs. Sarah Jenkins (who lived until 102 years of age, serving people on the by ways, teaching children without school houses, feeding the hungry), Bennett provided the skills and knowledge to effectuate my passion for service and leadership. As junior class president, I led the "Sleep-In" on President Isaac Miller's lawn. We were demanding a later curfew (curfew was 9:30 p.m. for freshmen and 10:00 p.m. for sophomores during the weekday and 11:00 p.m. on the weekends); fewer bed checks; fewer vespers; no required wearing of hats and gloves to chapel; allow wearing of pants to class and many other requirements some of which we later realized were developmental and cultural skills. My classmates would probably agree that we appreciate and practice much of what we protested against during those days. We later realized that "freedom without responsibility: is no freedom at all."

Bennett College offered internships far ahead of many institutions. Almost all psychology majors usually spent a summer or semester at Howard University and interned with a local agency (I worked with Housing and Urban Development when there was only wooden and boarded up housing surrounding Bennett), and had graduate fellowships. Graduating a semester early, I continued activism in the community, managing the Uhuru Bookstore (first Black bookstore) and later began my forty-year nonprofit career. Working as an aging administrator for ten years, I have been CEO of Piedmont Health Services and Sickle Cell Agency for thirty years.

My allegiance remains to social causes, empowerment of the underserved, and education for our children and people. Although a rebel who did not attend her own graduation, I realized the benefit of the college experience.

I Love Bennett College. From serving as a local chapter president for the Greensboro Alumnae Association to later president of the Bennett College National Alumnae Association and member of the Board of Trustees, the gifts I received from Bennett energized me to ensure that other young women had the same opportunity. Although neither daughter (Ladisa Onyiliogwu or Davida Robinson) attended Bennett; both attended HBCUs (historically black colleges and universities). Others in my family who graduated from Bennett were my baby sister, Lydia Ashe Mullin, my niece Felicia Ashe, and my great niece Aisha Jefferson (now a Bennett professor).

My commitment to education continues from pre-K through higher education, having served on the UNC Board of Governors for 10 years and most recently in the North Carolina Senate, where the "voting Belles" of Bennett were major supporters. My words to them, "I started where you are- in the political campaign of a state legislator."

Glenda Dodd Caldwell '72
13223 Mallard Landing Road, Charlotte, N. C.
28278
(704)969-7913   gdc1220@aol.com

I knew very little about Bennett, although I lived about a half hour from Greensboro, N.C. Some of my high school classmates were attending Bennett's summer sessions and later learned that a number of relatives had attended Bennett. Upon arrival, to my surprise, I was met by my great aunt (Rosanna Dodd Barrett) who was the dorm matron for Pfeiffer Hall, I had not seen for quite some time. Also, a cousin (Shelia Hairston) who I had not seen since we were children was also in the same dorm. As a side line it is important to continue the family reunions and stay in contact.

However, my formal introduction to Bennett came when my high school counselor, Mrs. Madeline Best, took some of us to tour the campus. Attending college was one of my goals, but not until that moment and the urging of Mrs. Best did I consider Bennett seriously.

Bennett opened a whole new world for me, the friends and experiences will always be irreplaceable. During my freshman year in Pfeiffer Hall I shared a small room with two roommates, Jennie Jones (South Hill, Va.) and Betty Wright (Creedmoor, N. C.), looking back its amazing how we got our things tucked away so neatly. We had a bunk bed and a single bed and of course being the last to arrive because I wanted to wait for my father to get off from work so he could accompany my mother and me, I ended up with the top bunk. My roommates were great; our friendship grew each day as we supported each other in our individual endeavors.

The following year we lost out on getting the largest room in Merner Hall that would accommodate the three of us comfortably. Jennie and I remained roommates and Betty was always close by, next door or on the same floor. How it happened that way I can't remember, but our friendship stayed intact.

The Memories:
- Slipping out the dorm and sleeping in the Student Union in protest for changes on campus.
- Attending Vesper in assigned seats and being marked for attendance. I sat in the row with Audrey Demps and Gwen Debnam.
- Racing back from wherever on Sundays to receive the last meal of the evening (a sandwich and an apple).
- Not walking on the grass. I still have a thing about not walking on the grass and my husband teases me about that.
- Nurse Trammel coming just the right moment at night selling fried chicken sandwiches and those delicious buns.

Nurse Trammell's Fried Chicken [73]
2 ½ lb. broiler chicken, cut into pieces
1 ½ c milk
Alston's steak or Lawry's seasoning salt
1 ½ c flour for coating   1/2 inch vegetable oil
½ stick of butter
Dip chicken into milk for battering.
Sprinkle chicken with seasoning salt.
Heat oil to 350 degrees before frying.
Cook chicken 15 minutes on each side.
Chicken is done when no fluids pop after being stuck with a fork.
(Courtesy of the Class of 1970)

We took our studies seriously. Often I would go into the stacks in the library where I could concentrate and have fewer interruptions. Others found their nook: on the lawn, on the benches, even other campuses, whatever it took for our excelling as Bennett Belles.

There were some fun and silly times:

-For breakfast every morning, Jennie, Betty and I would race to the dining hall in anticipation of beating two upperclassmen, the Bibb sisters, to be first in line. It was as if we were in competition. We never made it.

-I can't forget the time when Betty, Jennie, Violetta Poston, Ann Watson and I decided to stroll over to A&T's campus on a Sunday afternoon. Violetta and Ann decided to wear their long wigs not even the color of their natural hair color, tossing them over their shoulders. The stares we got did not phase them one bit.

-Some Friday or Saturday nights a bunch of us in Player Hall would fill Raynorda Brown's room, sitting on the beds and on the floor to watch TV. Raynorda had a big screen, but it turned out to be more of a fellowship time, with talking and much laughter.

Pledging Alpha Kappa Alpha Sorority was also a highlight during my time at Bennett. A new group of friends, we were a line of twenty with only three big sisters to keep an eye on us. On May 8, 1971 we became chartered members on Bennett's campus.

I didn't always take advantage of some of the opportunities presented, but Bennett College is where I grew and developed the confidence that was needed to move on. Before graduation, I was offered a job in New York (the Borough of Manhattan) and within one month, I moved to Newark, N. J. with relatives and commuted to New York each day. Within a year I got a city government job in New Jersey, retiring after thirty years of service, and along the way received my Masters' Degree in Public Administration.

Because of the lessons I learned and the things I encountered at Bennett is why I wanted my daughter during her campus tours in North Carolina (we were living in New Jersey) to visit Bennett, believe me there was no pressure. She had already been offer full scholarship to the University of Minnesota.

After her credentials were reviewed, a Presidential Scholarship was offered. After weighing the pros and cons she chose Bennett. My daughter, Dr. Melody Caldwell is a 2002 graduate of Bennett College and a graduate of Virginia –Maryland Regional College of Veterinary Medicine, at Blackburg, Virginia.

Wanda Denell Cobb Holmes, M.Ed. '75
Tulsa Community College - NE Campus
3727 E. Apache Street, Suite 1102, Tulsa, OK 74115-3151
918-595-8487   Cell: 918-269-7677
Fax: 918-595-8492 Email: wholmes@tulsacc.edu

From a Chrysalis to a Butterfly

First of all, I give honor to my Lord and Savior, Jesus Christ for the opportunity to thank Bennett College for an excellent holistic and relevant educational experience. I dedicate this entry to my husband, Ernest Holmes III; daughter, Dena Denell Holmes-Marshall; son, Ernest Edward Holmes IV; mother, Earnestine Davis Cobb; father, David Cobb; and granddaddy, John Franklin Davis.

My story starts in Kinston, North Carolina, where I stood on the shoulders of my parents and relatives. Like a kaleidoscope you can see the positive, brilliant and magnificent colors of my personality. These colors reflect the wonderful legacy of my family. The green is Granddaddy John's leadership. He is the smartest man I've ever known. When he spoke everybody listened and did it!

Now the red is Grandma Lena's big heart full of love for children. She was always glad to see me with biscuits and a pot on the stove cooking something good no matter when I came. The teal represents Aunt Josephine's frankness. She tells you like it is…clear and to the point. I've grown to appreciate this trait even more as I've gotten older.

I receive many compliments because the blue is Uncle John's keen sense of fashion. He could stop traffic all decked out from head to toe. Listen for the pink which is Aunt Queen's poised diction. She speaks with an elegant accent from the North. She lived so many miles away from our southern roots. In my youth, I marveled at the sound of each word she spoke.

The tangerine is Aunt Mary Lee's youthful stamina. She always looked younger than her years while getting so many things done on their farm with a welcoming spirit. I hope you notice the lavender is Aunt Lena's creativity. As a published poet, she touched lives with the written word and embraced the role of a peacemaker.

Magenta is the color that represents Aunt Beatrice's thriftiness. She shops with a strategic plan and gets the best deals. When I was younger, I thought she could get blood out of a turnip.

Unmistakable the bright yellow color is Momma Earnestine's strong will. You see when she set her mind to do something…It was done!

I stand steadfast because the bronze is Aunt Chanie's perseverance. She pressed on steady and determined no matter what was going with a joyful attitude. The white is Aunt Hilda's compassion. She seeks always to be inclusive and extends herself to make everyone feel like they really belong.

Now the gold is Aunt Dianne's endurance. She's been like second mom and a connecting force in our family, like the Rock of Gibraltar. Last but not least, the sea green blue is my father's adventurous spirit. You see the naval career waves always took him to distant and exotic places. That is so much a part of me that even now I can't wait to go and try something new.

Along with my family members I had several other strong role models like St. James A.M.E. pastors and church members; David Lenhardt, recreation administrator; Mrs. Ray-Holmes, elementary teacher; Mrs. Sample, yearbook advisor; Mr. Miller, high school tennis coach; Mrs. Gee-Malloy (Class of 1955) junior high, math instructor; and Mrs. Rhem, chorus director that also helped shape my life.

I started school at Our Lady of Atonement Catholic School and then transferred to the city's segregated public schools to continue my education. The Civil Rights Movement was in full force for quite some time, but Kinston was slow to change. However, without much notice everyone was thrust into a city wide de-segregation of the public schools during my very last year of high school. A family tradition was lost because I could not be an Adkin High School graduate. I was forced to be a member of the first graduating class of Kinston High School in 1971.

Even though my senior year was nothing like the one I dreamed of for years I still had a blast! I even got poetic justice when I was selected again to be a cheerleader. You see after cheering for years, the advisor decided single digit sized girls would represent the team in my junior year. A couple of us were dismissed. To all my fellow sisters and your daughters, love the skin you are in…and be a victor. Not only did I cheer, I reign with amazing Patrick Bell as Most Athletic, co-editor of the yearbook, Valhalla for outstanding students, student council, tennis team and chorus. To top it all off I won two scholarships and was a part of a recreational basketball, volleyball and swim shows. These are my blessings and testimony! I just want you to know if you believe and hold steadfast you will be victorious. God can give you the desires of your heart. He did for me, and He'll do it for you!

Even though we were all together with new books and more resources then we ever had before in the segregated school system, something was missing. I missed the tightest and engaging black teachers who would check you like your momma and daddy no matter inside or outside the classroom. Plus, they would teach you life lessons that would groom you for greatness with the book or the rod. Without hesitation, they had your back like a mother hen if anyone from the outside tried to harm you in anyway.

I intentionally applied to several historically Black colleges aiming to get that supportive environment back again. After receiving all my acceptance letters, I chose to attend Bennett College for Women. In the chrysalis stage I started at Bennett which offered a cocoon suspended with the rich traditions of wearing the freshman beanie, challenging curricula, service learning, chapel services, dress code, laundry services, curfews, mandatory attendance academic and cultural events, dances, pledging, and social activities.

From the first day I stepped on campus I knew it was the perfect place for me. Eager to absorb more knowledge and explore career possibilities I balanced books and fun. Always keeping in mind that I had to do well and failure was not an option.

Many of my firsts happen at Bennett. My first airplane rides to St. Louis, Missouri and Miami, Florida in order to attend workshops along with Ginger Bell (Class of 1975) and two faculty members. When I rode the train from Greensboro to Atlanta to see Janice Hatch Atkins (Class of 1975) get married, that also was a first.

Now let me tell you one of the firsts that marked me for life with some of my Bennett sisters. Remember earlier I told you the blue in me was my Uncle's keen sense of fashion. Well, during my sophomore I purchased my first pair of leather boots. They were yellow. Later on that year I pledged Delta Sigma Theta Sorority, Inc. Little did I know that the color of those boots would inspire my line name. As part of the Fifteen Fiery Females, I was called "Little Sister Chicken Feet." During the thirteen weeks I introduced myself proudly as "Little Sister Chicken Feet Number Seven."

I got a dance that is so unique I am gliding and sliding my way to Delta heaven. Even though time has long passed, I still had inquiries about the boots. At my 35th Class Bennett Reunion I had some sisters still asking about those yellow leather boots. Later on I thought about the boots. Girl, if I saw another pair I'd buy them in a heartbeat and proudly wear them today. Yes, there are more firsts but let us move on and give honor to whom honor is due.

The honorable Bennett College for Women prepared me extremely well. I am very grateful for the transformation and elevation that my beloved college gave me, being the first in my family to graduate from college. I worked for Kinston Recreation & Park Department; taught and coached in North Carolina, Montana, the Philippines, and California. I earned a Masters of Education with honors from the University of the Philippines while teaching science for the Department of Defense Overseas Dependent Schools.

Presently, I am the Director of the Tulsa Community College Upward Bound TRIO Program. This position gives me a wonderful opportunity to inspire greatness in potentially first generation students to successful complete a four year college degree. Talk about coming full circle, I am a butterfly. Bennett gave my wings and taught me how to fly! Now every day I get to do that for others, what a life!

Dyora Thomas Kinsey '75
P.O. Box 792, Fort Knox, KY 40121
dkinsey5@verizon.net

Bennett College was rough for me, but in the end, my saving grace. As a military brat, I remember crying at my Dad's announcement of our move to N.C. "They treat Blacks awful in the South," I remember saying.

My big city ideals didn't match my inexperience in life. Some may pin the label arrogant, but the correct terminology reflects that of most military kids–a protective environment from everyday hardships and prejudices.

My Detroit, Michigan-born parents, Lt. Col. (Ret) Donald and Armelia Thomas, Jr., were instructors at NC A&T State Univ. and Bennett College. Yet, this did not shield me from some of the streetwise and stylish women who ate me up. It is survive or drown…from the start.

Bennett College became a partnership school to A&T's Air Force ROTC program in the early 70s. My Dad was the Assistant Professor of Military Science there. He commissioned me and two others as the first women from Bennett to enter the Air Force as active duty officers in 1975.

Dr. Isaac Miller and Dyora Thomas

Life as a woman in ROTC was no different than any other, as independent Black females in the 1970s...challenging. But, I will say - I loved my Utopia! In retrospect, that was just about the best time of my life: surrounded by Black men who made you feel like a queen; rough women who made you aware of your shortcomings; caring women who took you under their wing - took you to the free clinics, helped you with homework, soothed you when you cried over some GOOD FOR NOTHING GUY and rejoiced with you when you found that GREAT LOVE. I met my husband while at Bennett and am still married after 36 years.

Of course, I love Bennett College: fond memories, teachers in a school small enough to get a message to you, when you were messing up - the GREATEST EXPERIENCE EVER! That is why my daughter, Dyora Michelle Kinsey is also a graduate of Bennett - all in the family! I thought the Lord gave me more than I could handle. I made mistakes, tried to cover them, got caught, and lived with embarrassment, but in the end, I came away with a backbone, a wonderful husband - all, from a short-term Utopia called Bennett College.

BELLES IN HATS AND GLOVES
THE 2009 WAY [74]

30th Reunion of the Class of 1979
Seated: Belinda Foster, Page Motley-Mims, Lisa Green
Standing: Deborah Tillman Love, Beverly Randolph Bowe, Karen Ferguson Nelson

1980s

Randye Jones '80
PO Box 281 Grinnell, IA50112
641-821-0188   afrodiva2003@yahoo.com

I had my first voice lesson my freshman year at Bennett College. to describe me at that time as a "diamond in the rough" would have been extremely kind. Mrs. Mary Jane Crawford was my voice teacher, and she had to get past a lot of insecurities since I had never sung alone before. This is not to say that I was an inexperienced musician. I had played flute—which I continued to play at Bennett—in band since the second grade and had sung in choirs both in Greensboro's public schools and at my church for longer than I can guess. I had simply never sung on a stage, or even a studio, alone before. And I had never felt so exposed.

Mrs. Crawford introduced me to a variety of songs in English, Italian, and French. Eventually, she must have decided that I was ready to learn opera. Before the end of my freshman year, I was scheduled to sing on one of the programs of opera excerpts Mrs. Crawford organized to give us experience singing before the public. It was an afternoon mostly of duets of standard repertoire for us voice students.

I was assigned the title role from Giacomo Puccini's opera, "Sour Angelica," and sophomore Margo Boone took the role of the Aunt. The scene involved a meeting between Angelica and the Aunt, who had come to get the nun's signature on a document dissolving any claims to her wealthy and prominent family. You see, seven years earlier the young woman was indiscreet and bore a son out of wedlock. In that day, unwed motherhood was an enormous embarrassment to the family and a matter to be hidden from the world—preferably behind the walls of a convent. After much pleading for news from her aunt, Angelica learned that her son, whom she had given up at birth and for whom she had sacrificed everything, had become ill and died two years previously. In deepest anguish, Angelica signed away her rights, and after the Aunt left, poured out her grief in an aria to her dead son.

We presented the program of excerpts in the parlor of Pfeiffer Hall. Our costumes were pretty makeshift. I wore a black choir robe with a black cloth draped over my head. Margo wore all black, including a long skirt and a gray wig. She leaned heavily on a cane throughout the performance. Our only other props were a small table, a chair, and the rolled paper that was the Aunt's contract. Mrs. Crawford played the reduced opera score on the parlor's aged piano.

We sang the excerpt in English, rather than in the original Italian, which made the performance accessible to the audience of mostly family and fellow students. Our rehearsals before the performance had gone well, but there was something magical about that afternoon's presentation.

Margo was truly imposing and totally the matriarchal Aunt. She handled the mezzo-soprano's music with the right touch of coldness. She sat in that high-backed chair with a dowager's aplomb and pronounced her intense disapproval of her niece with total disdain.

And I, for those ten minutes felt like I *was* Sister Angelica. As I sang, "Dying Thus Without a Mother's Blessing," it was my son who had died without knowing the comfort of my arms or my tender kisses.

My mother still remembers my scream when I was told the child was dead. She said it was heartrending. I only know I was not the only one crying real tears by the time the scene was over.

www.artofthenegrospiritual.com

Natalie V. McLean '80
Chaplain Bennett College
900 East Washington Street
Greensboro, North Carolina 27401
336-517-2334   nmclean@bennett.edu

Chaplain Natalie V. McLean, '80

I now know my journey to become chaplain of Bennett College began before I was born. (Even my brother said he prayed I would become chaplain of Bennett). It was my intent to become a pediatrician or a kindergarten teacher upon my entry into Bennett, but I came to realize that God had a different path for my life.

Having grown up in Greensboro in the home of a Belle, I believe it was my intent to attend college elsewhere. I grew up hearing Bennett stories not only from my mom, Joye Stanley McLean-Bridges, '54 but also from my uncle, Dr. Knighton (Tony) Stanley, who served as chaplain during a portion of Dr. Willa Player's tenure as president.

In 1976 Bennett offered early admission which meant I could enter Bennett after completing my junior year of high school. Dr. Dorothy Harris approached my mom with this offer and mom actually bribed me to attend by saying, "If you don't like Bennett after your first year, you can transfer to another school." I took mother at her word.

My first year at Bennett was filled with adjustments and transitions including meeting a fellow Belle – Melissa Graves Heyward - who became my lifelong friend. During that year, I grew in knowledge as I allowed myself to be open to what Bennett had to offer, but at after that year I transferred to a majority institution where my brother, Victor, was enrolled as a student.

I soon realized the structure that Bennett provided was best for me.

l.-r.: Melissa Graves (Heywood), Julia Williams (Gee), Natalie McLean

I graduated from Bennett on May 4, 1980; Dr. Willa B. Player was our commencement speaker. I have come to appreciate that experience as age and wisdom began to travel together.

Upon receiving my bachelor's in biology, I planned to attend medical school but in my senior year, Dr. Rao taught a course on research methods which really sparked my interest in scientific research and lead to an 18 year career.

Following graduation from Bennett, I was unable to secure employment and mother suggested that I attend graduate school at North Carolina A&T State University. I remained in the biochemistry lab at A&T for three years following the completion of the program. Afterward, I took advantage of an opportunity to attend graduate school at Meharry Medical College. At the end of the first semester, it became abundantly clear a doctorate in biology was not my heart's desire. So I spent the next four and a half years conducting research as a technician in a biochemistry lab. In 1990, I knew it was time to return home.

My time in Nashville was punctuated by a restlessness that I could not describe, understand or shake. I made various physical changes which included changing jobs, relationships, losing weight, and I even thought that coloring my hair would resolve my dilemma and restore a sense of calm. This outward modification was so dramatic that my mother did not recognize me when she came to meet me at the airport! But still the "dis-ease" remained.

My generation grew up with parents who maintained the same job until retirement, so the idea of leaving a position because you sensed a different calling was not always well received.

There were notable turning points on my journey to the chaplaincy at Bennett. Upon my return to Greensboro, I took a temporary placement with a local pharmaceutical chemical company. Their line included hair care products and cold remedies. My responsibility was to test the amount of phenol in each batch of cough drops; if the amount was out of range, we were to inform those on the production line so formula adjustments could be made.

After a short period of time, I came to realize this position was no longer suitable for my interest. This incident was a further indication that my path was about to turn. Approximately three months into the work, my brother called with excitement in his voice to ask how I liked my new job. My response was completely unexpected because I burst into tears and told him the job was absolutely boring! There were times when I actually hoped the amount of phenol in the cough drops was out of range just to break the monotony! Unfortunately, I did not heed this warning and continued to pursue positions in biological/ chemical research.

On November 1, 1990 after a successful interview, I accepted a position as research technician for the UNC-Chapel Hill; ten days later, I realized I should leave my post; yet I remained for 10 years! In the course of that 10-year period, God's call became more evident.

The restlessness came to a peak in July 1993. While sitting in the sanctuary of my home church, looking toward the pulpit, I said, "Lord, what would You have me to do?" I heard the voice of God say, "Preach the word!" My initial response was excitement because I now knew my path. Then I said, *"WHAT DID YOU SAY?"* Again, I heard, "Preach the word." Even though my generation represents at least the fourth of those called to Christian ministry, I would not have entrusted me with such a work! So I set out to disprove God's call by seeking signs which He used to confirm His will for my life.

At the death of a church member, I went to offer comfort to the family. As we sat in her den, Mrs. Gilbert took me by the hand and looked me dead in the eye and said, "I have been praying for the Lord to call you to preach." When I received the call, only two persons knew – my pastor and my best friend. I did not respond to Mrs. Gilbert's statement but thought, "God this is **not** funny!"

I was licensed to preach by Providence Baptist Church in February 1995, and ordained in 2003. Although I am the first woman offered this opportunity in my congregation, thankfully, I am not the last! In between these milestones, I attended Duke Divinity School while working full time as well. Mommie died in August 1999 shortly before the beginning of my third year of seminary, which was not an easy transition to make. But God sustained me through all of the aftermath of her departure as He answered my prayers to be allowed to complete the master's program without having to work and have the resources to care for myself until the next door opened.

In the winter of 2000, my job left me which was the answer to my prayer and I had the opportunity to settle mother's estate before my next assignment. Even though my heart was no longer inspired by scientific research, I applied to several companies but to no avail. I submitted applications to Bennett on two separate occasions with the hope of teaching in the biology department. As of 2011, the department has not contacted me to fill a position. Yet, when the previous chaplain was reassigned, she encouraged me to apply for her vacated position. I interviewed with then Vice President for Student Affairs, Emilye Mobley, who made arrangements for me to meet President Johnnetta Cole. I was hired on August 2, 2002, and offered my first invocation on August 7 – my first day as Chaplain of Bennett College.

God has a way of directing our paths and confirming His good and perfect will for our lives. While in college my best friend Rev. Melissa Graves Heyward and I sat in the back of the Chapel and timed how long the chaplain prayed. God has a sense of humor. He called the both of us into the Christian ministry and sent me back to Bennett.

Coming home to Bennett is a source of great joy in my life. As I begin my 10th year of ministry at Bennett, it is my humble and sincere prayer that the service I have rendered and continue to offer this beloved community is pleasing to God and uplifting to those in need.

<u>The Black Madonna</u> [75]
Annie Merner Pfeiffer Chapel

Wanda Edwards Mobley '83
Director of Public Relations/Communications Bennett College
336-517-2267   wmobley@bennett.edu

"What in the world is wrong with you!!!?"
"I just got my letter from Bennett College. I'm in!"
My father looked at me and said, "Okay, but stop acting foolish. Where is Bennett?"
"In Greensboro."
"Where is Greensboro?"
"I don't know, but we can find it."

The day arrived for new students to arrive on campus. It was a Sunday and my father, mother, and sister brought me to Bennett College. To this day, I don't know the route we took to get to Greensboro, North Carolina. All I know is it took us about four hours to arrive and today, I can make the trip in less than two hours.

After we unloaded the car, my parents met my roommate, Myra George, from Bishopville, S.C. They got back in the car, gave me $25.00 and said, "Do your best. We love you. If there is anything you need, call us." They were gone.

I stood for a moment or two thinking to myself, this is it. I am in college now. So many said I wouldn't make it, but yet, so many knew I could. I knew my parents and family believed in me and I knew that I could not disappoint them.

I went to my room and talked with my roommate. Other students arrived and soon, I was okay.

My instructors and the administrators reminded me of folks back home. They hovered over me. They reminded me of things I needed to do. They wanted to know if I was okay and how things were going. They expressed their expectations and they offered their assistance.

I was in a place called Bennett College and this place was good and kind to me.

I graduated from Bennett College in 1983…grateful for my time and grateful for the people that I had met. I was grateful for the discipline and grateful for no short cuts. I was grateful that I graduated on time and grateful for the friends that I had cultivated. Just grateful. I was a new person and everyone at home sensed that I was bigger, more confident, eager, and thoughtful. Bennett College had launched a new direction for me. It had instilled in me a sense of pride and who I was, was important. I had the power to shape my destiny and I had the support to dream my wildest dreams.

Fast forward. I came back to Bennett in 1988 as an employee. I left in 1991 and returned for the second time in 1996. This time, I think I am here to stay; at least I will retire from Bennett before I start my second career as the part-owner/operator of an intergenerational center. My passion is shaping the future of young people and honoring the works and experiences of my elderly.

Bennett College is in a good space. I am again grateful for being in this good space. As the Director of Public Relations/Communications, I take great joy in sharing the "good news" of this phenomenal institution. We have such great promise and as I meet and look into the eyes of our students, I see and remember me. It is an unexplainable emotion because as I see them, I see me as them. So as I was extended a great opportunity, I extend the same opportunity to them. They can achieve. They can dream. They can overcome barriers and challenges. They can change the world for the better. They can sustain sisterhood. They can give back. **They can**....

My granddaughter, **Amiya Davis**, is four years old. I have already introduced her to Bennett College. I will admit to you, the readers of this Volume II, if she does not attend Bennett College, it will cause me some grief because I want for her all that Bennett College has to offer.

I am satisfied. I am a Bennett Belle.

In Memoriam

Susie Williams Jones
(1892-1985)
Submitted By Gwendolyn Mackel Rice '61
Acceptance for the 2008 Susie W. Jones Award [76]

"This honor means a great deal to me as it named for a woman whom I have admired since I was a child. I first met Mrs. Jones on the occasion of my sister Audrose's graduation in 1949. What a special occasion that was for me! At that time we lived in the Jones Hilton, the Merner Marriott, or the Barge Sheraton. It was my first introduction to outdoor theater—Shakespearian or Greek plays outdoors, the choir concert—such a special weekend. A few years later, Mrs. Jones and Dr. David D. Jones visited our home in Natchez, Mississippi and I recall how gracious and engaging she was to my younger sister Marilyn and me (the others were away.) Though I had already been Bennettized by my older sisters, the final die was cast for me to attend Bennett during their visit. Mrs. Jones and my mother corresponded frequently until Mrs. Jones' death.

When I think of Mrs. Jones, I always picture her walking from her home, now alumnae house, to the chapel. She seemed always pensive and indeed prayerful, no doubt praying for us. But she always stopped to speak and to share a word of encouragement. On several occasions, she called me to her home, I believe to check up on me for my parents-to be sure I was on the straight and narrow but always the perfect, gracious, kind woman that we all loved."

1990s

*Golden Class of 1940 Entering the
Bearden Gate* [77]
*Alice Patterson Patience (center)
May 1990*

Welcome given by Alice Patterson Patience at the 1990 BCNAA Luncheon

Dr. Scott, members of the faculty, alumnae, and friends:

In 1940, 46 young women graduated from Bennett College. We weren't any different from the members of the Class of 1990 who will graduate tomorrow.

Upon graduation, we were scattered across the United States, taking our hopes, ambitions, dreams, and expectations with us. Even in that restricted time period, we believed that we could make a difference. That was 50 years ago. You do a lot of living in 50 years.

We grew older, held jobs, got advanced degrees, fell in love, married, and reared children. We lived through wars. We watched legal segregation disappear. We witnessed the emergence of Black civil rights and the assassination of a good man. Through it all, we remembered what life had been like at Bennett College.

In time, we sent our beloved daughters to Bennett so that they, too, could experience that special feeling of being a Bennett woman.

Today, we bring you greetings from that long ago graduation class. Like West Point, which is extremely proud of its "long grey line," we are extremely proud of the ever increasing line of African American women who call Bennett College "Alma Mater."

From the Class of 1940, Dear Bennett, greetings.

Lequetta Johnson Lunsford '92
4416 Gray Wolf Way, Greensboro, NC 27406
(336) 854-4589   lequetta1969@yahoo.com

Lesheryl Wootson & Lequetta Johnson

When I arrived at Bennett from Somerset, N.J., in the fall of 1988, I really didn't know what to expect from this small all Black women's college. My parents were dropping me off after our annual summer vacation in Georgia. It was a very hot day, but the campus was so beautiful and calm and it was as if no one were there but us.

As we ventured to do a self-tour around campus we met a family from Miami, Florida. I was like, "Wow! How did you hear about Bennett way down there?" As we greeted and talked for a while, we discovered that we both would be staying in the same dorm, "JONES HALL," as we went our separate ways not knowing that I had a friend for life (Ralphaletta Evans-Hall).

Jones Hall Front Steps (1988)
l.-r: Paula, Ralphaletta, Bridgett, Katrina,
Mildred, Courtney, Rhonda, Sophia, Nicole, Kimberly

To be honest, Bennett was not my first choice, but I wasn't sure where I really wanted to go. In high school I was in an organization named the MLK Players. Being that I attended St. Peter's HS, a Catholic school from the 4th grade thru high school and the majority of my friends attended the local public schools, I knew I wanted to go to a HBCU.

Each Easter/spring break the MLK Players would take rising juniors and seniors in high school on a college tour. We would travel from New Jersey to Alabama touring and visiting all of the HBCUs in between. We would have so much fun, but our senior year seemed more serious because we were going to have to make a choice to where we were going to attend school that fall.

Totally confused, my mom was talking to one of my former teachers, Ms. Sandra Curry, and she mentioned to my mother about Bennett saying that she and her daughter Janie Curry were both alumnae of Bennett and would love it if I would consider. With a little persuading, I decided to give it a try, but was determined that if I didn't like it I would definitely be transferring the following year.

Needless to say I made it and those four years went by really fast. I couldn't believe it was over. Of course, it had helped that NCA&T was directly across the street and that I had several "home girls" who also attended Bennett at the same time. (Tangela Napier-Jordan, Janae Simmons-Tucker, and Crystal Morgan). That only led and continued the legacy of what had come before us and what was to follow.

Belles of Harmony

The Belles of Harmony was basically the gospel choir. We were formed in the fall of '88 under the direction of Rev. Barbara Woods, campus Chaplin (1988-1992). We would have church services every 2nd and 4th Sunday on campus and we would sing at those services.

Once a month we would have a night and invite other gospel choirs from the surrounding schools (A&T and UNCG, etc.) to come and fellowship in a Christian environment to sing, read poems, skits, etc. We would also go to local churches and sing during their revival services and we toured twice up to New York, stopping in Maryland, Virginia, Philly, and Jersey! They are still active on campus, but I am not sure if the name is still the same.

We were pretty much self organized and never got much recognition from the school.

One of the things I loved the most about being at Bennett was the sisterhood that you got from your friends and the little/big sister relationship you gained during your freshmen and junior years. I have so many long life friends that come from so many parts of the world Maryland, DC, Durham, Cincinnati, Philly, Miami, LA, just to name a few I will always be so grateful to Bennett and what it means to me for the rest of my life!

Bottom l.-r.: Lequetta Johnson Lunsford, Ronita Johnson *(with baby sister and future Belle)*
2nd row: Nathalina Talbert, Damita Wilson, Garnet Pinder Miller
3rd row: Trina Vincent, Kimberly Williams, Connie Phillips Spruill, Seantina Collins, Shana Chambers

Gina N. Trimble Jordan, CPC, CPC-H '93
3112 Kings Pond Road, Greensboro, NC 27407
(336) 297-9259 Email: Kalexj@bellsouth.net

Mother-Candice Smith, Husband-Marvin Jordan, Gina Trimble Jordan '93

I, **Gina Trimble Jordan,** am from Cincinnati, Ohio. My mother, Candis M. Smith, was very active in the community and it was through the community, I was introduced to Black Achievers. Black Achievers taught us about becoming successful adults and how to do that through attending an HBCU. Brenda Madison (one of my many mentors) and her friend Betty Tuggle started a Black College Tour. During my junior year at the School for Creative and Performing Arts, where I majored in Visual Arts and Technical Theater; my counselor knew I wanted to be a Pediatrician, so she gave me pamphlets on Washington University in St. Louis, Mo. and Mars Hill College in Asheville, N.C. (I liked this one because of the beautiful pictures of the mountains).

My mother and my aunts had graduated from the University of Cincinnati, but I was determined not to stay home. After attending an informational, my mom and I signed up to go on the Black College Tour which took two buses; one bus went south and the other went east. My friends and I always talked about going to Howard University. At that time Black students from our school who wanted to be "famous" went to Howard University. My four best friends and I chose the East Coast Tour. Our first stop...North Carolina!

We stopped at WSSU, NC A&T, Bennett College, NCCU, Shaw Univ., Hampton Univ., University of Maryland Eastern Shore, Virginia Union, and Howard University, but the college that stood out to me the most was Bennett College. When we got off the bus and walked in front of the Chapel, there was a serene feeling of warmth and home. I made a mental note that this was my first choice!

As the tour went along, NCCU became my first choice (they had cute boys), then Hampton University became my first choice (the campus was so beautiful and I loved the history.), and finally we made it to Howard University. Well, to make a long story short, our bus was almost hijacked and the hotel where we were to stay, the Howard Inn, had a rat problem. We were done with Washington, D.C. and Howard University. Of course I chose Bennett College!

<u>Freshman Year 1989-1990</u>: My father Donald Trimble was not happy with my choice! He did not want me to leave home, but I was happy with my choice. I would be the first one in my family to leave home and the first one to attend a black college. My mom, dad, Uncle Vernon, and my Uncle Duke drove me to Bennett. And again, once I stepped foot the campus I had that same feeling of warmth and home. I had my white dress, my black dress, and my Cincinnati pride!

I lived in Jones Hall and my freshman roommate was Jackie Drummond from Brooklyn, N.Y., and how could I forget where she was from? She told me every chance she got! At the President's Welcome Dinner, my parents and I sat with Dr. Levi Walker who looked just as scared I did because it was his first day at Bennett. I would later find out he would be my advisor. My major was biology.

During our first dorm meeting, I met Wilma Clark from Winston-Salem, N.C. She would become my confident and walking buddy. We would walk downtown to Woolworth to get our snacks and other supplies. During fall break, I had a chance to go home with Wilma and her parents treated me like I was one of their own. I will never forget that weekend.

My English professor, a Bennett Belle, and my work study leader was Ms. Penny Hall. She would become my mentor, confident, mother, and most of all, my friend. Whenever I needed someone to talk to I knew I could go to her…and talk to her I did!

This was the year I experienced my first taste of North Carolina weather…Hurricane Hugo. The entire campus was on lockdown that day and it sounded like a tornado were circling the campus. All of us were summoned to sit in the main hallway. The front doors were shaking, the big magnolia tree in front of my window was trying to get inside the room, and then the lights went out! I had received a 5-way flashlight at Christmas from a boyfriend, which I thought was a joke initially, but it wasn't. Needless to say…I and the rest of Jones Hall were THANKFUL for the gift. My family back home was in a panic, they wanted me home! Especially my dad!

__Merner Hall__

This was also the year of the Merner Hall fire. It was around 1 p.m. I had the window open as I lived under that big magnolia tree and loved the breeze. Lying on my bed, I was studying when I started to smell smoke. When I looked outside, there was so much smoke I couldn't see the Quad. I jumped up and ran out of Jones Hall towards Merner, but everyone was told to stay back as the smoke was so thick. A friend of mine from

Cincinnati named April Hamilton lived in Merner. After the fire, she left and never came back to Bennett.

I had family in Greensboro, my cousins Mary and Vinn Fields, whose home would become my home away from home and campus. My "uncle" Vinn had read me my rights about NOT going to Gus' on Gorrell Street and if he caught me...well you know the rest! Needless to say, I NEVER step foot in that store. My "aunt" Mary "taught" me Greensboro. She would pick me up from campus, drive on the other side of Greensboro to go "grocery shopping" and when finished, she'd say drive me home! She didn't know I was a human map!

In the spring of 1990, through a mutual friend, I met Marvin B. Jordan, a junior at NC A&T. Of course he and I didn't "click" at first, but, as time will tell, we became great friends and started dating. Through Marvin, I met my best friend and true sister who would become my life line to Bennett College; LeQuetta (Kita) Johnson from Somerset, N.J. who was a sophomore.

Sophomore Year 1990-1991: I lived in Player Hall and my roommate was Janice Durr from Cincinnati, Ohio. Spent more time with Marvin...when I wasn't studying of course! Every school break, I hung out with Kita and a few other Bennett juniors, we would start out at someone's house in Washington, D.C. and end up in New York City! Once, we drove to Atlanta, Ga. for Morehouse College's Homecoming and when we found out Miss Bennett would be the only Bennett Belle, we quickly made a banner and cut into the Parade.

Our rule was: work hard Sunday–Thursday and then we can party Friday and Saturday. If your work was not done, you could not go! We kept track of each other, because school came first and none of us wanted to go home. We also started the Belles of Harmony gospel group this year, under the direction of Rev. Woods. We traveled from Maryland to New York.

Junior Year 1991-1992: I lived in Player Hall and my roommate was Ebonie Folk from Plainfield, N.J. Everyone in our dorm loved to hang out in our room. Ebonie's favorite color was purple and mine was blue. Our room reflected that down to the color of the telephones. We loved biology and physics classes. We would laugh at the way Dr. Rao pronounced certain biology words; he knew this and would continue to repeat them. Then we got a new professor, Dr. Michael Cotton. We challenged him as best we could and for that he made sure we learned everything he could throw at us.

Best Buddies
Lequetta and Ebonie

Senior Year 1992-1993: Ebonie and I made sure we paid our dorm deposit at the same time so we could live in Player Hall and in the same room. Kita and my other traveling buddies had graduated and Ebonie and I were trying to buckle down to make sure we graduated on time and with honors in biology. My senior year did not turn out the way I would have wanted. Let's just say if I had to do it over again, I would have taken organic chemistry at NC A&T and not Bennett. Though I graduated with a biology degree from Bennett, I didn't get to "walk" across the lawn with my classmates.

In June of 1995, I married my college sweetheart, Marvin B. Jordan. We have two school-aged children (Kaylin and Cameron) who are just enjoying life, as they should. I am a Girl Scout leader and a member of Delta Sigma Theta Sorority, Incorporated. I am a Medical Coder/Biller, but I am currently giving back to Bennett as their Walmart Mentoring Coordinator. I have been tasked to find mentors for the First Generation Emerging Scholars through a scholarship program provided by Walmart.

Karen Martin-Jones Ph.D. '98
1164 Hampton Park Dr., High Point, NC 27265
336-307-4251 kmdst12@gmail.com

Reflecting on my experience as a Bennett Belle brings about joy, excitement and sisterly love. The relationship between Bennett and me began a little differently than the traditional student.

The story goes like this: I was a young twenty year old, single, pregnant female from Sedalia, N.C., who had to transfer from North Carolina Central University to Bennett College to be closer to home. When I came to Bennett, a part of my spirit was broken and embarrassed. I felt ashamed of my situation. However, with God and through the help and motivation from my mother, the admissions staff and my professors, my confidence and self-esteem began to turn. I began to develop the confidence, determination and boldness that I once had.

At the end of my first semester at Bennett, I took my last final exam, went to my car to go home and my water broke (God is an "on-time God."). The next day I gave birth to a beautiful baby girl who would forever change my life for the good. I returned to Bennett the next semester and was even more determined to make it. I had someone who was depending on me to be great, and I could not let her down.

I am a strong believer that if you genuinely pour your all into a person, transformation occurs between you and the individual you are helping. I am a product of that, thanks to my natural family and my Bennett family. Not only did I graduate from Bennett with a BS in Chemistry, but I went on to further my education. I graduated from NC A&T State University in

Computer Science and later with my Ph. D. in Leadership Studies.

After graduating from NC A&T State University, I worked in Corporate America for five years as an engineer and team lead in Maryland. I moved back to N.C. and married the love of my life and later had two more beautiful girls. Upon returning to N.C., I received a teaching position at ECPI. About a year after working for ECPI, I received a phone call from one of my former professors, Dr. Ponting, asking me if I would be interested in teaching at Bennett. I immediately reflected on how great Bennett had been to me and responded with an emphatic, "YES!"

I was under the impression initially that I would be teaching a couple of classes. However, Dr. Ponting informed me that he wanted me to come on full-time. Without deliberating on the decision, I immediately gave ECPI my two week notice. When I stepped back onto the grounds of my Alma Mater this time from a different perspective, a professor, I felt an overwhelming, indescribable joy.

Jeff, Kennedy, Ariana, Karen, Taylor

Although I was older and wiser, my love of Bennett was the same, if not deeper. I felt a desire to pour into these young women the same encouragement, determination, love and knowledge that I had once received when I was a student.

I will forever be indebted and grateful to Bennett College for all she has done. All of my steps have been ordered by the Lord, my coming to Bennett as a student and later receiving a job offer when I wasn't even looking

The relationship I had and continue to have with Bennett will forever be etched in memory and in my heart. My mission and goal is to continue to aid Dr. Malveaux in her quest to take Bennett College from "Good to Great" and to educate, celebrate, and produce twenty-first century global leaders and thinkers.

Nadirah Goldsmith '99
La Belle Shoppe
900 E. Washington St., Greensboro, NC 27401
336-517-2216 Ngoldsmith@bennett.edu

"Did you get your application in to Mr. "So and So" (Director of Minority Affairs & Recruitment), Nadirah? Once you do, be sure to tell him that you are interested in the Overnight College Trip," said Maketa Collins, a freshman at Mansfield University.

Free round-trip transportation, two nights and all meals included on this all-expense paid college trip four hours away from the city of Philadelphia; my kind of adventure.

Mr. "So and So" had personally driven the motor coach all the way from the University to Philadelphia to collect the 35-40 students from various inner-city high schools who were selected for this mini college experience. Upon arriving on campus at Mansfield, connecting with Maketa and being taken on a personal guided tour and introduced to her college community, she escorted me to the cafeteria. After selecting my lunch, I returned to my exclusive tour guide and before my eyes sat a mesmerizing vision I could barely contain. Truly I was caught off guard by a beautiful surprise: honey bronzed complexion, crisply dressed in Carolina blue, with the most beautiful sleepy and seductive eyes. Mike Jackson introduced himself as a graduating senior. Surprisingly, I felt like I had arrived at Mike Jackson's University and now all I could think about was how I needed to desperately enroll.

As the time of our visit shortened and the time of departure arrived for us, I reflected on what I had experienced at this predominately white co-ed university. As I tried to spend time with Mike and investigate his requirements, the freshmen already in enrolled in his program worked to keep us separated. From what I had already witnessed, these young women had begun to lose perspective of why they had actually enrolled, sadly becoming bitter, distracted and painfully heartbroken; ultimately losing their way. Painstakingly, I observed a high school female student on the college trip with me exploit herself over the brief period of two nights with the boys from our group as they relentlessly insulted and talked openly for all to hear of their encounters with her on the bus as we departed the campus. These early experiences are what shaped my hearts desires to study at an undergraduate school for women.

It was the beautiful postcards filled with sisterhood that inspired me to attend Bennett College without even visiting, as my desire was to study at an institution where I would feel safe, worthy and exalted as a young African American female. I arrived on a lonely day in January (1995) before any of the enrolled students arrived.

As my aunt and my sister supported me through the registration process, I finally arrived at the last station which was the business office. My expenses were now being calculated against my loans and grants and I was then told that I had about $1,000.00 that would not be covered by financial aid. As my heart dropped and begin to palpitate in panic that I would have to return home with all my belongings, the business office rep suggested that I arrange a payment plan of $200.00 a month although I didn't know how this would happen since my mother was recovering from drug abuse with very little income.

Once my registration was complete, Aunt Paula and Tameka helped me to move my belongings into my new room on the second floor of Barge Hall. Once all my items were removed from the rented car, lovingly they announced it was time for them to get back on the road and make their journey home.

Suddenly and unexpectedly the trauma of being left alone in a foreign city, on an empty college campus with no family within 450 miles hit me like a ton of bricks. I cried and pleaded for my family not to leave me as they did their best to comfort me that everything would work out and that I would be ok. I realized that I had no choice but to try to believe in their words since they would inevitably have to leave and return home. Once I said goodbye, I unpacked my stereo, connected it and let the sounds that reminded me of home soothe and calm my fears while I unpacked the remainder of my items and arranged my room accordingly.

As I became hungry, I courageously journeyed from my room to the cafeteria trying to ignore the stress of a $1,000.00 balance to pay by the end of the semester. Once I selected something to eat, I sat down this time alone at the college that I had chosen to attend, with no beautiful surprises around to get caught up with and without any sisterhood to show me around or introduce me to the community; the exact opposite of my Mansfield University experience.

As I completed my lunch, I got up to look for where to dispose of my dishes and tray when a student finally emerged into the cafeteria. Disoriented, I asked her where was I to dispose of my lunch dishes and as she showed me she asked me what was wrong. As I began to respond about my concerns, fears and worries, I begin to sob uncontrollably while this student took me in her arms and consoled each and every one of my fears, including why there weren't any students presently on campus, when they'd begin to arrive and most importantly how many students receive financial aid and how a number of them have balances left to resolve.

Autumn Cutler served as my personal tour guide on that unforgettable day and Bennett College ever since. Bennett has been an immeasurable force in shaping my life. Not even one week later from my first day at Bennett, did I remember that I had a $1,000.00 scholarship that I had been awarded from participating in the President Clinton Summer of Service program during the summer of 1993. By the grace of God, everything worked out just as my family had expressed to me and I graduated with a BA in Psychology in May of 1999 with honors.

Bennett, my Beloved Alma Mater, will live in my heart forever and will undoubtedly live on and play a major role in my legacy.

BOOKS WRITTEN BY CONTRIBUTORS [78]

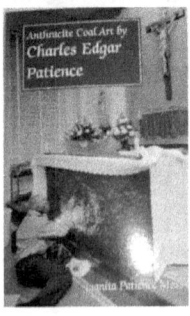

Books Written by
Fannie Lillian Miles Bellamy'58

Lillian M. Bellamy
Nonfiction writer
Dorrance Publishing Co., Inc.
1-800-788-7654
Home 1-703-938-0661

Melba Moore Stars At Phenomenal Bennett Women Banquet

The second annual Celebration of Phenomenal Bennett Women was a tremendous success with over 260 people in attendance on May 15, 1999. Eleven alumnae were recognized for their outstanding contributions to their communities, in their professions and to Bennett College. The award recipients were Hattie O. Bailey '38, Jean B. Braxton '65, Cynthia F. Hardy '74, Glenda Harris '73, Yvonne J. Johnson '64, Laureen G. Jones '79, Paula A. Patrick '90, Glendora Putnam '45, Geraldine K. Rayford '49, Judge Elizabeth A. Riggs '63 and Mary R. Scarlette '54.

Melba Moore, the renowned actress and songstress, captured and held the audience's attention as she performed her one-woman show: "Sweet Songs of the Soul: A Journey in One Life." Telling the story of her life from age four to present, Moore sang, talked, and brought the audience to the brink of tears, then back to laughter within her two-hour performance.

While it will be difficult to top this year's program, the Committee, under the leadership of Dr. Mary Jacobs and Sandra Johnson Walker, is already meeting and making plans for the year 2000. The Third Phenomenal Bennett Women Awards Banquet will be held on May 11, 2000. You now have the opportunity to submit nominations for alumnae you believe should be recognized for their contributions. Complete the Nomination Form and return to the Office of Alumnae Relations by February 29, 2000. Please consider the criteria for each award before submitting your nominations. (See page 30 for nomination form.)

Hattie O. Bailey '38

Jean B. Braxton '65

Cynthia F. Hardy '74

Glenda Harris '73

Yvonne J. Johnson '64

Laureen G. Jones '79

Left: Dr. Gloria R. Scott (left) presents a gift to Melba Moore

Below: Mary Jacobs, Melba Moore and Sandra Johnson-Walker

Paula A. Patrick '90

Glendora Putnam '45

Geraldine K. Rayford '49

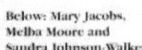

Judge Elizabeth A. Riggs '63

Mary R. Scarlette '54

2000s

Brandy A. (Jones) Osimokun 2000
barristerbrandy@yahoo.com

2011 President of the Metro-D.C. Bennett College Alumnae Chapter

Jan Erik Vold said, "If you gave me several million years, there would be nothing that did not grow in beauty if it were surrounded by water." My experience at Bennett College has been surrounded by very beautiful, life changing moments, all involving one common element, WATER.

If there were two things that I was certain of during my high school years, it was that I was going to attend Spelman College and that I was going to become an attorney. So, when Bennett College alumna Janis Badson McElrath '78 discussed the prospects of Bennett College with me, I was dead set against it. I applied just to suit my mother Raye.

Then I visited Spelman to which I already had been accepted and the spirit of sisterhood and family on the campus was less than stellar as the students ranted about how Bennett was beneath them. Was that enough to change the image that I had of Spelman and what my experience at that college might be like? Nope. With a lot of devious tactics, I caused anything Bennett sent to my house to mysteriously disappear. Somehow, my mother always seemed to find it.

The visitation weekend came around for Bennett and my mother decided that we would drive from Delaware, my home, to Greensboro through the night in order to arrive by day break. My childhood friend, Nina, drove non-stop for seven hours pumped up on No Doze. We arrived a few hours before the formal visitation program began and needed somewhere to freshen up since we were only in Greensboro for the day. The only place we could find was the "one room, one bathroom" bus station on Lee Street.

Well, you can only imagine what happened next! We went into the bathroom one at a time and took bird baths in a clogged up sink. I was so embarrassed, but at least we were half-way clean. When we checked in at the college later on that morning, Yolande Johnson told us that she had been looking for us because she had put a room aside for us to freshen up. We were invited to sit in the chapel for a formal program where they announced those who had received scholarships from the college. The last name that they called for a full scholarship was Brandy…**Hunter**. I was two seconds from standing up, but thank God, I didn't. I guess there were more than one Brandy there that day.

Just as we walked out of the program after it was over, Ms. Johnson ran after me apologizing profusely. She said I was the recipient of a tuition scholarship for the first year and they forgot to mention my name. Ms. Johnson's kind gestures throughout the day, students who never persuaded me not to attend Spelman but to find the best fit for me, and along with the scholarship, washed away any doubt that Bennett College was the school for me, despite my earlier loud protests.

After deciding to attend Bennett College, I couldn't wait to start as a freshwoman to continue the legacy of strong college educated women in my family and to make my mark on the campus like the many Belles who came before me. However, right before I left for school, my mother and I participated in a Yuruba rite of passage womanhood ceremony, where I was bathed in a river of ritualistically wash away all my childhood habits and to start my journey as a woman. I was excited about my new-found journey and independence until my mom and grandmother, affectionately called "Nini," unpacked the van and were about to pull off from Bennett's campus. Tears like the River Jordan began streaming down my face uncontrollably. Through my tears, I questioned whether I made the right decision. Would I make new friends? I cried so hard that Nini and the mother of my new Bennett sister and now life-long friend, Fenice, began to weep. Soon, my tears had caused a chain reaction and other mothers outside the dormitory started weeping. My mother remained stoic and reassured me that I would make friends and have a great experience. That wasn't my first cleansing experience and it would certainly not be my last. I later learned from Nini that my seemingly cool mother cried from North Carolina to Washington, D.C. after I was no longer in sight.

My freshwoman year went on without a hitch. When my sophomore year came around, we had relied so heavily on all my scholarships from the first year that we weren't financially prepared to pay for the next, despite the fact that Nini had already given us some money she had put aside for me for college. It still wasn't enough. A week before I was to return to Bennett, my mother was walking around like she was carrying the weight of the world on her shoulders.

"These fools are about to cut our water off for a thousand dollar back bill from when we were sharing water with the Ismael family. I'm going to pay your tuition, but I can't pay both bills. So hurry!! Go buy the largest K-Mart trash cans you can find."

She ordered me (despite my, "Mommy, no" wailing) to fill the purchased trashcans with water before the shut-off time. I pleaded with her not to make that decision because I could not go back to school knowing that she and my brother would have no water. She said it was not my decision to make.

Nervously, I got a hose, filled four huge 50-gallon trashcans full of water, stored them in the kitchen, and then left for Greensboro on a borrowed tank of gas and a prayer That water incident left me with a tattooed impression of the sacrifices that were being made for me. I had to not only go to Bennett and do well, but to take Bennett and her ideals with me always. By God's grace, our water was shut off only briefly until a payment agreement was negotiated, but my mother was willing to take that chance.

I decided in my junior year that I was going to run for "Miss Bennett College" to continue my service to the Student Government. The campaign was difficult because friends were turning against friends due to a raging was between some Christina groups on campus questioning sorority life as a form of idolatry and the sororities, particularly members of Delta Sigma Theta, Inc. Anyway, right before they announced the winners, my friends and I had a discussion that there would not be any crying of being sore winner losers.

The moment came and they announced that I was the first-runner up, "Ms. Royal Blue and White," and not "Miss Bennett College." I held it together, smiled and graciously walked back to my table. When I sat down and looked at my friends, all I could see was a bunch of tears, snotty noses, and lips quivering as they took on every emotion that I was feeling. It was unbearable so I excused myself from the table and went into the bathroom stall and started sobbing. I couldn't understand why my Christianity was being judged because I had joined a sorority and why people couldn't understand that I just wanted to give back to Bennett all that she had given to me. I pulled myself together and came out of the stall and all my friends were waiting there with tissues, and we cried together.

It is because of that kind of genuine support and friendship that we are still all very close today, still sharing all of life's tears of joy and pain. I called my mother and explained everything that had happened that evening, still getting choked up. She asked me a very direct question. "Did you run for "Miss Bennett College" to be in Ebony magazine or to make a difference?" I said, "Make a difference." She said, "Well, you don't need a title to do that."

She was right. I continued to work hard academically and in terms of my service to the college all the way through my senior year. Typical of my alma mater, I received notification that I would be the valedictorian for my class a few days before graduation and responsible for delivery of a speech at the

Baccalaureate. I was still feverishly trying to come up with this speech that I was to present in only a few hours when my mother kept asking me what I was doing. I never let on that I was the valedictorian and told her that I had to finish up a last minute paper. At the Baccalaureate, when they announced that I was the valedictorian and that I was on my way to law school, I could see the tears streaming down my mother's face.

That was the best gift I could ever give her for all of her sacrifices from the time I was born until that very moment. All of those indelible memories of my journey leading up to and throughout my matriculation at Bennett College were a purification of thoughts, healing of my body and lifesaving moments involving WATER that shaped me into the woman, mother, friend, wife, and attorney that I am today. When my mother could finally get to me after the Baccalaureate, she hit me upside my head so hard for not telling her that it brought a tear to my eye. This was my last tear at Bennett College.

MARCHING SONG [79]

Bennett College, where e'er thy daughters may have wandered through the years,
Loyal voices are ever raised to praise thee and to join our cheers,
For the mem'ries of the past are ever sacred to us still,
And the ivied walls of thy classic halls our hearts with fervor fill.

CHORUS
March on, Bennett College, loved from sea to sea,
On to greater glory, on to victory;
Sing our song of triumph, wave the White and Blue;
March on Bennett College, wave the White and Blue.
We are proud of you.

INAUGURATION OF THE
14TH PRESIDENT OF BENNETT COLLEGE
FOR WOMEN

DR. JOHNNETTA BETSCH COLE

Trustee
Dr. Maya Angelou
Greets Dr. Johnnetta B. Co

2003

Marissa Jennings
Class of 2003

As a native of Los Angeles, California, one can only imagine my transition from the West Coast to Greensboro, NC. I always tell people, I did not choose Bennett College for Women, but Bennett College chose me! I was not interested in attending Bennett College for Women but, my mother then, the Director of the Black College Tour in Los Angeles, insisted I looked at what Bennett College had to offer. I decided to give it a shot and if I did not like the school after one semester I was going to transfer to another school. I remember telling my big sister Kathryn Earley. "Oh, I am not staying here. I am transferring." She replied, "Girl! Bye! You're not going to transfer. You're going to graduate from Bennett in four years." Little did I know she was right!

I graduated with a class that depended on each other. I NOW realize this. The class of 2003 is very unique and full of life. WE weathered many storms, hurricanes, and when we graduated, there was nothing but CALM waters. The class of 2003 had FOUR presidents in the FOUR years we attend Bennett College for Women: **Dr. Gloria Scott, Dr. Althea Collins, Dr. Fuget and then Dr. Johnnetta B. Cole.** I don't think any other class can say they experienced four presidents.

Although the face of the presidency changed every year, the soul and sisterhood remained, with some help from Dean Mary Ann Scarlette. We learned very quickly that we were all we had and in order to be successful we had to depend or each other. We had to challenge each other in the classroom, support each other when we were home sick or heart broken, frustrated when we did not get the grades we thought we should get, encourage each other when we felt low, prayed with each other, laugh at and with each other, respect our differences and protect each other.

There was a rule we never spoke of, but we all understood. What happened on Bennett College campus remained on campus. No airing dirty laundry. In other words, keep family business family business and don't let us hear someone who was not a Belle speak ill of a Bennett Sister. Please believe that we stood up for her even if she might have been wrong.

I remember the road trips to our brother school Morehouse in Atlanta. Creating the slogan. *Bennett College! Morehouse College! Know your History!* Preparing for the freshwoman step show, by taping the windows of Jones Hall basement with newspaper, pulling out the dress or skirt for Thursday ACES programs, making sure when I left Bennett College campus I left with someone or somebody knew where I was going, and participating in my first protest. Walking out of a classroom and standing on the President's lawn in the rain because we believed we deserved adequate books, stellar professors, livable dorms and healthier food in the cafeteria. This protest taught me to speak my mind and stand up for my rights. The protest taught us to be BOLD. I believe this is the very reason why, I can advocate for women and girls rights on Capitol Hill. I am not afraid to meet with CEOs or Members of Congress. I believe Bennett helped me understand that I am a leader, I have a voice and deserve to be HEARD. While attending Bennett we also experienced the horrific day of 9/11. The feeling again of sisterhood strengthened. Not understanding what was going on, being away from family and depending on each other to process, America was under attack. I think we forget sometimes, but we were still young ladies.

I must admit that without Professor Dr. Charmaine McKissick Melton, I would not have graduated on time. Professors like her made my experience delightful. Not only was she an educator, she was our advisor, big sister, aunt, momma, friend and someone I could count on teaching me the truth about mass communication. She explained what we truly needed to know to compete in the working world. She was proud of us and we were proud of her. If we did not listen to one lecture, we left, learning that when you set a goal you can obtain it. We watched with our very own eyes, Dr. Mac become a Doctor.

Dr. Charmaine McKissick Melton
(Photo courtesy of Joy Scott 2003)

We watched her start off as Mrs. Mac and transition to Dr. Mac. Her knowledge kept us hungry and, Yes, sometimes we would have three separate one-hour classes, back to back with her. Our classes were not just a class time, it was also bonding time. If we did not go to class, she would send word that she is looking for you and you BETTER COME TO CLASS. I believe she is the very reason why I have been successful in the communication arena, working with Tavis Smiley, Congressman Melvin L Watt, BET Network, serving as publicist for book *Go, Tell Michelle: African American Women Write The New First Lady* and now talking a bold stand and launching my own business. To this day I still call on her for advice. I often wonder if other students received this type of concern and help from their professors.

Dr. Johnnetta B. Cole was our last president during our matriculation at Bennett College for Women. I remember when she announced that she was going to have office hours for students. She wanted to hear what we the students had to say and she made her office available. I made sure I got on the list because I had a few things on my mind. When we met she said, "Marissa, what would you like to talk about?" And I said, "Everyone says I should know you, but I think you need to know me." She laughed and said, "Is that so, and why should I know you?" My response,

"Because I am going to run something one day." She smiled, "Shut the door," and this was the beginning of her mentorship to me.

She listened to the plans I set for myself for after I graduated. By the time our meeting was finished, she had a list of things for me to do and one of them was to send her my resume. Dr. Cole helped me get my first job in Washington D.C. She listened to my goals and she reached out and helped. Everyone does not have the opportunity to meet with the president of their college, but I did at Bennett College.

We often say God has His plan for us. Dr. Cole had written me a note when I was just a young girl while she was president of Spelman College. My grandmother did not go to a Black college, so she went to "Senior College" at Spelman College. When my grandmother completed her classes, she asked Dr. Cole to write a note to me and the note said, *"Marissa, I will see you in the Class of 2003."* I still smile because neither Dr. Cole nor I knew that we would really meet to develop a relationship in 2003. She had the right time but WRONG place!

My experience at Bennett College for Women is absolutely priceless. What can not be bought or sold are the relationships I developed at Bennett. I still speak to my Big Sisters. We live all over the country and some times out of the country. Our conversations have remained the same laughter, tears, failures, success, prayers and more prayers and now new conversation, kids, and marriages. Our bond has brought us through several experiences, but I must admit these women kept and keep me inspired.

I remember Neda Brown suggesting that I join Model United Nations as a freshwoman. I had no clue what I was getting into but, believe it or not this experience taught me about international relations. I participated in Model United Nations every year I attended Bennett College. Without a simple suggestion from Neda, I would not have a true knowledge of other countries failures, success and laws. I am so proud of Neda Brown because not only did she share with me the opportunity with Model United Nations but she continues to share with her sisters.

l.-r.: Marissa Jennings 2003, Big Sisters Neda Brown 2001 and Kathryn Earley-Moore 2001 With Her Daughters

I watched Neda graduate from Bennett College, be sworn in the State Department by Colin Powell, and then work in the White House. I remember being so excited that I was working across the street from the White House at the Red Cross of America and Neda Brown, my "Big Sister," was across the street! I remember her saying, "Let's meet after work in front of the White House." Here we are setting up meeting spots after work and just a few years ago were saying "Meet me in front of the cafeteria." This relationship was established while attending Bennett College for Women and continued because we encourage and hold one another accountable for our success.

These are my priceless moments and memories that are cherished, respected and full of laughter and love. I will never say, that attending Bennett College was picture perfect, but it was a perfect picture for me!

<u>The Long Walk, Bennett College With Pfeiffer Hall in the Foreground</u> [81]

<u>The Long Walk by Dr. Linda Brown '61</u> [82]

In Memoriam

Dr. Willa Beatrice Player

(1909-2003)

FIRST BLACK WOMAN TO HEAD A FOUR YEAR COLLEGE

Dr. Willa Beatrice Player [83]

Five College Presidents, One Ex-president, and a Bishop Pose With Dr. Willa B. Player in 1955 [84]
L.-r.: Drs. Harry V. Richardson, Gammon; Mordecai W. Johnson, Howard; F. D. Patterson, former Tuskegee president; Dr. Player; Dr. Warmath T. Gibbs, A&T; Bishop Edgar Love; Martin D. Jenkins, Morgan; James P. Brawley, Clark

Dr. Willa B. Player will be remembered not only for being the first African American woman to be president of a college, but she will always be praised for her courage in hosting Rev. Martin Luther King, Jr., when no other Greensboro group would. On February 11, 1958 he spoke in the Annie Merner Pfeiffer Chapel to an overflow audience of hundreds, with students sitting on the floor just to be there.

According to her niece, Dr. Linda Brown, Dr. King's speech on that February evening planted the seed for many of the protests that followed in Greensboro. Dr. Player considered that event one of her crowning achievements. [85]

When the sit-ins began at the Woolworth's lunch counter in downtown Greensboro, both A&T and Bennett students demonstrated. Dr. Player stood behind her students when some were arrested and jailed. She visited them and made sure they could keep up with their academic responsibilities. Arrangements were made for professors to hold classes and to administer exams for the students. She was their "Bennett Ideal."

October 14, 1955 [86]
Dr. Willa B. Player is Formally Installed President by Bishop Edgar A. Love

INAUGURATION OF THE 15th PRESIDENT

DR. JULIANNE MALVEAUX [87]

Dr. Julianne Malveaux was inaugurated as the 15th President of Bennett College for Women on Saturday, March 29, 2008.

Inauguration Convocation [88]
Saturday, March 29, 2008

During the installation of Dr. Julianne Malveaux as the 15th president of Bennett College for Women, the <u>mace</u> was carried by its designer and the chief marshal, Professor Alma S. Adams. Approximately 35 inches in length and made entirely of metal (copper, bronze and brass), the mace has a tapered shaft with an engraved globe placed at the bottom (symbolic of the college's international link with the world).

Mounted vertically at the top of the mace is the seal of the college in a deep two sided golden brass color with raised detail and a textured background. Two black and two white dowels represent the college's diverse community support. The four posts hold a tapered hollow metal "trapezoid." Beneath the seal around the top of the "trapezoid" is the college's purpose (EDUCATION FOR WOMEN). The "trapezoid" bowl section below the dowels is embellished with a series of Akuba figurines (West African symbols of womanhood) that are affixed to magnolia leaf outlines (one of Bennett's symbols).

The <u>president's medallion</u> is a 1½ inch custom made brass replica of the Bennett College seal featuring the college's symbol, the bell. On the left side of the bell is found the date of the college's founding in 1873 and on the other side the date of 1926 when the college was reorganized as Bennett College for Women. The president's inauguration date is engraved on the back of the seal.

"The president's name and initial date of service are engraved on a raised rim plate above the college's seal as a center balance of support for the other plates. Rectangular shaped plates joined at the top and bottom of the chain with custom designed attached rings bear the Akuba image (a West African symbol of womanhood) and serve as the connecting links between a chain of Adinkra symbols. Inscriptions indicating the names of the college's previous fourteen presidents and their dates of service appear on the back of Akuba plates. Adinka symbols of West Africa link each plate and prominently adorn the chain of the medallion, highlighting three key Adinka symbols: (SANKOFA AKOMA, NTOSO, GYE NYAME). The three 1/8 inch thick symbols are repeated throughout the chain and are integrated with additional models of seven other Adinka symbols."

In Memoriam

Dr. Isaac Henry Miller, Jr.
(1921-2008)

Dr. Isaac Miller, Jr. became the 11th president of Bennett College after the retirement of Dr. Willa Beatrice Player. According to the College's archives, "The trustees selected Dr. Miller in 1966 because he understood the changing times and also realized the value of the Bennett experience."

At that time America was filled with young people who were symbolizing their rebellion against the "establishment and the status quo" and their convictions were reflected in their dress, hair styles, and actions. In the midst of all of that, Dr. Miller pledged that "Bennett would continue to go forth in excellence."

In 1970, Dr. Miller established an office of Alumnae Affairs whose director would serve as liaison between alumnae and the College. Although several informal alumnae chapters were in existence, what was needed was a formalized national organization. When he retired forty-three active alumnae chapters were contributing over $250,000.00 annually.[89]

Alumnae Employed at Bennett 2009 [90]
<u>Seated:</u> *Yamuranai Kurew '94, Addie Harrison '80, Julia Scott '78.*
<u>Standing:</u> *Natalie McLean '80, Penny Speas '86, Jocelyn Biggs, '94, Audrey Franklin '72, Nadirah Goldsmith '99, Bridget Patterson '07, Esther Terry '61, Krystal Toney '07, Linda Brown '61, Yolande Johnson '83, Karen Martin-Jones '98, Wanda Mobley '83, Rhonda White '85*

$5,000.00 Check Presentation October 2, 2009 [91]
l.-r: Stanley Viltz, Suzanne Douglas, Donna Richardson Joyner, 3 Home Depot Staff, Dr. Julianne Malveaux, Dr. Esther Terry '61, Dr. Millicent Rainey, Dr. Glendora Putnam '45

GROUND BREAKING 2009

The Rendering of the New Global Studies Building [92]
Alumnae Breaking Ground – l.-r.: *NAA President Dr. Lisa A. Johnson'81,
Alma Stokes'64, Wanda Edwards Mobley'83, Roslyn Smith'61,
Honorable Yvonne Jeffries Johnson'64, President Julianne Malveaux,
Mesha White'09, Dr. Andrea Harris'70, Dr. Joyce Martin Dixon'81*

Bennett Belles [93]
*L.-r.: Charmel Holland'11, Delresha E. White'13, Evelyn White'12,
Honorable Yvonne Johnson'64, Dr. Malveaux, Lauren White'10,
Courtney Ward,'10, Erica Harris'11*

Bennett College Board of Trustees [94]
l.-r.:Mary Reed, Dr. Talia McCray'90, Dr. Anne Sassaman, Honorable
Yvyonne Johnson'64, President Dr. Malveaux, Dr. Cynthia Hardy'74,
Robbie Perkins. Cynthia Marshall

BCNAA 2008-2009 Contribution [95]
Dr. Lisa Johnson, President of the BCNAA, Dr. Julianne Malveaux,
President of Bennett College for Women

2010s

BEVERLY EAVES PERDUE

05/12/2010

Juanita —

Thank you for the beautiful signed copy of Tell Me Why Dear Bennett. W...

<u>2010 Commencement Speaker</u>

<u>Governor Beverly Purdue</u> [96]
*(Thanks to courtesy of
   Dr. Alma Adams
   (Photo by Reba Burruss-Barnes)*

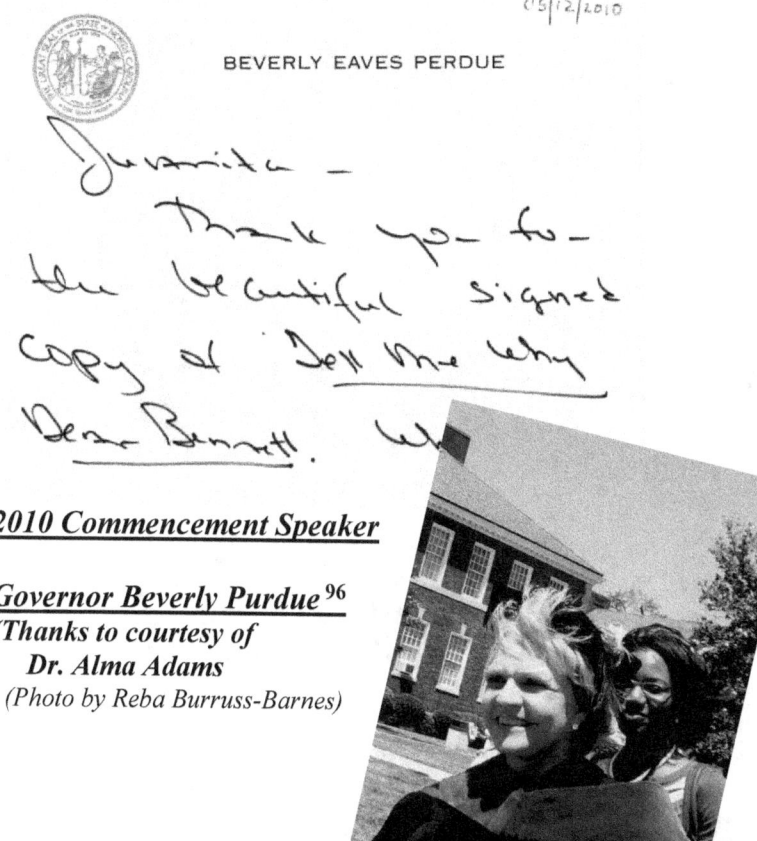

CONTRIBUTORS RECEIVING COPIES OF
TELL ME WHY DEAR BENNETT: VOLUME 1
Alumnae Weekend May 2010

Emily Davis 2004

Elizabeth Patterson White '70 & Ivenetta Smith 2006

Center: Dr. Esther Alexander Terry '61, Right: Dr. Rhonda Jackson White '85

Dr. Yardley Hunter '75

FRG Leader
Theatre Teacher

Toi Rice-Jones 2010
Member of Alpha Kappa Alpha Sorority Inc.
toitwo@gmail.com   toitwo@aol.com

Toi-Rice Jones &
Husband 2nd LT Mario Jones

August 2011

Dear Bennett,

    It seems like yesterday that my grandmother, Gwendolyn Mackel Rice '61, first brought me to you. It was a gloomy, rainy fall day when we met. However, despite all that gloom your beauty shined through and that is the day I realized why my Grandma Gwen '61, Aunt Audrose '49, Aunt Lyvonne '53, Aunt Marilyn '61 and my Cousin Michelle '91 love you so much. I know that is one of the reasons why I fell in love with you. I not only fell in love with your beauty, but with your Sisterhood as well.

    My Grandma Gwen and her Bennett Sisters, Aunt Dee [Dolores Finger Wright] and Aunt Maggie [Margaret Bailey Urquhart], made me realize how special your Sisterhood is by how they talked about their Bennett years and life after graduating from Bennett. I was in shock that they still stayed connected years later and I wanted that type of Sisterhood. I was so happy when it was my turn to walk through the Bearden Gate. I never knew that those four years would challenge, develop, and inspire me in is so many ways.

There were times when I wanted to give up and times when I felt lost, but you gave me big sisters who lifted me up and inspired me. My big sisters gave me lectures, encouraged me to continue on and implored me to set high goals and expectations for myself. I gained my own personal relationships with some of my grandmother's other classmates. I can't forget about Roslyn Smith giving me advice and steering me in the right direction. I always loved how she always came and supported me at different functions in which I was involved. Provost Dr. Terry really helped me to keep on pushing when I wanted to give up when I was struggling in class during my last semester. Both of us were smiling ear to ear when I walked across the stage.

I remember many times when my sisters and Ms. Audrey Franklin [alumnae affairs director] came out and supported me at my plays. It felt good having my Bennett sisters there when my family members could not make it. They would always clap and cheer for me even when I was backstage as the Stage Manager. I also loved the day you gave me my little sisters. I was ready to pass all of the knowledge and wisdom that my big sisters gave me to other younger Bennett Belles.

One of my favorite days with you was the day of the probate show of Zeta Xi chapter of Alpha Kappa Alpha. My Zeta Xi Sisters and I looked so pretty in our pink and gorgeous in our green. There are days when I miss going to the chapel for ACES every Tuesday and Thursday dressed in our business attire. I enjoyed being motivated by the range of guest speakers. They kept me informed about what was happening in the world and in our local community while at the same time pushing me to become that change in the world.

I have a special place in my heart for my theatre professors. Once again I was blessed with professors who *challenged and molded me into the best theatre scholar I could possibly become. They gave me opportunities to network with different people in the theatre field. I loved how I was able to see so many professional plays in the Greater Greensboro area. The knowledge gained has allowed me to teach theater to children on the Army base where my husband is serving.*

You have prepared me for so much in this new chapter of my life. Now I am happily married to an Aggie man and we have a one-year old son. We live in Korea where I am embracing the Korean culture as well as the military lifestyle. I try to do as much exploring and volunteering as possible. Bennett has also prepared me to lead. Now I am a volunteer leader for the military spouse support group. Yes, Bennett, this Belle is now a wife, mother, career woman, and community activist.

Bennett, I can never say that I love you enough. You saw my potential, planted seeds of patience, strength, endurance, wisdom, knowledge, grace and selflessness. Bennett, your confidence in me changed me from a girl into a woman. All I want to do is to make you proud.

I LOVE YOU!!

The Nellouise Watkins Faculty House
Gift of Dr. Nellouise Watkins Former Mathematics/Computer Science Professor [97]
l.-r.: Dr. Malveaux. Dr. Watkins

The Institutional Advancement Team 2011 [98]
1st. row l.-r.: Iris Ramey, Associate Vice President, Anthony Neal, Vice President
2nd row: Audrey Franklin '72, Director of Alumnae Affairs; Sharnelle Alexander, Prospect Research Analyst; Norma Wilson, Advancement Services Coordinator
3rd row: Patty Cone, Grants Compliance Coordinator; Scott Abdul-Salaam, Major Gifts Officer; Danielle Williams '90, Community Relations Coordinator; Wanda Mobley '83, Director, Public Relations/Communications

Yasmine Bowens 2011
Graduate of Bennett College for Women
Major: English, Writing Minor

Now, I can talk about the friends I have met there and the wild and crazy times we have had, but so could every student who has ever walked through those doors and stayed long enough to build the friendships with their sisters. So what I am going to do is briefly speak about the opportunities that I, a native of Utica, N.Y., was afforded as a student at Bennett because I believe it is important for young women, whether potential Bennett Belles or elder Bennett Belles to know just how far Bennett has come and where Bennett is going.

As a sophomore I was granted the opportunity to work as an office assistant of then Director of Global Studies, Cinnamon Hunter, who just happened to be my Spanish I and II professor. Under her guidance and persuasion, I decided that I would study abroad in my senior year. After all, I was working in the office so I had first-hand experience in learning the process to study abroad, after writing essays, helping other Bennett Belles get their paperwork filled out and things of that nature.

So during the spring semester of my junior year, I busied myself in preparation for studying abroad. I went to London, England through the NYU London abroad program and had a wonderful time over there, expanding my intellect base and increasing my thirst for knowledge and exploration. Being overseas for the first time as a twenty-one year young woman was exciting and the friendships that I have made while over there with other young students from different colleges made the experience that much more fun and pungent.

Also, as a junior at Bennett I was able to be a part of the pioneering Honors Program, directed by Dr. Linda B. Brown, one of the most amazing and influential professors that Bennett College is blessed to have on the faculty-in my opinion, of course.

So as an honors student, with then a GPA of 3.96, I was able to travel as a student representative to the National Association of African American Honors Program convention that was held in Miami, Florida, along with another Belle, Briana Barner. This opportunity was definitely an eye opener, but also one of the most memorable because I had so much fun getting to connect with other black students who are just as focused and intellectually talented, whom I would have never met had I not been in the Honors program at Bennett. Then of course when the Honors Dorm on campus was built I was able to reap the fruit of my labor to live in a brand new dormitory with my fellow extraordinary and brilliant sisters.

Senior year was a blast, starting off with living in London for the fall semester, then graduating summa cum laude with a 3.8 GPA, having dinner with the illustrious President Malveaux, and then being afforded another opportunity to go abroad and experience another culture, was just the right way to end such a transformation period in my life.

Lanisha Brown & Yasmine Bowens 2011

Never in my wildest dreams would I have dreamt of doing the things that I have been afforded to do. Bennett College for Women is a place of opportunity, if you choose to take advantage of the resources and opportunities that are there. No one will are professors who are watching you, who see the possibilities in you and will work with you to see that you succeed. This is why I love my Alma Mater, these are the memories that I will take with me and I hope that after you have read this you will soon make your own. The possibilities are endless: just dream, work hard and see how far you will go.

Simone Lucresia Janniere 2011

s_janniere@yahoo.com

Commencement May 7, 2011
(Photo courtesy of Great-aunt Valaida Wynn Randolph '62)

Senior Day for me was not like the traditional student. I participated on three separate occasions. I had robed my "unofficial" Big Sister, Brittany Walker, in 2008 and my "official" Big Sister, Nitrecus Simmons, in 2009. At both of those events I cried after promising both of them I would not. In 2011 when it was time for my senior day I reassured my little sisters not to cry because it was a day to remember and should be celebrated with smiles. That morning as I began to prep for my special day all I could think about was that these would be some of my last memories here at the place I have grown to love with all of my heart.

I dressed for the occasion in the traditional white dress, flesh tone pantyhose, closed toe black shoes, and pearls. With my robe in hand I walked into a gymnasium full of woman who each had a journey that soon was coming to an end. We lined up and began to process through the gymnasium, down Gorrell St., through the Bearden Gate, and across the campus. I remembered taking this walk for *Convocatum Est.* four years prior, but this time my heart beat was to a different tune, a greater feeling of success!

As I walked into the chapel I remember seeing faces both new and old. I took my seat and began to look around for all of my little sisters. Our service was filled with many speeches, laughs, and memories, but the main occasion began when the robing actually started. One after the other I watched my classmates being robed by their little sisters and I got those same butterflies I did when I first met mine two years earlier. My little sisters robed me, gave me my rose and I did not cry.

As we stood on the chapel steps to sing our song, I grabbed the hand of my roommate from my freshwoman years and sang, sang, and sang. At this point I felt myself beginning to tear up and after seeing one of my little sisters crying in the crowd, the tears fell. The peculiar thing to me was that my tears weren't because I was sad, but because I survived my four years at Bennett College and had left my mark.

Golf Tournament During Family & Friends Weekend 2010 [99]

President Julianne Malveaux along with sister Mariette, students and staff send the tournament golfers off with smiles. (L to R) Rita-Rae Conley '11, Tiffani Bryson '11, Ebony Edwards '11, Dr. Malveaux, Mariette Malveaux, Mary Joe '13, Simone Janniere '11, Tonisha Coburn '11, Danielle Williams '90, *Community Relations/UNCF Coordinator,* and Iris Ramey, *Associate Vice President, Institutional Advancement*

Zipporah Angela Sanders 2011

zipporah_s@yahoo.com
Journalism Major

l.-r.: Eny Olusanya, Zipporah Sanders,
Angela Workeman

During the spring of 2006, I went on a college tour with my Upward Bound program. We went to many colleges, learning about their history and what they had to offer us as students. I remember visiting Bennett's campus and paying no attention to the tour guide because the college was for all girls. I went home and told my mother that I loved all the schools except for Bennett. I was quick to find out that, although I had my own plans, God had already set my path for me. I had crossed Bennett off my list when, in reality, it had everything that I needed in a college: small class sizes, hands-on learning opportunities, strong sense of community, and the chance to know my professors well. Every year while I was at Bennett I understood more and more my purpose for being there. My experiences at Bennett College have increased my confidence and have helped me to understand the social, economic and political realities facing women today, and most importantly have provided many opportunities for improving and practicing my leadership skills as an African American woman.

"*My family is my backbone.*

Being the first to graduate in my family was the reason I woke up every morning, rain or shine, to go to class. My mother saw something I me that I didn't see in myself. She would cry with me every year when I needed the money to continue school and every time God would make a way. I will never forget when in my junior year I packed all of my things and drove down to Bennett when I didn't have the money or even a place to stay. I knew that my journey at Bennett College was over, but my parents would not give up that easily. They came to North Carolina on faith and in the end I got all the money I needed, and a new apartment. I can't say "thank you" enough to my family for standing by me through all the hard times and for that I am so grateful.

"History repeats itself."

In my senior year in the spring of 2011, I was able to give the student at the Upward Bound program (which first introduced me to Bennett) a tour of the College. I was able to tell another female about the history and my personal experiences throughout my four years, leaving her with no reason to doubt that Bennett College for Women is the right choice.

l.-r.: Angela Workeman, Norquesha Martin, Zipporah Sanders,

OUR LEGACY LIVES ON THROUGH OUR TRADITIONS

"Held in the Annie Merner Pfeiffer Chapel of Bennett College, the Senior Day Convocation commenced as the sophomore class prepared their big sisters for the journey of graduation. Entering the chapel in professional white attire, each senior received her robe, a red rose, and a tearful hug as her little sister ceremoniously pinned the graduate." [100]

THEN-----1963
(Photo courtesy of Tisha Harris'63)

NOW----2011

Charnee' Pearson-Starling 2011
122 Kenilworth Ave. NE,
Washington, DC 20019

Miss Bennett College 2011

According to Webster's dictionary a dream is "A series of deep images, ideas, emotions, and sensations occurring involuntarily in the mind". Dreams mainly occur in the R.E.M. stage (rapid-eye movement) of sleep; that is, when brain activity is high and signaled by continuous movements of the eyes. At times, dreams may occur during the other stages of sleep. However, the dreams tend to be much less memorable and less vivid. Dreams can last for a few seconds, or as long as twenty minutes or in my case…one full academic school year. Nevertheless, I'm delighted that something that was once a dream was set forth into reality for me!

As I reflect on my past years at Bennett, dating back to August 2007, I vividly remember practicing in Coronation 2007-2008 as Miss Biology under the reign of Chemaye Herring. During her tenure she transformed from being a freshwoman who already understood the role of royalty through the lineage of her older sister, former Miss Bennett Carah Herring, a role model, a sister, and now my Miss Bennett College legacy. I remember being that freshwoman who looked up to her and said to myself "I too will become Miss Bennett College for Women." My freshwoman dream to become Miss Bennett College was fulfilled during the second semester of my junior year as the student body elected me to represent them as the official ambassador of Bennett College in the upcoming academic school year as Miss Bennett College. I was elated with joy!

On October 2, 2010 the night of my coronation ceremony, I did not stand before everyone just to accept a title and a crown but also the challenges and responsibilities of serving and leading the student body as an example during a pivotal time of taking the Bennett College Family, Back to the Basics and revisiting "her-story.: During my entire senior year, I was ever so privileged, humble, and grateful to accept the title but also to accept the role of leadership, service, and sisterhood in which it signifies. I was honored by the loyalty and faith that my sisters had in me. My prayer throughout my reign was for God to lead and guide me safely through this journey of committed legacy of Bennett excellence.

During my senior year I was ready to show the transformation from freshwoman Charnee' Pearson-Starling to senior Charnee' Pearson-Starling. This was a vital year as I epitomized Charnee' who is a young woman of great quality. I breathe in STRENGTH, DEDICATION, and HUMILITY. While exhaling LEADERSHIP, GROWTH, and SUCCESS. I can make a mistake and smile through embarrassment because I am comfortable in my own skin. I have unconditional love for myself. I am able to catch people in awe with my poise, my elegance and grace. There is something about the way I speak. I speak with meaning, ready to start a movement. I have a voice of determination, and courage, letting everyone know I mean business. I am accountable to my sisters and the first to service mankind. I am able to bring people up when they are down with my inspiration. I am able to persevere through challenges and celebrate others through successful endeavors. I am a young woman who upholds the principles of leadership, honesty, integrity and fidelity. I am a leader in my own right and does not allow anyone to define who I am, but myself. A Queen is a Queen recognized, not by what is in her pockets, her past, or what she looks like, but what's in her heart.

I was once told that at "Bennett you pay for education but your experiences are free." During the end of my tenure, I was asked if I would like to submit a submission to compete for a spot in Septembers Issue of Ebony Magazine to represent Bennett College in the annual HBCU Campus Queens competition. For this competition they would only select the Top 10 HBCU Campus Queens to grace the pages of the magazine. With online voting in full effect, it was a race to see who would obtain enough votes to represent their college or university in Ebony Magazine.

Behold! With more than 2 million online votes that were cast for the HBCU campus queens, I, **Charnee' Pearson-Starling, Miss Bennett College 2010-2011**, was one of the Top 10 HBCU Campus Queens! With humility, I rose to the occasion and held my head up high as I was proud to represent my HBCU as I continued to walk in the path of greatness and carry on the legacy of service and sisterhood!

If someone were to pay me for my experiences at Bennett, I would kindly decline the offer! I wouldn't trade my experiences in for the world! From receiving my big sister Carmen Murchison to becoming a big sister to Denise Burnett, Andrea Henry, Lenora Hill, Jillian Lynum, and Laterria Whitener, and holding bonds with them as well as my other Bennett Belle Sisters that will always and forever be unforgettable.

One thing for sure, two things for certain, my journey was not an easy one, but it was all worthwhile. I watched myself transform into a beautiful young adult. I witnessed the young girl who met the young woman that I would become. I know that this journey would not have been successful without my Lord & Savior, my parents, Ms. Rachel Pridgen, Ms. Cristina Moriera, and Crystal Mattison, just to name a few. To those who were not mentioned, charge it to my head and not my heart. To all those who have supported me, I thank you.

To Alma Tarpley, Margaret Dean, Maggie Matthews, Ruth Artis: Thank you for allowing me to stand on the shoulders of giants when all I did was try to keep my balance. Now that I have entered to learn, I have now departed to serve.

To the future, I encourage you all to strive for excellence in academics, strive to serve with love that is rare to find, strive towards showing sincere sisterhood, but most of all strive to be the epitome of the Bennett Ideal and take your crown of service, leadership, sisterhood and become vigorous leaders of today. I encourage you all not to lose sight of your dreams.

In the words of Disneyland, "Remember...
Dreams really do come true."

2011

"Embrace the Past, Engage the Present, Endow the Future"

Bennett College
invites you to join us
for the
Naming and Ribbon Cutting
of the
Intergenerational Center
as we
Honor the Donor
Dr. Joyce Martin Dixon

Saturday, October 1, 2011
at 11:00 AM

600 East Gorrell Street
Luncheon 12:00 Noon
Global Learning Center
521 East Gorrell Street
Greensboro, North Carolina

*RSVP: Sharnelle Alexander at (336) 517-2105 or salexander@bennett.edu
by Friday, September 23*

October 1, 2011 [101]
Dr. Joyce Martin Dixon '56 (7th from l.) along with the program participants cuts the ribbon to officially dedicate the Martin Dixon Intergenerational Center.

L.-r: Demetria Craven, Dr. Lisa Johnson '81, Rev. Arnetta Beverly, Rev. Dr. Frankie Jones, Dr. Treana Bowling, President Julianne Malveaux, Dr. Dixon, Yvonne Johnson '64, Dr. Millicent Rainey, Alma Stokes '64, Keyona Smith 2012

On the cusp of the nationally recognized Intergeneration Week, Bennett College for Women celebrated the ribbon cutting and dedication ceremony of the Martin Dixon Intergenerational Center. The preschool facility is named in honor of the family of Dr. Joyce Martin Dixon '56 and to recognize her generous one million dollar donation in May 2011. Her donation marks her as the largest alumna donor in the history of Bennett College.

Interestingly, the building sits on the very spot where her father's two-chair barber shop had stood many years ago. He was known for his kindness throughout the community. According to Dr. Julianne Malveaux, Dr. Joyce Martin Dixon "has not only lifted up this place and her father, but she has also lifted up the future."

FOUNDERS' DAY CONVOCATION

OCTOBER 2, 2011

The Honorary Doctorate Degree of Humane Letters [102]
CNN Anchor Soledad O'Brien
*l.-r.: President Malveaux, Provost Esther Terry '61,
Dr. O'Brien, and Board Chair Charles Barrentine.*

Dr. Soledad O'Brien and Bennett College Students [103]

Miss Bennett College and Her Royal Court

Keyona Frances Smith, Miss Bennett College

Keyona Smith '12 is a graduating senior, biology major from New York City. Her vision as she serves as Miss Bennett College is to provide the KEY to unlocking sisterhood. During her reign, she hopes to help unite the student body and to encourage them all to reach their full potential in love and in life.

After graduation, Keyona plans on continuing her education by getting her PhD in Applied Physiology and Kinesiology. After obtaining her degree, she hopes to help find solutions to the many motor challenges that individuals with disabilities face. She also hopes to make such a difference in the world that she will be awarded a Nobel Peace Prize for her research.

Toshaleza Majadi, Miss Freshwoman

Toshaleza Majadi '15 is double majoring in mathematics and mechanical engineering and is from San Diego, California.

Toshaleza's career goals are to maximize her capacity to develop impactful STEM programming for underserved youth. Within the math department at Bennett, she will develop a theoretical foundation in mathematics. She wants to see the world and give a helping hand across the globe.

Lydia Blanco, Miss Royal Blue and White

Lydia Theresa Blanco '12 is a senior broadcast and electronic media, journalism and media studies major from San Francisco, California. Lydia serves as the publicist for the Belle Media Group where she orchestrates readership, advertisement, and public relations for the phenomenal publications produced by student journalists.

After graduation, Lydia would like to attend the University of Southern California for a Master's in Specialized Journalism then go on to Central and Latin America and teach poetry and photojournalism to Afro-Latinos and document her travels. She believes that being at Bennett College has taught her that passion outweighs recognition.

Kenyona Smith
Miss Bennett College 2012

Brenda Keels,
Miss Sophomore

Brenda Jacqueline Keels '14 is a political science major from Washington, DC. The oldest of five children born to a single parent, Brenda has remained on the Honor Roll and plans to take her academic achievements to new heights. Her passion for helping others inspired her to run for Miss Sophomore. She has the privilege of writing a memoir that will be published in the second volume of "Tell Me Why Dear Bennett" by Dr. Juanita Moss '54.

After graduation, Brenda plans to attend Columbia University School of Law and become an attorney.

Mikea Nelson,
Miss Junior

Mikea Nelson'13 is a biology major from Washington, DC. An honor student, Mikea is a member of Alpha Lambda Delta Honor Society. She has also held the positions of Miss DC and Maryland Association and at Bennett, she served as Player Hall Council President.

Mikea hopes to one day become a ranking pediatrician in the United States by incorporating educating patients as she tends to their health needs. She lives by the saying, "a blessing is not a blessing unless you bless someone else."

Ashley Sherrill,
Miss Senior

Ashley Courtney Sherrill '12 is a Psychology major, global Belle, and active community servant, from Detroit, Michigan. In the past three years, Ashley has been inducted into seven honor societies and has studies abroad in India and completed a research internship in London, England.

After graduation, Ashley plans to attend graduate school to attain her PhD in clinical psychology. She aspires to work for the FBI as a Forensic Psychologist.

Brenda J. Keels 2014
Political Science Major from Washington, DC

Brenda.Keels@bennett.edu

I am the oldest of six children to a single parent who taught me all she could considering that she was 17 years old when she got pregnant, didn't graduate high school, and had suffered the death of her own mother months before giving birth to her first child. Although some would say that my background turns the odds against me, I can gratefully say that I wasn't deprived of any opportunities. My mom was determined to make sure I would grow up with the knowledge and poise I needed to become a strong, elegant, well educated African American woman. My mom was certain that what she couldn't teach me, Bennett would be able to: thus, encouraging me to attend Bennett College for Women.

In the beginning I took Bennett College for granted. I was sure I wanted to attend an all-women's HBCU, however, I wasn't sure of Bennett. A couple of months before graduating high school and after being accepted into Bennett, my mom and I went to Greensboro to participate in the "Belle Beginnings" program. The "Belle Beginnings" program provided me with a great impression of Bennett. I got the chance to meet staff, stay in a dorm room, eat in the campus dining hall, sit in on a college class, and sample a potential sisterhood that would last forever.

After participating in the "Belle Beginnings" program, speaking with Bennett Belles and months of researching, I was certain that Bennett was for me. Any former uncertainties were put to rest by my future Bennett sisters.

The first to go to college in my family and not knowing what to expect, I packed my things and headed to Greensboro to start my college career at Bennett College for Women. I felt anxious, excited, and optimistic. Entering Bennett College during the fall of 2010 was a most interesting time... good and bad. America would have had its first African American president in office for two years, the "BP Oil Spill" would put a further dent in the already struggling economy, and an earthquake in Haiti would result in the death of thousands of people.

While at Bennett I started to experience feelings that I had never felt before. Somehow when I walked through the Bearden Gate in my white dress, I developed the idea that I was invincible. I felt like I could accomplish anything that I could dream up. I had the courage to learn, think and say things the old me wouldn't dare. The motivation and support that I received from staff, my sisters, family, mentors and alumnae have given me the courage to work harder towards my goals.

At an ACES (Academic Culture Enrichment Series) Program, Dr. Julianne Malveaux gave a sermon about having faith, but also working hard to accomplish goals. This particular sermon taught me that having faith without hard work is pointless. At that moment I decided that my faith had to be accompanied by "works," which meant that I needed to take advantage of as many opportunities as possible.

While taking a class called "Women in Politics" I was able to gain a firsthand experience of politics from a woman's perspective. The class was taught by Dr. Alma Adams: who at that time served in the North Carolina House of Representatives. Taking Dr. Adams' class provided me with many new experiences. I was able to meet politicians, canvas neighborhoods, and participate in a live candidate's forum. As a political science major opportunities such as these are very relevant. This is just one example of the many opportunities at Bennett College. Belles aren't limited to any one opportunity.

Although I am the oldest of five girls, Bennett taught me the meaning of sisterhood outside of my family. I had never experienced this type of relationship with women my age. While growing up in Washington D.C., I had become accustomed to rude behavior, jealousy, and even deceit from my peers.

I first experienced the genuine love of my Bennett sisters at a "Sister Chat" that took place in my "freshwoman" residence hall. During "Sister Chats" we were able to talk about our problems or anything that we needed to get off our minds. At first I as hesitant to the idea of expressing my feelings to complete strangers until one of the upperclassmen who led the chat shared a story. The story she told was about how she lost a parent and how her roommate encouraged her to stay in school. Seeing this showed me how much these girls really cared for one another. On many occasions my sisters loaned me a shoulder to cry on as I have to them. Bennett gave me the lifelong gift that is sisterhood!

Because of the sisterhood, opportunities and academics offered, I am proud to be a Belle. There are no other colors I'd rather wear than our honored royal blue and white. Young women around the world united for purposes that are **Education, Sisterhood**, and **Bennett**.

" May we never smirch the good
Gendered here in sisterhood;
May we ever choose a-right,
Guided but by honor bright;
Ever lovelier shalt thou live,
As thy daughters freely give;
Ever glorious a-bove,
Testimonies of our love."

2nd verse of "Alma Mater"

THEN-----A physical education class in the college bowling alley in the 1950s.

TODAY--- On the same spot in the Student Union Building

Grand Opening of the Bennett Boutique [106]

EPILOGUE

THE BATON HAS BEEN PASSED

OUR race for excellence began with Lyman Bennett's initial gift of $10,000.00 to purchase property to build a school in Greensboro, N.C. for the children of the newly freed slaves.

Years later, the baton was passed into the altruistic hands of Mr. and Mrs. Henry Pfeiffer whose generosity helped to erect several buildings, including the Annie Merner Pfeiffer Chapel in 1941.

Most recently, philanthropist and alumna, Dr. Joyce Martin Dixon, graciously accepted the baton by her generous gifts to Alma Mater.

Many others, as well, have carried the baton of generosity through the 19th and 20th centuries. OUR race for excellence will continue as alumnae continue to carry the baton in OUR own individual ways, and then pass it on to the new Belles of the 21st century.

Hopefully, many will be so inspired when reading the memoirs and achievements of the Belles who have shared in these two volumes of *Tell Me Why Dear Bennett*.

BENNETT COLLEGE'S STATE OF THE ART SCIENCE LABORATORIES

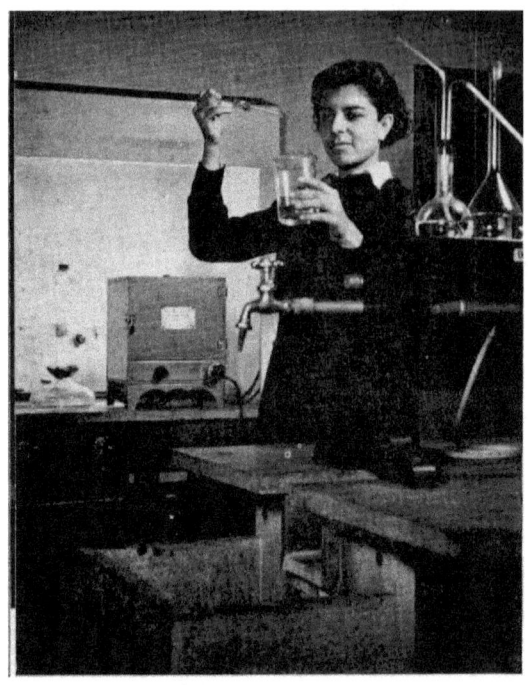

THEN-----1938 [107]

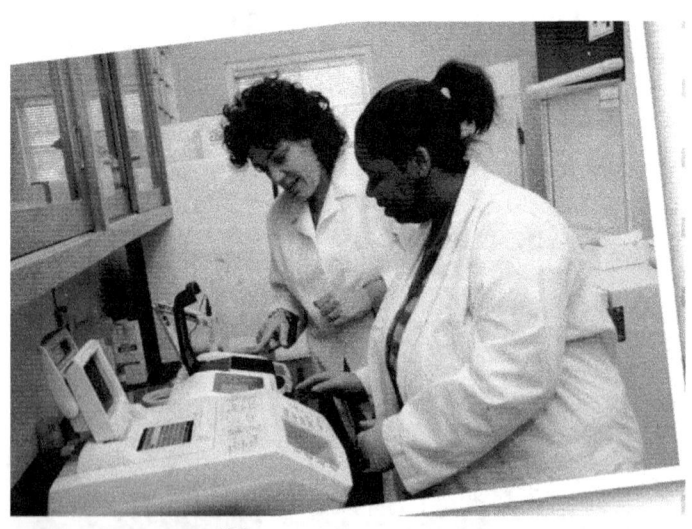

NOW------2011 [108]

AFTERWORD

Excerpts from:

BENNETT IN 138 YEARS: A CONVERSATION FOR MY SISTERS [109]

"Where have we been and where are we going?"
by Tiara Kennedy'11

"Bennett Chaplain Reverend Natalie McLean, who graduated from Bennett in 1980, says we as people are not consistent in passing traditions from one generation to the next. 'We have left our young people," McLean said, "to seek direction from other sources, such as peers, who have had similar experiences and chances, and various forms of media, which are not dedicated to lead us into the truth about ourselves."

And the truth is, without the tradition, there would be not Bennett College...Some of these traditions include Convocatum Est, Big Sister/Little Sister ceremony, the Lyceum Series, and ACES.

Tiara Kennedy '11

Special Assistant to the provost Yolonde Johnson '83 sums up what she believes has kept Bennett going for 138 years. "First, the Christian foundation and principles; then it is love for the school."

President Dr. Julianne Malveaux says Bennett meets a critical need in the African-American community. "We were founded in the basement of a Methodist Episcopal Church to educate the descendants of formerly enslaved people," she says. Dr. Malveaux said in order to see Bennett through another 138 years, we must continue the tradition overall, we must not forget out history or our present individual responsibility to Bennett College. And whenever you forget, just ask yourself: **Where would I be if 138 years earlier no one had thought about me?**

THEN----- 1938
<u>Attending A Tea Party in the Home Economics Department Parlor</u> [110]

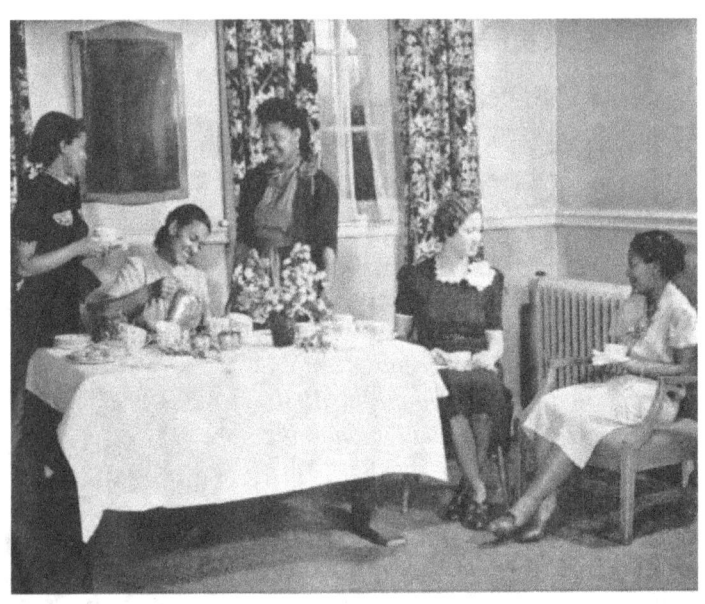

NOW----2011
<u>Attending the 19th Annual UNCF Golf Tournament</u> [111]

END NOTES

1. *The Belle Ringer*. The Spirit of Bennett, Spring 2011, p. 2.

2. *The Belle Ringer*. Breaking Ground At Bennett College, Fall/Winter 2011, p.2.

3. *The Belle Ringer.* Tell Me Why. Letter from the Editors, Fall/Winter 2011, inside cover.

4. *Ibid.* p. 4.

5. *Ibid.*

6. 2009-2011 BCNAA Officers. *The Belle Ringer*, Fall/Winter 2009, p. 3.

7. The Spirit of Bennett via campus buildings:
   (Carolina Hall, Bennett hall, Carrie Barge Chapel, Kent Hall, John Race Administration Building, Global Learning Center, Nellouise Watkins Faculty House, Honors Residence Hall, Intergenerational Center, Bennett 2020 Master Plan).
   "The Spirit of Bennett, Celebrating 85 years as a College for Women," Inside back cover of *The Belle Ringer*, Co-editors: Audrey Franklin '72 and Wanda Mobley '83, Spring 2011.

8. Rosetta Libian Lloyd Mackel, *Rosetta: An Autobiography,* mother of four alumnae and grandmother of one, 1987.

9. *The Belle Ringer*, Vol. 15, No. 4. June-July 1985, p. 16.

10. *The Bell Ringer*, Oprah, Spring 2007, p. 8.

11. Norlisha Jackson, "Saving More Than She Spent," *The Belle Ringer* 1999, p. 8.

12. *The Bell Ringer*, Breaking Ground: No Borders, No Limits. Fall/Winter 2010, p. 25.

13. Bennett College song sheet, 1939.

14.. Dr. David D. Jones' first class of four-year graduates, the Class of 1930. Cover of *The Belle Ringer*, The Spirit of Bennett Spring 2011.

15. Members of 1930 class, the first after Bennett became a woman's college, returned for their 25th class reunion and won the cup for having largest percentage of attendance, *Bennett College Bulletin,* Fall 1955, p. 18.

16., Members of the 1930 class, *The Belle Ringer*, The Spirit of Bennett Spring 2011, p. 3.

17. Mrs. Dorothy Strothers Kennedy's memoir is found in *Tell Me Why Dear Bennett: Memoirs of Bennett Belles: Class 1924-2012,* p. 22.

18. Trustee Rose Mae Withers Catchings was born Greensboro, N.C., and reared on Bennett's campus where her parents were faculty members. A tribute by Esther Canty-Barnes is published in the first volume of *Tell Me Why Dear 2012,* pp. 24-26.

19. Mrs. Henry Pfeiffer and Dr. David D. Jones., *The Bennett Banner*, Vol. 6, No. 4, Greensboro, March 1936, p. 1.

20, Members of the Bennett College board of trustees. *Bennett College Bulletin,* Fall 1955, p. 5.

21. Class of 1935 in reunion. *The Belle Ringer* 1990, p. 5.

22. Student Government Cabinet. *The Bennett Banner*, December 1937, p.1.

23. "Boycott of 1937." *Greensboro News and Record*, February 4, 1994, article in full in Appendix of *TMWDB*, pp.389-393.

24. The "Greensboro Four" are Ezell Blair, Franklin McCain, Joseph McNeil, Jr., and David Richmond.

25. Alice Patterson Patience'40, *Bittersweet Memories of Home,* Book I, pp. 18-21.

26. Bennett College Song Sheet, 1939.

27. Patience, *Bittersweet Memories of Home*, Book I, pp. 18-21.

28. *Wilkes-Barre Times Leader,* Wilkes-Barre, Pa., circa 1943.

29. "Honorees '91," The Susie W. Jones Award was given to Edith Taylor Sheppard '46.

30. Photo identification by Virginia Jeffries Brown '[48], Ouida Rush Hodnett'[50], and Lillian Clarke Lockery '[50].

    1. Carrie Kellogg Ray (Director)
    2. Dorothy Blue
    3. ?
    4. Patsy Blanchette
    5. ?

6. Virginia Wagstaff
7. Rose Ann (Cayenne) Johnson
8. Geraldine Hill
9. Verona Pulley
10. Matilda Chavis
11. Marilyn Motley
12. ?
13. Vivian Greenleaf
14. .Vira Kennedy
15. ?
16. ?
17. ?
18. ?
19. Annie Herbin
20. Wilma Harris
21. Sharon Webber
22. Ouida Rush
23. Irma Weathers

DK- Dr. Rose Karfiol   PR- Paul Robeson

31. Linda Brown, *The Long Walk*, p. 162.
    President Jones brought Mrs. Eleanor Roosevelt to Bennett during World War II and on March 20, 1945, she spoke to the Homemaking Institute on "The Veteran Returns to His Family."

32. *The Belle Connection*, Issue 2, November/December 2003, p.15.

33. Betty Walker '49, *Alumnae Directory 2010*, Harris Connect, p. A7.

34. Class of 1949. *The Belle Ringer*, Fall/Winter, 2009, p. 15.

35. Bishop Robert E. Jones was Dr. David D. Jones' brother (corrected from Volume I),

36. A gift from Gwendolyn Harris Blount '52. *The Belle Ringer*, Breaking Ground at Bennett College, Fall/Winter 2009, p. 8.

37. Helen Newberry McDowell'[24] is surrounded by 1st memoir book contributors at the Metro-D.C. Chapter's White Breakfast on November 7, 2009.
   Seated: Juanita Page Cooke, Joyce Pullum Gray, Helen Newberry McDowell, Irene Powell Carter, Juanita Patience Moss, Joy Scott
   Standing: Joyce Dunn Garrett, Ernestine Herbin Gray, Roberta McGuinn Polk, Kenya Samuels Gray, Geraldine Hughes Kiser, Charlene Sanders Jones, Othelia Hughes, Hazeline Taylor Harris, E. Adell Taylor Dowdy, Angela West Thompson, Lisa Johnson, Annie Green Ponds, Edna Fitts Holsey, Adelia Hammond Williams.

38. The Bennett bell was a gift of Lyman Bennett, a white businessman from Troy, N.Y. He donated the first $10,000 for the founding the school and died from pneumonia while raising money for the bell.

39. Mr. William Cooper was the organist in 1951-52. *The Belle Ringer*, December 1952.

40. Betty Washington'53, *Alumnae Directory 2010, Harris Connect, p. A-11.*

41. *"In Memoriam"* for Ellease Colston. *The Belle Connection,* Fall 2008, p.8.

42. Golden Class of 1954 photographed by Robert Bell prior to the 2004 Commencement in the Coliseum.
   1st row: Ina Eleanor McCarther, Juanita Patience Moss, Alma Fitzgerald Fowlkes, Doris Drummond Gupple, Judith Jackson Adams
   2nd row: Dorothy Dixon Morrow, Rosa Fargas, Grace Whaley Chambers, Marjorie Gay-Jones, Janet Cain King
   3rd row: Mildred Copeland Simms, Mary Ann Rogers Scarlette, Eugenia Duncan Johnson

    4th row: Janice Dejoie, Emma Cheek Odim, Dr. Marion Lee Bell'53 (President of the National Alumnae Association), Gene Davis
    Top row: Frances Allison Gabriel- Harris, Peggy Hall James, Sydney Roberts

43. *Greensboro News and Record*, September 1950.

44. One of the original debaters from Wiley College in the 1930s, Dr. Hobart Sidney Jarrett served as Professor and Chair of Humanities Division at Bennett College from 1949-1961 after which time he moved to Brooklyn College. Before leaving Greensboro, he had been ombudsman for student demonstrators and chief negotiator for opening the eating facilities that the sit-ins had won there.

45. The Carrie Barge Chapel predated the Annie Merner Pfeiffer Chapel which was dedicated in 1941.

46. A painting of Dr. David D. Jones in the narthex of the Annie Merner Pfeiffer Chapel.

47. "President Jones' Philosophy Appears in Murrow's 'This I Believe." *The Belle Ringer*, Vol. XX, No. 3, December 1952, p. 1.

48. *Ibid.*

49. *Bennett Banner*, June 1940, p. 1.

50. *Bennett Banner* December 1952, p.1.

51. Linda Brown, "To Light One Candle," *The Belle Ringer*, Spring 2007, p. 7.

52. *Afro American,* "No time for tears," 1957.

53. "Long-Forgotten Tape Brings King's Words Back to Life," *The Washington Post*, METRO section, B1, Friday, February 26, 1999.

   Dr. Martin Luther King's 72-minute oration was given on February 11, 1958, without notes before an audience of more than 1,500 people in the overcrowded chapel and basement. The title of his oration was "A Realistic Look at Race Relations."

54. Compilation photos of Golden Class of 1961, copied from the Golden Class 2011 Souvenir Book.

55. The wrought iron Bearden Gate was given to Bennett College by the children of a former dorm matron, Mrs. Catherine Kennedy Bearden of Greensboro. It is opened only for academic processions for Founders' Day, Senior Day, Baccalaureate, and Commencement, but kept closed at all other times.

56. The Golden Belles of 1961, *News from the Oasis* May-June 2011, p. 2.
   Front row l.-r.: Millicent Allen White, Dolores Finger Wright, Dorothy Groves Chambers, Constance Colston Oliphant, Laura Plummer Marshall, Joyce Pullum Gray, Helena Howell McCorkle, Shirley Dismuke Graham, Linda Brown, Carolyn Brown Edwards, Von Deleath Moore Kersey, Roslyn Smith, Esther Alexander Terry.

   2nd row: Doris Luck Fullwood, Eleanor Lotson Canty, Elishama Madison-Withers, Johanna Polanen, Minnie Sims Holmes, Shirley Degraffenreidt McQueen, Marva Lucas Douglas, Gwendolyn Mackel Rice, Karen Leach Wilson, Ida Jeanne Robinson Brown, Jacqueline Daise Lee, Hattie Green Price, Daisy Robinson McIlveen, Nettie Baldwin, Elisabeth Daise, Barbara Miller Moore, Patricia Hargrove Lockett.

57. Bennett Belles Participating in Downtown Greensboro Boycott 1960. Front cover of *The Belle Ringer,* Spring 2010, Co-editors: Audrey Demps Franklin '72 and Wanda Edwards Mobley '83.

58. Women of Substance Circle inductees with Dr. Malveaux and student escorts during Family and friends Weekend 2011.
    Standing: l.-r.: Mikea Nelson, Toshaleza Majadi,
     Dr. Iris Jeffries Morton '61, President Malveaux, Melanie Campbell, Brenda Keels (Miss Sophomore)
    Seated: Mildred Mama Dip Council

59. Bennett College National Alumnae Association's Awards were given at the All-Bennett Banquet, Saturday, May 8, 2010, *Belle Ringer*, Fall/Winter 2010 p. 2.

60.   *The Greensboro Four*

<u>Birthplace of the Civil Rights Movement</u>

Four students at North Carolina A&T State University conducted the first lunch counter sit-in on February 1, 1960 at the Woolworth Store: Franklin McCain, Joseph McNeil, Ezell Blair, Jr., and David Richmond.

"*Sometimes taking a stand for what is undeniably right means taking a seat.*"

Presented to the City of Greensboro by Radio Stations WEAL and WQMG on February 1, 1990.

Huff Art Studio

61. *Bennett College Yearbook 1963.*

62. Excerpts from the *Times Leader*, Charles H. Bogino, Wilkes-Barre, Pennsylvania, Monday, June 8, 1992.

63. North Jersey Alumnae Chapter (ca. 1990) during its annual Cotillion.: l.-r. Wilma Giles Marshall '65, Patricia Jamison, Barbara Dawkins '73, Mollye Lisa Spruel Thompson '67, Johanna Lee-Wright '74, Esther Canty-Barnes '76, Juanita Patience Moss '74, Annie Ward '75, Barbara Williams Williams '68, Yulonda Green Cunningham '85

64. *Bennett College Yearbook 1963.*

65. *Ibid.*

66. *Ibid.*

67. *Ibid.*

68. *Bennett College Songs,* p. 3.

69. *The Belle Ringer*, Fall/Winter 2010, p. 15.

70. *The Belle Ringer*, Tell Me Why Dear Bennett, Fall/Winter 2011 p.13.

71. *The Belle Ringer,* Breaking Ground at Bennett College, Fall/Winter, 2009, p. 14.

72. *Bennett College Yearbook* 1970.

73. "Nurse Trammell's Fried Chicken," *The Bennett Beacon*, 1970, Bennett College Alumnae, Issue 03, April 2010, p. 4.

74. *The Belle Ringer*, Class of 1979 at 30th reunion, Fall/Winter, 2009, p. 15. (Deborah Love's memoir is found in the first volume, pp. 313-314.)

75. The "Black Madonna" is a beautiful stained glass window created by the late Eva Hamlin Miller commissioned by Dr. Gloria R. Scott for the 50th anniversary of the Annie Merner Pfeiffer Chapel.

76. "Tribute to Mrs. David Dallas Jones ('Miss Susie')" from Gwendolyn Mackel Rice, the 2008 recipient of the Susie W. Jones Award.

77. On the way to Commencement on the Quad, the Golden Class of 1940 enters the Bearden Gate. *The Belle Ringer.* Inside cover, Spring/Summer 1990, Vol. 20, No. 3.

78. Books by Contributors:
    1st row: *Thriving and Surviving,* Julianne Malveaux
    The Long Walk, Linda B. Brown '61
    Black Angels, Linda B. Brown '61
    2nd row: *Growing up Nigger Rich,* Gwendolyn Y. Fortune '46
    Weaving the Journey, Gwendolyn Y. Fortune '46
    Family Lines, Gwendolyn Y. Fortune '46
    Created to Be Free, Juanita Patience Moss '54

    3rd row: *Annie Mae and the Preacher,* Sandra Philpott-Burke '70
    Watch Words: Thoughts on Race, Water and War, Beatrice Perry Soublet '65
    One Sunny Day, Hideko Tamura Snider '56
    Tell Me Why Dear Bennett: Memoirs of Bennett College Belles, Juanita Patience Moss '54

4th row: *Bittersweet Memories of Home,* Alice Patterson Patience'40
Anthracite Coal Art by Charles Edgar Patience, Juanita Patience Moss '54,
Forgotten Black Soldiers Who Served in White Regiments During the Civil War, Juanita Patience Moss'54

Books by Fannie Lillian Miles Bellamy'58
My Love Affair With The French. Fanning Island, Anaka's Post Boule Tour of South Africa, China and Places, Jacques: Le Chien Terrier.

79. Bennett College Song Sheet, ca. 1939.

80. *The Belle Ringer,* The Inauguration of our 14th President, Oct. 9-12, 2003, p.12.

81. "The Long Walk," a postcard sent from Frances ("Tuppie") Jones Bonner'39 to Alice Patterson Patience '40 in 1939.

82. Linda Brown, *The Long Walk. "The 'long walk' represents endurance, determination, deliberate and careful building toward the ultimate goal. It is made of flagstone, carefully pieced together in a puzzle which makes one straight line from the idea, to the work it takes to bring the idea into being."* p. 12.

83. *Bennett College Bulletin,* Cover Photograph, Fall 1956.

84. *Ibid.* p. 9.

85. "Rights Fighter Willa Player Dies." *Greensboro News and Report,* Friday, August 29, 2003, p. 6B.

86. *Ibid.* p. 4

87. Commencement Exercises 2008, p. 24.

88. Inaugural Convocation for Dr. Julianne Malveaux, 15th President.

89. *The Belle Ringer,* Spring/Summer 1990. Vol. 20, No. 3, p. 7.

90. Alumnae Employed at Alma Mater Bennett College in 2009, inside front cover of *The Belle Ringer*, Co-editors: Audrey Franklin '72 and Wanda Mobley '83, Fall/Winter 2009.

91. "To help students think holistically about themselves, The Grow Green Get Fit Garden of Hope was partially funded by a $1,500.00 grant from Home Depot and a parcel of land for students to grow fruit and vegetables that be eaten raw. A garden will be on Washington and Medley streets, next to the Maintenance Building." *The President's 2009-2010 Annual Report: Ground Breaking,* p. 16.

92. Alumnae participating in the "ground-breaking" ceremony at Bennett College, Front Cover of *The Belle Ringer, F*all/Winter 2009.

93. Belles participating in the "ground-breaking" ceremony of the new Global Studies Building, *The Belle Ringer* Fall/Winter 2009.

94. Trustees participating in the "ground-breaking" ceremony of the new Global Studies Building, *The Belle Ringer*, Fall/Winter 2009.

95. "This is the first time under Dr. Malveaux's administration that the alumnae gift totaled a million dollars. According to Audrey Frankin'72, Director of Alumnae Affairs, 'This gift is significant given the economic turbulence of the country. The Bennett Alumnae really wanted to raise their voices and give

their treasures to say we care about Bennett and her future.'" *The Belle Ringer,* Fall/Winter 2009, p. 7.

96. Governor Beverly Purdue was the 2010 Commencement speaker.

97. The Nellouise Watkins Faculty House during Capital Improvements Project Dedication, Family and Friends Weekend, October 2010, *News From the Oasis,* October 2010, p. 2.

98. Institutional Advancement Team, *The Belle Ringer,* Spring 2011, p. 4.

99. Tournament Golfers, Family & Friends Weekend 2010 Photo Gallery, *News from the Oasis*, October 2010, p. 4.

100. Robing Tradition on Senior Day, Joyce Collins Clarke robes her junior/senior sister in 1962. (Photo courtesy of Tisha Harris '63)

101. Bennett College Dedicates the Martin Dixon Intergenerational Center, *The Belle Ringer*, Tell Me Why, Fall/Winter 2011, p. 26.

102. CNN Anchor Soledad O'Brien receives the Honorary Doctorate Degree of Humane Letters. *The Belle Ringer*, Fall/Winter 2011, p. 8.

103. *Ibid.*

104. Miss Bennett College and Her Royal Court, *The Belle Ringer*, Tell Me Why, Fall/Winter 2011, p. 24.

105. *Ibid.* p. 25

106. 2009-2010 The President's Annual Report, Breaking Ground, p. 17

107. *The Way of Life at Bennett College.* 1938.

108. "News from the Oasis." A newsletter from Dr. Julianne Malveaux, President of Bennett College. Dr. Cristina Moreira, Assistant

Professor, Biology and Project Director, VA-NC LSAMP with Prestina Smith 2010.

109. Tiara Kennedy '11, "Bennett in 138 years: A Conversation for My Sisters," *The Belle Ringer*, Spring 2011, p. 5.

110. *The Way of Life at Bennett College*. 1938.

111. *The Belle Ringer*, Fall/Winter 2011, p. 8.

112. Class of 1938. Back cover of "The Way of Life at Bennett College."

113. Attired in their traditional white attire, the Class of 2015 enters the Chapel for Founders' Day Convocation during Family and Friends Weekend 2011, *The Belle Ringer*. Tell Me Why, Fall/Winter 2011. p. 8.

114. *The Way of Life at Bennett College*. 1938.

115. 2009-2010 The President's Annual Report, p. 15.

116. *The Belle Ringer*. Fall/Winter 2011, back cover.

THEN--------CLASS OF 1938 [112]

TOMORROW---- CLASS OF 2015 [113]

SOURCES

"25 for Jones." *Newsweek.* January 7, 1952.

"Boycott Ahead of its Time." *Greensboro News and Recorder.* February 4, 1994.

AFRO-American Newspapers. Archives and Research Center. "No Time For Tears," 1957.

All-Bennett Banquet Booklet. Saturday, May 8, 2010.

Alumnae Directory. Harris Connect, 2010.

Baker, Richard T. "To A Bennett Girl." *The Epworth Herald.*

Bennett College Bulletin. The Way of Life at Bennett College, Vol. XIII, No.1. 1938.

Bennett College Bulletin: Catalog Issues 1952-1954, Vol. XXII. No. 1, February 1952.

Bennett College Bulletin (Summer 1954).

Bennett College Bulletin (Fall 1955).

Bennett College Bulletin (Fall 1956).

Bennett College Songs. Bennett College. Greensboro, N.C.

Bennett Yearbook 1963.

Bennett Yearbook 1965.

Bennett Yearbook 2008.

Brown, Linda. *The Long Walk: The Story of the Presidency of Willa B. Player at Bennett College,* Danville, Virginia; McCain Printing Company, Inc., 1998.

"Celebrating Our Legacy of Excellence." 2nd Annual White Breakfast, North Jersey Chapter of Bennett College for Women NAA. April 9, 2005.

Commencement Exercises 2008. Bennett College For Women.

Greensboro News and Recorder. "37 Boycott Ahead of its Time." February 4, 1994.
_____ "Freshman View the Campus," 1950.

Inaugural Convocation. Dr. Julianne Malveaux, 15th President, March 29, 2008.

"Lucy Sadler Interview." Alvah Taylor Beander '73 and Juanita Patience Moss '54, Coleman Falls, Virginia, 2002.

Mackel, Rosetta Libian Lloyd. *Rosetta: An Autobiography,* 1987.

Moss, Juanita Patience. *Tell Me Why Dear Bennett: Memoirs of Bennett Belles: Class of 1924-2012*, Heritage Books, 2010.

News from the Oasis. A Newsletter from Dr. Julianne Malveaux, President of Bennett College, October 2010.

News from the Oasis, May-June 2011.

Obituaries:
    Gwendolyn Harris Blount
    Shirley Cundiff Bethea

Bishop Joseph Bethea
Peggy Jeffries Foman
Mable Vivian Hargrave
Helen Ellison McDowell
Gilberta Marie Jeffries Mitchell
Dr. Willa B. Player
Edith Taylor Sheppard
Audrey Wynn Spence

Patience, Alice Patterson. *Bittersweet Memories of Home*, Wilkes-Barre, Penna.: Wilkes University Press, 1998.

Smith, Pauline Waters. *By God's Grace: A Personal Testimony.* 2007.

Norlisha Jackson. "Saving More Than She Spent," *The Belle Ringer*, 1999, p. 8.

The Belle Connection. Issue 2, November/December, 2003.

The Belle Ringer, "The Inauguration of Our 14th President Dr. Johnnetta Betsch Cole." October 9-12, 2003.

The Belle Ringer. Breaking Ground at Bennett College, Fall/Winter 2009.

The Belle Ringer. Oprah, Spring 2007.

The Belle Ringer. Spring 2010.

The Belle Ringer. Tell Me Why, Fall/Winter 2011.

The Belle Ringer. The Spirit of Bennett, Spring 2011.

The Belle Ringer. Vol. 15, No.4, June-July 1985.

The Belle Ringer. Vol. 20, Spring/Summer 1990.

"The Class of 1961: An Amazing Journey Through 50 Years." May 2011.

The Montclair Times. Rose Withers Catchings, ca. 2002.

The Oregonian. Hideko Tamura Snider. August 8, 2011.

The President's Annual Report. Breaking Ground, 2009-2010.

Tributes to "Miss Susie." A Celebration of Life for Susie W. Jones, October 1-6, 1985. *The Belle Ringer,* Vol. 15, No. 4, June-July 1985, pp. 2-6.

Wilkes-Barre Times Leader. "Friends mourn area woman who fought for civil rights." Audrey Wynn Spence, June 8, 1992.

Wilkes-Barre Times-Leader. Dorothy Walker Smith at Bennett College, ca. 1943.

THE LITTLE THEATRE, BENNETT COLLEGE, GREENSBORO, NORTH CAROLINA

THEN----1938

<u>Studying in the NEW Holgate Library</u> [114]

NOW------2011

Studying in NEWLY RENOVATED Holgate Library [115]

INDEX

CONTRIBUTORS	PAGE
Banks, Audrose Mackel '49	126
Beander, Alvah Taylor '73	65
Bellamy, Fannie Lillian Miles '58	197
Berry, Lisbeth Ellen Edwards '39	97
Bowens, Yasmine 2011	341
Boykin, Vernelle Clements '70	271
Brayboy, Jeanne Martin '51	55
Brown, Virginia Jeffries '48	122
Burnette, Clara Whitmore '51	137
Caldwell, Glenda Dodd '72	277
Campbell, Betty Washington '53	148
Carter, Irene Powell '45	113
Cook, Veda Patrick '70	268
Cooke, Juanita Page '52	145
Dixon, Dr. Joyce Martin '56	177
Dixon, Faye Ann McClain '66	248
Eakins, Peggy Patrick '67	250
Fargas, Rosa '54	152
Franklin, Audrey Demps '72	11
Goldsmith, Nadirah '99	309
Gray, Joyce Pullum '61	207
Greene, Sylvia Rock '49	128
Hamilton, Claudia Wells '50	131
Harris, Sylvia (Tisha) Fish '63	227
Holmes, Wanda Denell Cobb '75	280
Humphrey, Zepplyn '35/'55	80
Janniere, Simone L. 2011	343
Jennings, Marissa 2003	321

Johnson, Carolyn James '61	215
Johnson, Dr. Lisa '81	14
Johnson, Jewel Merritt '66	248
Jones, Randye '80	287
Jordan, Gina N. Trimble '93	302
Keels, Brenda J. 2014	357
Kennedy, Dorothy Strothers '30	78
Kennedy, Tiara 2011	363
Kinsey, Dyora Thomas '75	284
Lunsford, Lequetta Johnson '92	298
Mackel, Marilyn Hortense JD '65	235
Marshall, Wilma Giles '65	237
Martin, Ida Johnson '56	182
Martin-Jones, Dr. Karen '98	307
McLean, Rev. Dr. Natalie '80	289
McQueen, Shirley Degraffenreidt '71	220
Mobley, Wanda Edwards '83	294
Morrow, Dorothy Dixon '54	156
Morton, Dr. Iris Jeffries '61	222
Moss, Dr. Juanita Patience '54	388
Neeley, Winzell (Wendy) Ervin '70	264
Nicholson, Brenda Morgan '69	263
Osimokun, Brandy A. Jones 2000	315
Pearson-Starling, Charnee' 2011	348
Randolph, Valaida Wynn '62	231
Rayford, Geraldine Kimber '49	44
Rice, Doris Evangeline Boyd	112
Rice, Gwendolyn Mackel '61	224
Rice-Jones, Toi 2010	337
Robbins, Josephine Hunter '56	184
Robinson, Dr. Gladys Ashe '71	274
Sanders, Zipporah Angela 2011	345
Scarlette, Dr. Mary Ann Rogers '54	164
Scipio, Alice Hayes '57	192
Simms, Mildred Copeland '54	134
Smith, Dorothy Walker '45	115
Smith, Roslyn '61	203

Snider, Dr. Hideko Tamura '56	186
Soublet, Beatrice Perry '65	242
Terry, Dr. Esther Alexander '61	7
Thompson, Mischelle '70	264
Thompson, Mollye Lisa Spruel '67	255
Walker, Betty Marie '49	129
Wall, Josefa Bethea '87	44
Washington, Dr. Lyvonne Mackel '53	150
Wells, Barbara Hickman '58	201
White, Elizabeth Patterson '70	268
Williams, Dr. Adelia Hammond '56	189
Williams, Modgie Enzlow '70	101
Willoughby, Ola Parker '42	109
Wilson, Karen Leach '61	218

2011 BCNAA WHITE BREAKFAST [116]

Pictured Contributors

Karen Leach Wilson '61, Valaida Wynn Randolph '62, Dr. Linda Brown '61, Dr. Esther Alexander Terry '61

COMPILER
Juanita Patience Moss '54

One of my fondest memories is that of singing in the choir at Sunday vespers. We would quietly line up in the narthex. The sanctuary doors would remain closed until the college bell ceased its pealing to call each Belle to her assigned seat.

The choir would sing the first verse of the processional hymn *a cappella*. Until I attended Bennett College I had never heard what would later become a lifelong favorite, ***"Are Ye Able," said the Master, "to be crucified with me?"***

The music from the organ would soar gloriously as the doors to the sanctuary were opened by the marshals on duty. The choir would sing again while marching in precision to the front while "Prexy" watched our every movement. We would climb the steps very carefully to finally take our places in the choir loft. I loved it and every time I ever hear the question, *"Are ye able?"* I answer, *"Yes, I am able."* My other favorite is ***"When I Survey the Wondrous Cross,"*** arranged in four part harmony by Dr. R. Nathaniel Dett in 1941 for the dedication of the new Annie Merner Pfeiffer Chapel. So majestic an arrangement!

Juanita Patience Moss, born and reared in West Pittston, Pennsylvania, attended Bennett College during her sophomore year (1951-52) when she formed lifelong friendships. Although financial constraints kept her from completing her education at Bennett, she remained affiliated with the alumnae, serving as president of both the North Jersey and the Northern Virginia Alumnae Chapters. A New Jersey high school biology teacher for 33 years, she received a BS degree from Wilkes University, a MA degree from Fairleigh Dickinson University, and an Honorary Doctorate of Humanities from Kings College. Profits from the sale of these two volumes are donated to the Alice Patterson Patience Scholarship Fund created for seniors in need of funds to graduate with their class.

ALMA MATER
(Words by Carol Cotton; Music by Edith Player Brown)

Bennett now our voices raise
Harmonies of grateful praise;
We thy daughters find thee fair,
Loyally thy colors bear.
Truth and honor in thy halls,
Faith and love within thy walls,
Ever dear to us thou art,
Firm within each loyal heart.

<u>*Chorus*</u>
Alma Mater, now we sing,
Hail the light that thou dost bring;
True we've been through the past,
True to thee while life shall last.

May we never smirch the good
Gendered here in sisterhood;
May we ever choose a-right,
Guided but by honor bright.
Ever lovelier shalt thou live
As thy daughters freely give,
Ever glorious above,
Testimonies of our love.

<u>*(Sing Prayerfully)*</u>
"Till the evening shadows fall,
"Till we heed our last clear call,
Mother---- may we offer thee
Lives of worth and purity.
Go with us throughout the years,
Smile on us in doubts and fears,
Bless us with thy tender care,
Mother----fairest of the fair!

www.ingramcontent.com/pod-product-compliance
Lightning Source LLC
Chambersburg PA
CBHW051625230426
43669CB00013B/2189